People are talking about...

People are talking about...

people and things in

VOGUE

Edited by Allene Talmey

PRENTICE-HALL, INC.

Englewood Cliffs, New Jersey

Text Acknowledgments

"The Cultural Schizophrenia of Luis Valdez" (The Great Valdez), by Stan Steiner. Copyright © 1969 by Stan Steiner. Reprinted by permission of Barthold Fles Literary Agency.

"Alice in Wonderland" and "I Won't Pay for the Trip," by Jonathan Miller. Reprinted by permission of Jonathan Miller.

"Francis Bacon," by Lawrence Alloway. Reprinted by permission of Lawrence Alloway.

"Hans Hofmann," by Harold Rosenberg. Copyright © 1965 by Harold Rosenberg. Reprinted by permission of Harold Rosenberg.

"Philip Johnson," by Cleveland Amory. Copyright © 1964 by Cleveland Amory. Reprinted by permission of Cleveland Amory.

"Marianne Moore Speaks," by Henrietta Fort Holland. Copyright © 1963 by Marianne Moore. Reprinted by permission of John Schaffner.

"Mastroianni," by Luigi Barzini. Reprinted by permission of Luigi Barzini.

"In Dreams," by Frank O'Connor. Copyright © 1967 by Harriet R. O'Donovan. Reprinted by permission of Cyrilly Abels.

"The Unique Ross," by Janet Flanner. Copyright © 1968 by Janet Flanner. Reprinted by permission of Janet Flanner.

"The Hidden Force of Black African Art," by Leopold Sédar Sénghor. Reprinted by permission of Leopold Sédar Sénghor.

Excerpt from *David Smith* by David Smith, edited by Cleve Gray. Copyright © 1968 by Holt, Rinehart and Winston, Inc. Reprinted by permission of Holt, Rinehart and Winston, Inc.

"A Major American Sculptor, David Smith," by Robert Motherwell. Copyright © 1965 by Robert Motherwell. Reprinted by permission of Robert Motherwell.

"The Genius of Chaplin" and "Nabokov," by Penelope Gilliatt. Copyright © 1966 by Penelope Gilliatt. Reprinted by permission of John Cushman Associates, Inc.

Excerpt from *Anti-Memoirs*, by André Malraux, translated by Terence Kilmartin. Copyright © 1968 by Holt, Rinehart and Winston, Inc., and Hamish Hamilton Ltd. Reprinted by permission of Holt, Rinehart and Winston, Inc.

"A Reference for Lady Chatterley's Lover," by Anthony Powell. Copyright © 1966 by Anthony Powell. Reprinted by Harold Ober Associates, Inc.

Excerpt from *Markings*, by Dag Hammarskjöld, translated by Leif Sjoberg and W. H. Auden. Copyright © 1966 by Alfred A. Knopf, Inc., and Faber and Faber Ltd. Reprinted by permission of Alfred A. Knopf, Inc.

"The Man Who Invented Modern Art Dealing," by John Russell. Reprinted by permission of John Russell.

Excerpt from *Letters to Georgian Friends*, by Boris Pasternak, translated by David Magarshack. Copyright © 1967 by Giulio Einaudi editore S.P.A., Torino; English translation copyright © 1967, 1968 by Martin Secker & Warburg Limited and Harcourt, Brace and World, Inc. Reprinted by permission of Harcourt, Brace and World, Inc.

Excerpt from *The Proud Tower*, by Barbara Tuchman. Copyright © 1965 by Barbara Tuchman. Reprinted by permission of The Macmillan Company.

Photograph Acknowledgments

The Hermitage Museum and the Kirov Ballet, by Bruce Davidson. Copyright © 1964 by Bruce Davidson and Magnum Photos, Inc. Reprinted by permission of Magnum Photos, Inc.

Ed Murrow and Fred Friendly, by Elliot Erwitt. Copyright © 1954 by Magnum Photos, Inc. Reprinted by permission of Magnum Photos, Inc.

Barbara Linthicum, by Philip Jones Griffith. Copyright © 1968 by Magnum Photos, Inc. Reprinted by permission of Magnum Photos, Inc.

Claude Lévi-Strauss, by Henri Cartier-Bresson. Copyright © 1968 by Magnum Photos, Inc. Reprinted by permission of Magnum Photos, Inc.

Irving Berlin, by Henri Cartier-Bresson. Copyright © 1962 by Magnum Photos, Inc. Reprinted by permission of Magnum Photos, Inc.

Faulkner photographs, by Henri Cartier-Bresson. Copyright © 1962 by Magnum Photos, Inc. Reprinted by permission of Magnum Photos, Inc.

Andrew Wyeth photographs, by Henri Cartier-Bresson. Copyright © 1962 by Magnum Photos, Inc. Reprinted by permission of Magnum Photos, Inc.

"The Man Who Invented Modern Art Dealing," photographs by Snowdon. Copyright © 1965 by Snowdon. Reprinted by permission of Snowdon.

Kansas Landscape, by Truman Capote, and photographs of Dick Hickock and Perry Smith, by Jack Curtis. Copyright © 1966 by Truman Capote. Reprinted by permission of Truman Capote.

Luis Valdez, by George Ballis. Copyright © 1969 by George Ballis. Reprinted by permission of George Ballis.

"Alice in Wonderland," photographs by Snowdon. Copyright © 1966 by Snowdon. Reprinted by permission of Snowdon.

Harold Pinter, by Snowdon. Copyright © 1967 by Snowdon. Reprinted by permission of Snowdon.

Marie Nyswander, by Snowdon. Copyright © 1968 by Snowdon. Reprinted by permission of Snowdon.

People Are Talking About . . . People and Things in Vogue edited by Allene Talmey

The material in this book was all originally published in *Vogue* © 1969, 1968, 1967, 1966, 1965, 1964, 1963, 1962, 1960, 1958, 1954 by The Condé Nast Publications Inc.

SBN 13-656876-9 Library of Congress Catalog Card Number: 76-86515. Printed in the United States of America *T*

Prentice-Hall International, Inc., London
Prentice-Hall of Australia, Pty. Ltd., Sydney
Prentice-Hall of Canada, Ltd., Toronto
Prentice-Hall of India Private Ltd., New Delhi
Prentice-Hall of Japan, Inc., Tokyo

Contents

Preface   This book swings comfortably between relevance today and relevant nostalgia. Within these pages are a series of diverting and superb photographs, plus a series of articles that are sometimes literature and sometimes the best kind of journalism, expert, limited, and often highly subjective. These articles, and the captions for the photographs, are reprinted here exactly as they first appeared in *Vogue* with no attempt to bring the material up to an arbitrary date, for the changes could never catch up with the realities of life, death, and book deadlines.

Acknowledgments   The unsigned short articles and long captions in this book were written by three *Vogue* editors: Kate Lloyd, Mary Roblee Henry, and myself. I owe a great debt to Mrs. Lloyd and Mrs. Henry as well as to Diana Vreeland, the Editor-in-Chief of *Vogue*, Priscilla Peck, and to all those others on *Vogue*—photographers, writers, editors—who through the years contributed ideas and spirit to the pages of the magazine. I owe special gratitude to Alexander Liberman, the Editorial Director of *Vogue*, who first saw the photographs, the writings, and the layouts on their way into the magazine, then gave additional care and advice in the making of this book. Among my unpaid creditors are Iva S. V.-Patcévitch, Chairman of the Board of The Condé Nast Publications, and Perry L. Ruston, President of Condé Nast.

Allene Talmey
New York, New York

…people and things in
VOGUE

Alice in Wonderland

BY JONATHAN MILLER

PHOTOGRAPHS BY SNOWDON

The subtle, lyrical, exact logic of the Wonderland child of Lewis Carroll has been netted. Again this unforgettable fantasy of childhood happens, this time through the poetic reasoned imagination of Jonathan Miller, who especially wrote, organized, and directed a new film of Alice *to be shown on British television on New Year's Day. Holding to Carroll, dropping Tenniel, Dr. Miller changed the dreams to marvellously fresh and detailed Victoriana.*

I believe it was Lillian Hellman who first put me up to doing *Alice.* Sitting on the edge of a New York cocktail din we somehow got around to children's books and agreed that *Alice* was a rich, sombre book full of special promise as a film. It had been done before, but they had always missed the point. They had been too joky, or else too literal. And certainly they had always come unstuck by trying to re-create the style of Tenniel's original illustrations.

Alice is an inward sort of work, more of a mood than a story, so that before it could be turned into a film we had to discover some new key with which to unlock its hidden feeling. Tenniel's drawings are fastened to the printed page. They belong to the world of ink and type and just refuse to translate into photography. All those animal heads and playing cards look fine on the printed page. On celluloid they look like awkward pantomime drag. So we had to go deeper into the text, under the scratchy texture of the print, to find some commanding image which would provide a picture, as inevitable for celluloid as Tenniel's illustrations were for paper.

What was Charles Dodgson (alias Lewis Carroll) about? What is the strange, secret command of *Alice's Adventures in Wonderland?* Nostalgia and remorse, of course. Like so many Victorians, Dodgson was hung up on the romantic agony of childhood. The Victorians looked on infancy as a period of perilous wonder when the world was experienced with such keen intensity that growing up seemed like a fall and a betrayal. And yet they seemed to do everything they could to smother this primal intensity of childhood. Instead of listening to these witnesses of innocence, they silenced them, taught them elaborate manners, and reminded them of their bounden duty to be seen and not heard.

Perhaps the adults were frightened and, long before Freud, knew the anarchic vigour of the child. Whatever the reason, they were two-faced about youth, secretly longing for the very condition which they took so many efforts to

SNOWDON

"What a curious feeling," said Alice. "I must be shutting up like a telescope." Although Dr. Miller chose for his cast some of the greatest British actors, he chose an unknown beautiful schoolgirl, Anne-Marie Mallik, for Alice.

stife and restrain. They were caught in a cleft stick between the incompatible claims of duty and sensibility. They knew very well that in growing up they must sacrifice the glory and the freshness of the dream. And yet they realized, too, that only by doing this, by ignoring the splendour in the grass, could they apply themselves to work, to duty, and to substantial public accomplishment.

For above all, the Victorians were prodigious workers with an almost obsessional sense of the dignity of labour. The world pressed down on them with a burden of serious obligation, and anything which interfered with the discharge of this obligation seemed like a frivolous intrusion. Life was short enough without having to waste time on the petty sensitivities of childhood.

Yet the Victorians knew, or suspected at least, the damage they were doing by hurrying on to maturity like this. Deep down, in moments of sentiment and remorse they realized that infant sensibility was more than a frivolous luxury—a core of precious spiritual vitality without which life was a meaningless drudge. It is significant that when John Stuart Mill fell into a depression in early manhood, he was comforted not by work, but by the poems of Wordsworth.

Alice is another Victorian's quest for consolation in childhood. Both books are about the pains of growing up. In *Wonderland* and *Looking Glass*, a sombre punctilious child reaches hesitantly toward her own seniority, realizing as she does so the terrible penalties of the adult state. Right at the start of *Wonderland*, she feels herself growing bigger only to feel with an awful shock that by doing so she can no longer get down the passageway and out to the garden with its cool fountains and bright flowers.

The journey which Alice then makes takes her deeper and deeper into the mesh of adult obligation—into a world where punctuality is the cardinal virtue and where disobedience is punished by having your head off. And the story converges on an occasion which is surely the epitome of adult responsibility—a trial. At the end it is not the Knave who suffers but Alice herself who is finally accused of having grown too big.

Everyone Alice meets on the way to this climax represents one of the different penalties of growing up. One after the other, the characters seem to be punished or pained by their maturity.

SNOWDON

4

*A*lice at the Queen's croquet ground:
"'You shan't be beheaded!' said Alice,
and she put them into a large flower pot."

The attendants at this furious gala are dressed like the ladies-in-waiting in
Velásquez's "Las Meninas."

**A**lice, at the beach: "Taught us Drawling, Stretching, and Fainting in Coils," said the Mock Turtle.

Alice listening to the Mock Turtle (Sir John Gielgud) and the Gryphon (Malcolm Muggeridge) who act like two hopeless Chekhovian uncles.

The Queen is infuriated, the King is brow-beaten. The Caterpillar is a fossilized pedant and the Duchess a bibulous old frump prompted by morals and mottos.

Even the congenial characters are bowed down with pathos and remorse. The Gryphon and Mock Turtle sink into senility with a few tattered reminiscences of their school days to comfort them in their shallow grief. The Hatter lives on riddles; the Dormouse snoozes into his dotage. The whole book is a panorama of corruption and decay.

The animal heads and playing cards are just camouflage. All the characters in the book are real, and the papier-mâché disguises with which Carroll covers them all up do nothing to hide the indolent despair.

Once this was clear, the way to make the film fell neatly and inevitably into place. No snouts, no whiskers, no carnival masks. Everyone could be just as he was. And Alice herself? Not the pretty sweetling of popular fancy. I advertized for a solemn, sallow child, priggish and curiously plain. I knew exactly what she would be like when I found her. Still, haughty, and indifferent, with a high smooth brow, long neck, and a great head of sphinx hair.

Seven hundred kids answered the advertisement and for three months I riffled through an album of bouncing, bonny Mods. It seems that every girl in England sees herself as Alice. Or at least some jolly sweet version of her. Half of them came in as holiday snaps, knee-deep in estuary water, with a bronzed brute of a father about to throw some coiled rope out of the background. But the real Alice, my little white whale, was elsewhere.

Then my Alice turned up. Just as I'd imagined her. She was the only child I interviewed out of the seven hundred who applied. She had no wish to become an actress, but her mother thought that a summer stint like this would do her good—bring her out a bit. She was too much with her books and a bout of jolly acting might bring some roses to her cheeks.

She was the reincarnation of Alice. In scene after scene she met the distinguished cast with the same indifferent courtesy with which in the story Alice meets everyone. Oddly enough this child required the least direction of all. Her nature supplied everything that needed to be done. She cruises through the film with prissy hauteur.

Not once did this girl do what I feared any child actress might have done. She never emoted, and best of all she never showed any surprise. She just spoke her lines and carried herself straight. As a dreamer, after all, Alice is the landlord of her estate and the characters are her tenants. She must come on like a stuffed Infanta, cold and gorgeous.

The film is very elaborate in its setting. This is not strictly true to the nature of dreams, most of which are rather slipshod about the details of décor. Dreams are only intermittently elaborate in visual detail. But I wanted to re-create, in addition to a dream, that bursting fatal ripeness of Pre-Raphaelite surrealism.

I wanted the child to move through a world where every detail threatened to blossom with some dreadful vision. Grass blades, dewdrops, bricks, silk brocade, violets, and lace. The awful pristine imminence of physical things. So in one set, for the Trial, my designer, a magpie genius called Julia Trevelyan Oman, loaded the scene with four thousand movable props.

It seems that the film contains the entire visual contents of the child's mind. Every object and surface she has ever seen and forgotten looms up with fatal clarity. We ransacked the Tate Gallery for all this. Pictures by Millais, Holman Hunt, Calderon, and Arthur Hughes were digested and assimilated into the décor. Everything to help re-create the nauseating intensity of the Pre-Raphaelite vision.

And then we prayed for heat. We petitioned for that special syrupy English summer heat when insects play cellos in the grass and oak trees stand stock still on their own doilies of mid-summer shadow. Because that's the sort of afternoon when Alice fell to drowsing. We wanted pollen and midges, long drugged silences, and the flash of sunlight off a laurel leaf.

Tall order for an English summer but we got it all. Except for the drugged silences. We didn't get too many of those. American bombers saw to that. Short of going to Ireland there seemed to be no hope of escaping the Strategic Air Command. Even at thirty-eight thousand feet a Boeing cuts across the Pre-Raphaelite scene with shattering irrelevance. But we steered a course between the flights, and only once does an aero-engine intrude. We pass it off as a hornet.

We toured three months looking for the right locations. As the summer opened we took off each day into the secret hinterland of rural England. It was ten years since I had been in the depths like this and I had forgotten how mysteriously rural much of England still was.

We took a wide sweep in each of the four quadrants of the compass. And I realized how different each one was—like a different temperament—or humour almost. There was the dry sedgy East. Tennyson country, with huge upholstered skies, cold marshes, and flights of honking swans. And the West, mythical and sleepy, drowsing under swaths of poppy-milk mist. And the Western rivers, too, sleek green and oily like small Limpopos.

This odyssey through England put me right in the mood for filming. *Alice* is saturated in an intense feeling for the English countryside. It's quite clear that Carroll understood the awful apocalyptic mystery of English nature—its terrible damp, mossy fecundity with hobbits and angels ripening like dragonfly larvae in the ooze.

If you stand for a moment quite silent, in an English orchard, say in Gloucestershire, on a hot afternoon in July, you can hear the *Alice* fauna creeping among the grass stems. That's why I filled the movie with dwarfs and midgets. I wanted the best human counterparts for all those jewelled regiments of vermin that crawl down at ankle level in the English grass. And we dressed the dwarfs and midgets all à la Velásquez so as to get Empire of Hapsburg insects.

We filmed in the midst of all this for about nine weeks. We forgot where we had come from, and when the end came someone suggested that we just carry on. No film in the camera. Sham takes and all—but just carry on, sinking deeper and deeper into the somnolent magic of Alice's last summer as a child.

American Genii

The six American geniuses here and on the next two pages have nothing in common except that each man is a genie, that each is an influence on our lives, that each can call forth from his inner life a large outer response. These genii, transforming mysteriously, have no touch of hyperbole about them. Always in full view, they are wonder workers.

ALAN HOVHANESS AND EDGARD VARÈSE

These two composers are giants, friends, and admirers of each other's work. The younger man, fifty-three-year-old Hovhaness, born in Somerville, Massachusetts, is gaunt, tall, gentle, aloof, a mystic. His music, he wrote recently, is inspired by the "orchestral sonorities of Tang Dynasty music and by Confucian temple music. I do not like box-shaped buildings, and I like to bend the tones of flutes and trombones." He was led to do this, he added, "after practising ancient instruments in Japan and Korea. I also believe in the raga and tala principles of South India which can bring a new mysterious beauty into the world." The unique spirit of Varèse, who will be seventy-nine years old this month, has been a force among musicians. As a young student in Paris where he was born, Varèse studied mathematics and science, has incorporated the principles he learned then in his advanced antiphonal compositions, some for wind and percussion, alternating with electronic organized sound. A revolutionary in music, one of the great original minds, Varèse has always remained a pioneer. When his "Ionisation," composed thirty-three years ago, was played recently by the American Symphony Orchestra, it sounded fresh and immediate, its shock absorbed. Although his music breaks like upheavals of volcanic mountains, the man is mild, willing, his face powerfully designed as though carved from the roots of an old, strong tree.

ROBERT LOWELL AND EDWARD ALBEE

Robert Lowell has loosely been called "perhaps the greatest poet now writing in English." At forty-seven, with half-a-dozen prizes and awards, with his new book of poetry, *For the Union Dead*, on its way to the best-seller lists, with his first play, *The Old Glory*, produced, Lowell is a tall, handsome, quietly harassed Bostonian with a powerful chin and a look of uncertainty. His poems are, however, sure, personal, often tender, brilliant with figures of speech, incisive, memorable, and specific: "the sailors and their pickups under trees with Latin labels," or this elegiac, "You wore bow-ties, and dark/ blue coats, and sucked/ wintergreen or cinnamon lifesavers/ to sweeten your breath," or, "You usually won—/ motionless/ as a lizard in the sun." Quite unlike Lowell is Edward Albee, a slight, reticent dramatist with a concealed charge of dynamite in every scene. A poet years ago, this thirty-six-year-old playwright has a fascination with destruction. After early poetry, he worked as a record salesman at Bloomingdale's department store, became a Western Union messenger, and then wrote his succession of plays, *The Zoo Story, The Death of Bessie Smith, The American Dream, Who's Afraid of Virginia Woolf?, The Ballad of the Sad Café*, and now his newest play, *Tiny Alice*, planned to open at the end of this month. Albee always attacks the nerves and sensibilities of his audiences, his weapons, bitterness, wit, some horror, a smidgen of the gruesome, a one-two blow.

IRVING PENN

JOSEF ALBERS AND JASPER JOHNS

Although forty-two years separate these two painters, both are world famous. Josef Albers, now a pink and white seventy-six, has been preoccupied for years with colour and perspective, his "optical art" exhibited over the world. To many people his most famous series is his "Homage to the Square," a remarkably beautiful extension of vision, hard-edged, kinetic, and sometimes dizzy. In the forty recent paintings at his New York exhibition, Albers showed only squares, sometimes three, sometimes four squares within one canvas, the colours receding or coming forward, all based on his theories expressed in his extraordinary book, *Interaction of Color*, published a year ago at a price of two hundred dollars. His dedication read: "This is my thanks to my students." Unquestionably one of the greatest teachers, with his influence spread in the Western world and Japan, Albers, now professor emeritus at Yale University, still has his professorial manner, talkative, delightful, witty and serious at the same time. In one of his writings, he wrote: "Thus art is not an object but experience. To be able to perceive it we need to be receptive. Therefore art is there where art seizes us." The art of Albers early seized Jasper Johns, born thirty-four years ago in South Carolina, who owns an Albers painting on glass, broken in eight pieces. Johns, too, has had an influence, is an uneasy father of Pop Art, but not a Pop artist. In his time he has painted beer cans, the objects of daily life, American flags, maps, and, in recent years, numbers, for he is fascinated by their shapes. He blurs and smudges his colours, likes these days variants of greys, of whites. Where Albers has tension, Johns has a controlled air of relaxation; where Albers laughs aloud, Johns smiles with pleasure. He has much to be pleased about. Collectors, museums, galleries all over the world, including Japan, want Johns. In fact, since 1957 he has had ten one-man exhibitions, been importantly shown seventy times with other artists. To explain what he does, he wrote a month ago that it consists of "putting marks and materials and objects on canvas. Letting painting be what it is. Letting it become what it will. Looking and thinking."

IRVING PENN

Francis Bacon, who is now having an extraordinary exhibition at New York's Guggenheim Museum, arranged by its curator, Lawrence Alloway, is an original, a discoverer of new ways with a memory of the old. (In the photograph here, taken in Bacon's studio, there is at his left a Rembrandt self-portrait reproduction.) To some people he is a shocker as a painter to some he is only an eccentric with a known compulsion towards gambling. To some he is bats. To others, however, he is by far the greatest painter in Britain. An isolated man, sometimes extremely attractive, sometimes curiously aloof, who wants to record the faces he sees, he is frequently surprised that certain spectators think of his paintings as screams of rage, for there is little of the rebel about him. He lives his unsettled life comfortably in disorder. With great candour he knows that he horrifies. Before the Guggenheim, the Tate Gallery in London gave him, several years ago, a show, oddly violent in reaction since his paintings are so quiet, mirages often of multiple images, of sliding, melting faces that make some spectators feel their eyes are out of focus.

Francis Bacon

A great, shocking, eccentric painter

BY LAWRENCE ALLOWAY

Some years ago, in London, I sat for my portrait. The artist was a slow worker, so I spent days looking at the back of the canvas on his easel. Since he was a friend of Francis Bacon's, I had something to look at during our sessions. He was painting on the reverse side of an abandoned work of Bacon's. There was, I remember, the shadowy outline of a figure, dark against a whipped-up background of blue and other colours. It looked like a mad scientist in a greenhouse.

Bacon appeared in London, after World War II, with a few turbulent and anguished paintings. The impact of these paintings was terrific, but rumour was persistent that the works shown were merely the tip of the iceberg. For every painting that he let out of the studio, there were said to be rows of discarded or slashed masterpieces. The canvas on which my portrait was being done was one of these works. A double drama became associated with Bacon: There was the struggle of a desperate man who destroyed most of his own work; and, there was, too, the violence of the imagery in the paintings that did survive—meat decomposing or people screaming.

For years Bacon was inseparable from rumour and legend His nonchalance towards the preservation of his own work, his pleasure in gambling, his visits to an André Gidean North Africa, were all threads in the story. (One anecdote I remember had an English art student sketching on a beach in North Africa. An Arab came up to him and opened the conversation: "Do you know Francis Bacon?") It is a characteristic of the successful twentieth-century artist to live in a goldfish bowl. Once an artist has been awarded a goldfish bowl of his own, his whole life becomes information that he shares with the world. The world troops through the studio today. Bacon, though the object of great curiosity, has managed to live in the goldfish bowl and

IRVING PENN

preserve a great deal of privacy. In fact, the violence associated with his name has acted as a screen behind which he could live and work as he wanted.

Bacon is in his early fifties, but does not look it. It is neither the regularity of his work habits nor the circumspection of his life that has given him his remarkable youthfulness. On the contrary, he has never spared himself, never been a man to take it easy. Bacon does not like abstract art and dismisses it casually as mere decoration —an opinion revealing the indifference with which Bacon protects himself from subjects that are of no interest to him. Nevertheless, he is the only painter of his age who continues to interest the younger artists in England, many of whom *are* abstract painters. No other painter of Bacon's generation in England (a mild lot) has displayed the particular qualities of nerve and obsession that seem to characterize the best modern painters in other countries.

An exhibit of more than sixty paintings by Bacon has opened at the Solomon R. Guggenheim Museum. Surrounded as one is at the Museum, by an abundance of large spectacular works, it is hard to remember that Bacon achieved fame first as a painter almost without paintings. Gradually, he has separated himself from the web of rumours and party talk that surrounded him, and, in the last few years, has become a very much more productive painter. At least he has allowed much more of his productivity to remain. At the Guggenheim, for example, though the show is retrospective, and goes back to 1946, at least twenty percent of the works were painted within the last three years. Bacon has made the transition from cult figure to major painter with his later work fully displayed, not shielded by being held back or destroyed. (American collectors, incidentally, were on to Bacon early, and the present exhibition draws on American, as well as European, sources.)

It used to be thought that abstract painting was difficult to appreciate and that figurative art was easy because it appealed directly to common experience. This argument was O.K. for the *early* twentieth century, but is no longer convincing in the changed situation of mid-century art. Good art and bad, difficult art and easy, are no longer identifiable with set styles, but only with the uses artists make of them. The work of Francis Bacon is among the reasons that this easy antithesis has to be abandoned. There is, for instance, little agreement as to what the subject matter of his paintings really is. There are nudes, but what are they doing? There are men in spaces that look like hotel rooms; or they may just be corners of Bacon's studios. The scenes are clearly displayed and yet not decipherable into verbal explanations. Bacon is fully prepared for this situation, or at least used to it, because he says: "Everybody has his own interpretation of a painting he sees. I don't mind if they have different interpretations of what I have painted." Certainly his critics have made full use of this freedom (which is, perhaps, rather insolently bestowed—like Apollo granting Midas' imprudent wish for gold). His figures of Popes have been explained as anti-clerical and as Freudian father-symbols; they have also been explained away as appealing to Bacon as a theme simply because the Pope wears such handsome colours.

Then there is the problem of his quotations from other artists. He has often paraphrased Velásquez's famous portrait of Pope Innocent X, but the quotation is not like the respectful evocation of a classical model because the artist feels he can not improve on it. On the contrary, one image begets another in Bacon's art and it is quite possible for him to continue, in the same picture, from the Pope to a reference to Eisenstein's film, *The Battleship Potemkin*. A screaming head, famous from the Odessa steps sequence in that movie, began to appear in his paintings in 1949. Thus, a famous painting is combined with a photographed image, so that the old and the new, the traditional and the modern are disconcertingly fused. Both art lovers and movie fans have been disconcerted.

Incidentally, the movie quotation, though from a *silent* film, makes Bacon a precursor of today's pop artists, with their references to images of mass communications. Bacon has persistently used original and unexpected sources for his art. Many of his figures and animals derive from such books as Eadweard Muybridge's *The Human Figure in Motion* and Marius Maxwell's *Stalking Big Game With a Camera in Equatorial Africa*. One was published in the 1890's, the other in the twenties, and undoubtedly Bacon relished the period-flavour of the photographs, as well as their status as records of

Bacon's "Landscape near Malabata," painted at Tangier in May this year, is one of his few landscapes. About it, Lawrence Alloway wrote: "The landscape is sucked into a kind of vortex, and surrounded by a screen, like the canvas windbreaks they put up on Côte d'Azur beaches or, perhaps, like the pens in which, three hundred years ago, royal boar hunts took place. The forms within this arena are blurred by wind or by movement, including the evocative human-looking smear in the foreground." (Published through the kindness of Marlborough Fine Art Limited, London.)

fact. He shows that no visual material, no human records, exist that can not be valid, if interpreted meaningfully.

Bacon's art has a way of connecting, knowingly but obliquely, with problems which have to be faced, at one time or another, by everybody interested in art. First, what is the rôle of the masterpiece? There was a time when nobody doubted its value. It was the great work which summed up all that an artist had been trying to say and it was undoubtedly destined for immortality. In one way, Bacon seems to aim at producing masterpieces, in the grandeur and ambition that his works display, but at the same time he seems to be destroying the ground for a masterpiece. By painting pictures in series, as he does, he seems to be saying that no single painting is sufficient to make his point. Thus, instead of destroying masterpieces, as his friends say he used to do, he repeats possible masterpieces in endless series and variations. The result is that his pictures need to be seen in groups, and, when they are, they look like successive stages from a film or a picture magazine (like, say, records of a suicide jumping off a building or a girl having a completely new hairdo).

A second problem which Bacon's art consistently raises has to do with the influence of photography on art. Of course, this is not a new theme, and in the nineteenth century, Delacroix, Corot, Daumier, and (the suddenly revived) Alphonse Mucha, were among those painters who were interested in the new medium. What Bacon has done is to bring his painting into relation with the mass of photographic images which fill the world today. And this means that his paintings, in this respect, share a common ground with ourselves. Today none of us escapes the influence of the visual explosion. In fact, it is through photography that we get much of our information about politicians, fashion, outer space, science, and Christine Keeler. Our image of reality is substantially shaped by photography. Bacon transfers the visual appearance of photographs into his art, and never more so than when he is painting freely. He has an evocative way of dabbing a dry brush, or twisting a wet one, so that, like heavily screened newsprint or out-of-focus photography, physical reality is evoked, but in a rather oblique form. In fact, Bacon told David Sylvester in a recent

interview on the British Broadcasting Company that to him "forms change continuously." He improvises as he works so that a painting, even though planned in advance to some extent, may not have a predictable outcome. It is not the least of Francis Bacon's paradoxes that however much he improvises in paint, he never loses contact with that blurred, gritty, yet persistently factual presence that photography creates.

Bacon's paintings are as stately as the portraits of ancestors in English country houses, even though the forms are evasive and hard to pin down. The composition of his paintings prepares us for an image in the Grand Manner, but when we look closely, its forms and composition seem to stretch, as in a distorting mirror, or dissolve out of focus. The result is that everything in Bacon tends to produce uncertainty, often of an ominous or breathtaking kind.

In a new painting of Bacon's *Landscape near Malabata, Tangier* his dazzling colour range, and the emotive power of his imagery, can be seen. The landscape is sucked into a kind of vortex, and surrounded by a screen, like the canvas windbreaks they put up on Côte d'Azur beaches or, perhaps, like the pens in which, three hundred years ago, royal boar hunts took place. The forms within this arena are blurred by wind or by movement, including the evocative human-looking smear in the foreground.

IRVING PENN

Bacon, in the famous disorder of his London studio.

Why does Bacon paint sinister and harrowing subjects? This is a question that, often asked, needs to be answered, although one is tempted to say, why not? After all, nobody demands "why bottles?" when faced with Giorgio Morandi's calm still lifes. One answer takes the whole affair out of painting and into the area of moralizing editorial writers. This argument sees Bacon as a mirror held up to the human condition, faithful recorder of a bad time.

However, there is another way to look at Bacon's subjects and that is to see them as the personal expression of a view of life—and death. To quote Bacon's own words: "Man now can only attempt to beguile himself, for a time, by buying a kind of immortality through the doctors." And, in his paintings Bacon represents life, its vulnerability and man's impermanence. Thus, one can say, it is the speed of change that is, in a way, his subject. Just as fashion styles are always on the move, visibly changing every few years how women look and, more slowly, how men look, so Bacon depicts man as subject to change, unstoppably. The human body is represented as if it were as topical and as expendable as clothes. This is not, by any means, a negative view of his life, but simply recognition of the facts of life.

Edward Villella

The Greatest American Male Dancer

BY RICHARD POIRIER

Those who watched a Bell Telephone Hour last March, called "Man Who Dances: Edward Villella," were given a rare and instructive glimpse of the physical agonies necessary to the grace of ballet. Dancing, it would seem, can be as physically punishing as any other contact sport. The cameras happened to follow Villella during the days when four of the New York City Ballet company's male leads couldn't dance because of injuries. There's scarcely a day when some part of a ballet dancer's body doesn't hurt him, and mishaps are frequent anyway, so that the situation Villella had to confront was unusual only in degree. The absentee stars were evidence that even an ordinary schedule of workout, practice sessions, and performances can be precarious, and Villella was required to go well beyond that by substituting in some of the most taxing ballets in the repertoire of the company. On November 19, 1967 he found himself committed to dance three major rôles during the matinee and evening.

In the afternoon, having finished "Tarantella," he went on to the bravura rôle in "Raymonda Variations," and there, to the audible distress of an audience of some 2,700, he fell in agonized muscular cramps. Ashen-faced from pain and with what looked like foolish courage he managed to finish the performance. But he then had to decide whether or not to risk permanent bodily damage, perhaps even his career, by going on in the evening. He decided to do so, against the advice of his wife, the dancer Janet Greschler, and despite the fact that he was

to dance what he himself regards as his single most physically demanding rôle, which no one else has even begun to learn, the "Rubies" section of the latest and most popularly successful of George Balanchine's ballets, "Jewels."

His decision, and his way of talking about it (rubbing his hurt leg, talking to it as if he'd been unjust to it, "Speak to me," he said) was like the decisions he makes second by second on stage: happily free from self-dramatizations, self-inflations, or temperament. In this he shows how much he is a dancer in the mode of Balanchine and of Balanchine's great company. He was being precise, calculating, tough-minded, and wholly unsentimental about the physical potentialities of his body and the needs of the company.

Edward Villella is now the greatest male dancer in the world, and he embodies the principle that makes Balanchine the greatest choreographer—that dancing is what it is and not something else, not drama, or literature, or business, though it might choose momentarily to involve itself with them, and above all not a way of life, however much it might affect the schedule of one's life. A dancer is what you are while you're dancing, and the better you dance the more intensely aware you become that it is not like anything else at all, and the freer you feel, therefore, about doing all kinds of other things without worrying about their effect on the seriousness of your dancing.

Villella is president of the Establishment Discothèques, Ltd. which means he owns part of the discothèque Arthur in New York and visits

Villella, the star of the New York City Ballet Company.

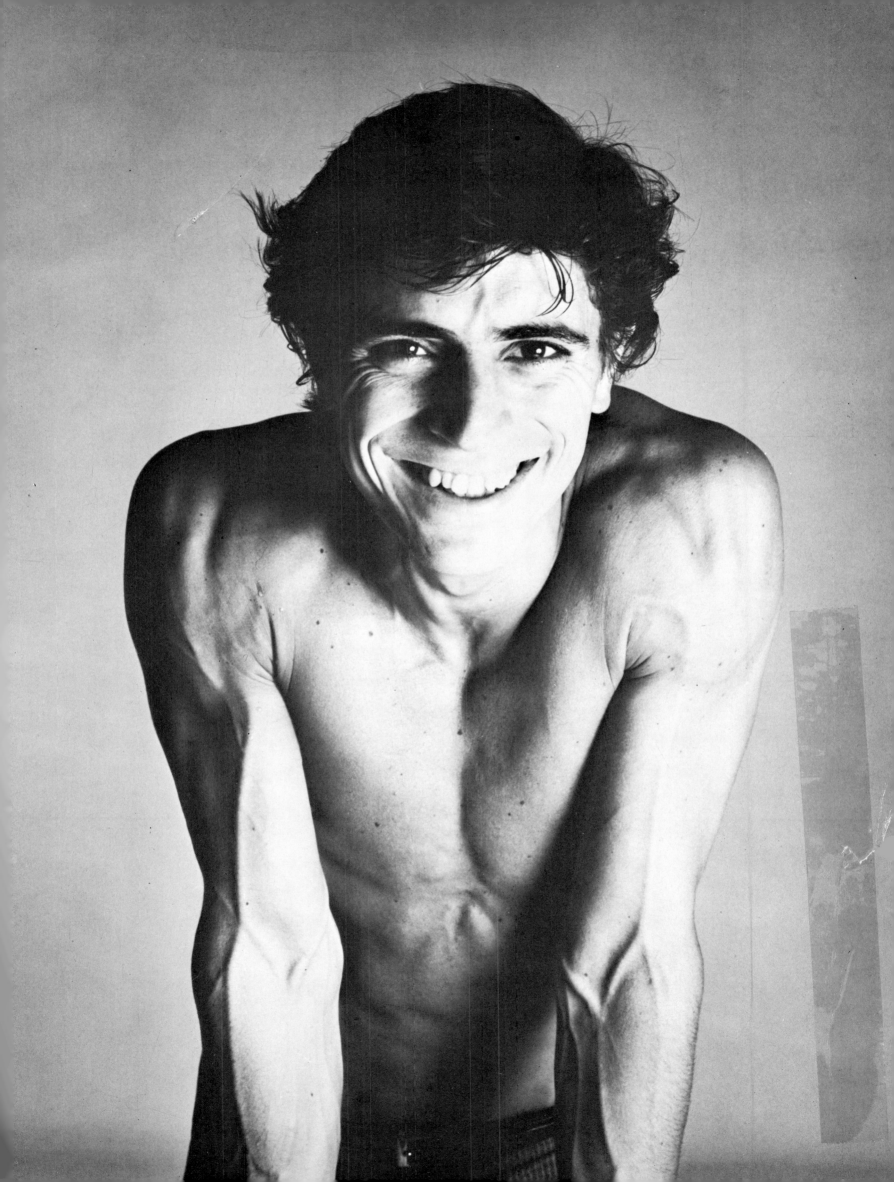

associated clubs that have opened in Detroit, Los Angeles, New Haven, and Washington, D.C. He can choreograph a television presentation of *Carousel* and also the brilliant and mysterious "Markissos" for the New York City Ballet, or be featured as an actor-dancer in *Brigadoon* while in his head he is working on the choreography to match Prokofiev's *First Violin Concerto* for a January première. Villella does all these things because his natural energy, ambition, and desire for money—he is married, thirty-two, and owns a house on the West Side —are simply up to them. He is also now a member of the National Council on the Arts and beginning to worry about two books he's promised to write, worrying characteristically about the *way* to do them, their proper shape and style. The first is to be a book about the experience of a principal ballet dancer, his approaches and techniques, and the second (mostly for younger readers) will be an account of his own experiences as a dancer.

Villella's interest in helping young people find their way to an appreciation of classical ballet takes him into still other activities, educational ones, sometimes for the Lincoln Center Fund and the New York State Council on the Arts. He's a remarkable teacher for many of the reasons that make him an unusually good conversationalist: he's really there, open and easy and a little amused at the situation in which he finds himself, and a bit inquisitive about the rôle playing of whomever he's talking to.

During a lecture demonstration at Manhattan's Metropolitan Vocational High School, the teenage boys were at first jostling and snooty, sprawlingly embarrassed, especially when they first caught sight of Villella in his ballet tights, and saw the pretty, cheerful, nicely ordinary face and pleasant body of Patricia McBride, his frequent partner. Ballet costumes are strange and were to these kids ridiculous. Villella enjoyed this reaction, because he too has felt it. To know that what you do or wear is very special for most other people can save what you do from weirdness and eccentricity: you don't claim too much for it by grandeurs, hauteurs, or literary amplifications. He was able to talk naturally to these kids about his body. It was as if he were an athlete, comparing the leap of a dancer to a leap for a ball in the outfield. Except that if a ballplayer were a dancer he would

have to think not only about catching something but, even while doing that, about the exact slant of his shoulders, the angle of his feet, the turn of his knees, the fall, say, of the fingers of his left hand.

In a sense ballet for Villella emerged from the sandlot. When, as a boy of ten in Bayside, New York, he was knocked out by a baseball and told by his parents to lay off the game for awhile, he took to walking with his sister to her lessons at the School of American Ballet. For want of something better to do, he soon joined her classes. He liked it, and so he began. But even after that, at the New York State Maritime College, where he earned a B.S. in marine transportation, sports were a part of him; he won a varsity letter in baseball and the campus welterweight boxing championship.

To elicit from ballet some of the pleasure of athletics is altogether more appropriate to it than are more genteel efforts to find in it the kinds of significance belonging to literature or pop psychology. Which isn't to dogmatize any kind of reaction. Ballet is like athletics, but it is something else, something more. It requires more stylized movement, a greater human muscular variety than do most sports, a submission of the body to the collective discipline of the music and of the other dancers.

During "Rubies," I unapologetically imagine watching the cavortings of a neighbourhood gang out of the late 'thirties. The boys frisk about, enjoying their own terrain, laying claim to it by celebratory leaps and bounds that press against its boundaries. They race, they seem to play various kinds of handball or basketball, they get now and then entangled with neighbourhood girls who want to be included, but on terms of which everyone is uncertain—whether they are being partnered for amourousness, a turn on the dance floor, or some inconclusive wrestling. Why the 'thirties? Because many of the dance movements by Villella, McBride, and the chorus are apparently allusive to dime and dance joints, dance marathons, to charmingly inexpert tries at jitterbugging or boogie-woogie.

Such imaginings greatly enhance the pleasure of anyone watching "Rubies," especially when the principals have the good looks and irresistible sociability on stage of Villella and McBride. But I'm assured by some people who dance in this part and in other parts of

"Jewels," that while on stage they aren't thinking about such characterizations at all. "But it's perfectly all right," said Villella reassuringly, "for you to think of them." While dancing, Villella isn't playing at being leader of the gang, proving his leadership by dynamic twists and turns, by movements that suggest he's cycling better than the rest or is better at skipping rope.

Instead he's thinking about the music, about his own body in relation to music, about what Balanchine has created by translating the music into the space and time of bodily movement. Continuity here is a matter not of "story" but of sequences, combinations of movement, and the dancers invent their small innovations that get settled into the piece for bodily convenience, pleasure, and communication between one dancer and another. But no one ever tells anyone in Balanchine's ballet company to move in order to characterize a dramatic rôle; you move to characterize the music.

Villella can not be understood as a dancer and can't himself talk for very long about dancing without honouring the genius of Balanchine. In relation to his dancers Balanchine is as punishing as he is generous. He is generous in making ballets for the particular bodies and temperaments of particular dancers. Imagine a young woman like Suzanne Farrell or a young man like John Prinz, the best of the male dancers of a group younger than Villella, receiving as a kind of gift a masterpiece fitted specifically to their dimensions and potentialities!

The repertoire of the New York City Ballet is more vital and changing than any in the world, and the requirements of the dancers are correspondingly greater, because Balanchine is always discovering new things about their bodies, inventing new things about the human body in general. His extraordinary burst of creativity in the past three or four years is directly the result, I suspect, of his having finally mined some of the human resources now available to him. "Rubies" was written for Villella, and is almost for that reason the most difficult of ballets for him when it comes to physical expenditure. Technically, he doesn't find the rôle especially difficult, even though his spectacular mid-air turns may make it look so to the audiences. More difficult for him from a technical point of view is a ballet like "Apollo," written originally

for Serge Lifar and later changed for d'Amboise, and easier in all respects are bravura rôles like the Tchaikovsky "Pas De Deux" and "Stars and Stripes," pieces that call mostly for tricks.

"Rubies" is shaped to Villella's technical capacities; he is not asked to do anything that he can not do, but for that very reason Balanchine wants to push these capacities to the limit of Villella's physical powers: his animal grace and boldness, his unrivaled capacity for quick acceleration and for elasticity in slowing down, his capacity to maintain coherence of movement, so that the unfolding of the whole dance takes on the excitement of a plot—what can happen now?

Villella's immersion in "Rubies," or in other starring rôles for Balanchine, is evident in his activities before an evening performance: at least ninety minutes of exercise class in the morning, two hours of rehearsal in the afternoon, a massage or whirlpool bath to relieve knots and pains, something to eat and a brief rest period, then a couple of hours warming up before performances, ending with practice of the part in an exercise room while the first section of "Jewels" is on stage.

And then it's his turn—to expend everything in concentrated bursts of energy that scarcely give him an interval to fall to the floor off stage, as he sometimes does, getting his breath and kneading his muscles with his hands before the next entrance. Coming back from his elegant curtain calls, he's winded, sweating from his whole body, but intensely eager for some kind of further engagement, juiced with accumulated excitements, ready to talk of what he's just done or about anything else, anxious to give forth, gasping for breath though he is, the enormous powers built up with too brief a time for their release.

"Jewels" is only one of the most "beautiful" of Balanchine's ballets, but it can probably claim to be the most illustrative. It's a kind of anthology by the Prospero of this magnificent group. Each of its parts echoes and retrospectively enhances the enormous variety of his work going back to 1924 and including the choreography for more than 150 ballets, eighteen musicals, and six movies. It anthologizes, too, the human resources presently at his disposal, each section being a gift to what are now his best dancers, an opportunity for the display of their powers: Violette Verdy in the first part, "Emeralds"; Villella in the second part, "Rubies"; and Suzanne Farrell in the third and last, "Diamonds."

The green serenity of "Emeralds" suggests not the jewel so much as a pastoral world, at once fresh and formal, inhabited by explorers transfigured from some more formalized existence. The suggestion is accentuated by the beautiful solo work of Miss Verdy, especially when she is allowed to dance to Fauré's "Pélleas et Mélisande." Her hands curl up past her neck, her arms extending in beautifully circuitous movements, as if celebrating some new discovery of their flexibility and grace, now of one arm, now of the other. Pastoralism is evident, too, in the exquisite duet of Francisco Moncion and Kay Mazzo, with its delicate stateliness of movement, and in the calm authority of John Prinz, at once courtly and crisp, during his *pas de trois* with Sara Leland and Suki Schorer. All these partnerings are immunized from the excited, youthfully unself-conscious eroticism in "Rubies," danced to Stravinsky's "Capriccio for Piano and Orchestra."

A way of looking at "Rubies," and for that matter at a series of Balanchine's ballets that would include such disparate pieces as "Serenade," "Episodes," and "Bugaku," a rôle to which Villella has set the standard for all subsequent interpretations, is that the work is about the effort to achieve some ideal physical and human harmony in partnering; in the duet between a man and a woman.

The eroticism of Balanchine's choreography, as Robert Garis was among the first to notice in any full way, really distinguishes him from other classical choreographers. In the comically grotesque, charmingly youthful duets in "Rubies" between Villella and the engaging Miss McBride, in the hilarious frolickings between Marnee Morris and the four men who are, as it were, Villella's pals and cohorts—Richard Dryden, Deni Lamont, Robert Weiss, and the highly promising Paul Mejia—one repeatedly sees men turning away from masculine sports toward a momentary romp with their women, an exploration, however, that soon breaks off for further showoff play on both sides.

In "Rubies" there are scarcely any pauses, as these sequences repeat themselves and get enacted through Villella's almost unbelievable changes of momentum, his control of turns and reversals, of jumps that veer off course, changes of direction, acceleration in movements whose power threatens to take him out of the environment of the group within which the movement takes or its special meaning. "Rubies" is full of engrossing *non sequiturs*—in the meetings between men and women and in the rapid changes of gesture that refer us now to one kind of social image, now to another.

Expectations aroused and sweetly delayed occur too in the dancing by which Miss Morris seems to be heading into a split, goes instead into a squat and from there to an exit stage right, while her boy playmates head off stage left in stylized chain gang fashion. "Rubies" is followed by the formal elegances of "Diamonds," with its long, romantically beautiful *pas de deux* in which one sees, in contrast to anything in "Rubies," both arms of the man, sometimes Jacques d'Amboise, sometimes the new dancer from Denmark, Peter Martins, joined in possessive gestures around the body of Suzanne Farrell. Through all this, as one watches d'Amboise, and remembers him when he was dancing more than he does now, or sees Martins, who is a mere twenty-two, or John Prinz emerging as a great dancer, it's evident that Villella's preeminence is by virtue of genius rather than default.

Irving Berlin

BY ALLAN BROAD

PHOTOGRAPHED
BY HENRI CARTIER-BRESSON

Irving Berlin, a coony, complex man conditioned for fifty years to almost unceasing acclaim for the rough yearn, the skill and pull of his acutely simple songs, the non-anonymous folk songs of the whole country, has confusingly run into bumps with his score for the new musical, *Mr. President*. In Boston in late August he suddenly got a touch of the critical whip. It flicked at his age, it flicked at the lyrics, it even flicked at his flag waving in "This Is a Great Country," a song to rouse every patriotic instinct with its impassioned lyrics and its marching beat. It is hard at seventy-four to get a battering. It was pleasant, however, to get a report from Russel Crouse, one of the co-authors of the book, that the Saturday matinée audience, primarily middle-aged women with grey-white hair, had lustily enjoyed watching Robert Ryan as the President tuck himself into bed, listening to Nanette Fabray as the President's wife singing "They Love Me" with just enough resemblance to Mrs. John Kennedy to make her cheeky lines have triple meanings. This stage President fortunately has only three true worries: Russia, his son's speeding, and the late hour his daughter comes home from parties. No Cuba, no Congress.

The story behind the opening nights in New York, Boston, and Washington is absurdly simple. After twelve years of idleness, following *Call Me Madam*, Irving Berlin found himself thoroughly bored. He had an idea for a musical with an outgoing President as the lead. He took his notion to his friends, Russel Crouse and Howard Lindsay, with whom he had worked on *Madam*. They liked the idea and from them the idea travelled a few blocks to Leland Hayward and thence to Joshua Logan. The first releases went out, and almost before plans were really in work, the benefit party agents climbed in. By last April, before Hayward signed the cast, the dates were set for some one hundred or more organizations to take benefits. Committee chairman organized luncheons and teas, began sending out notes suggesting early applications for seats. Just about this time the Lieutenant Joseph P. Kennedy, Jr. Institute and the Kennedy Child Study Center for Retarded Children took *Mr. President* as a benefit in Washington, with dinners arranged before and a supper dance afterwards, the seats $100 each. After full-page advertisements appeared in the newspapers, the money came mailed in from all three cities. Almost before the cast went into rehearsal, the Boston and Washington engagements were sold out. New advertisements asked people to stop sending money.

During the summer, the five principals, Berlin, Logan, Crouse, Lindsay, and Hayward sat on the blue brocaded seats of the empty Lunt-Fontanne Theatre listening to eager auditioners. It was pretty relaxed, especially the afternoon the belly dancers tried out, the afternoons when the applicants, thin and young, sang for the part of the President's son. Standing under the big work light, the boys, diffident, apologetic for somehow not being prepared, sang their own choice of songs, almost always for some tactless reasoning, a tune from the song bag of Richard Rodgers, often "Mountain Greenery."

No one sang from that treasury of standards, the bulging bag of Irving Berlin. No one sang "Alexander's Ragtime Band," "A Pretty Girl Is Like a Melody," "All Alone," "Always," "Blue Skies," "Easter Parade," "White Christmas," "How Deep Is the Ocean?"

It was odd. They seemed to ignore the small, dark-haired man, with the jutting jaw, the black-rimmed glasses, the chunky smile, the tanned glow, the obvious happiness at being back in the theatre, even if the business is less fun than it was in the old days with Sam Harris and Flo Ziegfeld. "There are too many lawyers in the machinery," Berlin said.

He had never heard of lawyers in show business when he started on the Bowery near China-town singing parodies of pop songs at the Pelham Café. Like many of his friends, he was a school drop-out. After two years in public school he quit when his father died. Irving was eight years old. In time he worked up to the Pelham Café, singing, clowning, waiting on table —the crew got nickels and dimes for tips with perhaps eight dollars thrown on the floor on Saturday nights. (Last summer on a photographic tour of his old places he told Henri Cartier-Bresson: "Everybody ought to have a lower East Side in their life.") He early drifted into writing songs—he needed them and he had no money to pay for them. He wrote character songs in Italian and Yiddish dialect. "No one was sensitive in those days. I can't get dramatic about poverty. Everyone I knew was poor. The parents worried but the kids had a hell of a good time. We didn't know about failure; you can't fail until you've been a success once. As I got some experience, I got some education. I can laugh now at some of my terrible songs. I sometimes wrote four a night, stealing bits and pieces from others. But not 'Alexander's Ragtime Band.' That is still good, still played after more than fifty years. I even saw the movie on the 'Late Show' a while ago. The work is harder now. You get on to yourself and you start being a severe critic. It stops you up."

In those early days, nothing stopped him up. The music publishing houses began using his stuff; he began getting a song or two into big musicals. For his first important show, *Watch Your Step*, starring Irene and Vernon Castle, he worked with Harry B. Smith, a bald, intellectual man who loved Dickens, rare books, and sim-ple-minded librettos. Charles Dillingham once put in the program credits of one of his shows: "Plot, if any, by Harry B. Smith." Berlin's songs had a fresh syncopated rhythm, played some-time as in "Play a Simple Melody," with the rag against the beat. Soon after came his big Gaby Deslys show, *Stop, Look and Listen*, which almost came into the world as *Chicken à la King*. Among the songs for that musical were the young and still lovely, "The Girl on the Magazine Cover," and "I Love a Piano."

From the great Charles Dillingham he moved over to another superb producer, Flo Ziegfeld, an eccentric, extraordinary man whose personal extravagances could only be equalled by his business ones. He once chartered a 110-foot yacht in Palm Beach that he never pulled anchor on. He wanted it only to allow his daughter to invite some children to play on it. One day near the end of the rehearsals for a *Follies*, Ziegfeld showed Berlin some costume sketches for the big show girls.

"I need a song to follow," Ziegfeld said, "got one?"

"Yeah." said Berlin. "A Pretty Girl Is Like a Melody."

The song went in without a Joseph Urban set, without any planning by Ned Wayburn, the director. When the *Follies* opened in Atlantic City, John Steel, with only a black velvet drop behind him, stood quietly and sang "A Pretty Girl Is Like a Melody" to instant success. The song is now a classic in the Berlin repertory.

The big days for Berlin were not his Ziegfeld and Dillingham years, but his years with his friend, Sam Harris, another Bowery boy. In his time Harris ran a wash tub into a city block of wash tubs. He pushed Terrible Terry Mc-Govern, a pug-nose who trained at roadhouses, into three fight championships. He even had a horse, Sadie S., that came near winning the Chicago Derby. He walked into show business by the back door and ended with a string of successes and his own house, the Music Box Theatre which he built with Berlin.

A solid, small man who had laughter lines like scratches across his rugged face—somewhat like Berlin these days—Harris had, like Berlin, something friendly and pleasant that had long resisted analysis. For both men, the romance of their show life came in building the Music Box Theatre.

HENRI CARTIER-BRESSON

Berlin with his old upright piano, which has a lever to change the board into whatever key he needs.

One Sunday late in 1921, after reading about a coming auction of some West Forty-fifth Street property, he called Irving Berlin, then high with success. Harris had a plan. He wanted to buy that property, build a theatre, and house there the biggest and best stock company in the land. Berlin agreed. They bought the land, and, dropping the stock company idea, began building the Music Box on a budget of $600,000. Somehow the cost ran up to a million, with Harris borrowing the last $400,000. Much as he borrowed for his first production, *Little Johnny Jones* in 1904, he borrowed for the *Music Box Revue* in 1922. To make even more impressive the gambling horror of his situation he engaged Hassard Short, the wildest spendthrift director in town, a man with an abnormal passion for rising stage elevators, for Rube Goldbergian mechanics. By the opening night Sam H. Harris was once again cleaned out—temporarily.

During the middle of the construction of the Music Box, Berlin was cleaned out. He went to Joseph Schenck, his closest friend ever since the days when Schenck was a drugstore clerk at No. 6 the Bowery, an address still remembered by Berlin. By 1921 Schenck was a movie power and it was to his office that Berlin went.

"Joe," said Berlin, "I'm in trouble."

"What's her name?" asked Schenck.

"We need money to complete the Music Box. John Golden says the boys think they are building a monument, but they're building a tombstone. You can have 50% of my 50%."

"Done," said Schenck. "Here's a check."

For the next months Berlin kept asking for more money and getting it. At last Schenck came to Forty-fifth Street to see the house. Berlin tried to thank him, saying, "We've done our best."

Schenck said flatly, "Irving, all I've put in this is some money, you've put your heart."

Along with their hearts, Berlin and Harris put there the famous *Music Box Revues*, the first of which cost about $180,000 only because its director had a compulsion for extravagance almost as great as Flo Ziegfeld's. (In those days most revues ran to about $50,000.) Later on, during the Depression, Harris put on *Face the Music* with Berlin's score which included "Let's Have Another Cup o' Coffee," and *As Thousands Cheer* in which Clifton Webb sang the Berlin song, "Not for All the Rice in China," Ethel Waters boiled up his song, "Heat Wave," and the whole works came to a big beautiful beige climax with "Easter Parade."

After the rouser of *As Thousands Cheer* in 1933, it took him seven years to turn up the steam for *Louisiana Purchase* in 1940, but only two years to do so for the miracle of *This Is the Army* in 1942, and then another four years before *Annie Get Your Gun*. It is his theory that his best scores have general songs that fit the plot situation. In *Annie*, he had, among others, "Doin' What Comes Naturally" and "You Can't Get a Man With a Gun" to prove his point. He has another theory that hotel bedrooms in try-out cities give him an inspirational push that is part desperation plus adrenal stimulation. Bizarre hurry drove him to write "You're Just in Love" to fill a miserable hole in *Call Me Madam* when Ethel Merman and Russell Nype were stuck on stage in New Haven. To fill a yawn in *Mr. President* Berlin wrote in "Empty Pockets Filled with Love" at the Ritz in Boston Because songs that sound like hits during auditions often droop in performance, Berlin once said "there is no such thing as a hit in a room." In his long show-tune span of forty-eight years, in his song-writing career that began fifty-eight years ago with his first published song, "Marie from Sunny Italy," Irving Berlin has never had a true flop. At times he's been cuffed around a hit; he's been bruised but never flattened. Now at seventy-four, resilient, bouncy, Irving Berlin is happy with a show in town. Blasting at critics is for David Merrick, but Berlin gets contentment just at the sight of a theatre filled again with audiences hearing Berlin's non-anonymous folk songs.

The Cultural Schizophrenia of Luis Valdez

BY STAN STEINER

In the vineyards of the San Joaquin Valley in California the children of the Aztecs stoop in the fields, like beggars. The migrants with torn clothes and worn faces picking grapes and onions hardly look like the sons of warriors. Who then are these men? "The last divine Aztec Emperor Cuauhtémoc was murdered and his descendants were put to work in the fields," said Luis Miguel Valdez, a young poet of the farm workers, "we are still there, in the fields of America."

On Highway 99 through the San Joaquin Valley one sees them; the dark faces of the children squeezed into the chicken wire on the back of pickup trucks, watching the highway rushing away, always. Where are they going? All they ever see is where they have been. In the words of Luis Valdez's song:

> Children are on the road in summers,
> winters and springs, crossing states
> and counties
> and cities that are foreign. Like
> swallows come
> down from the heavens they give
> themselves
> flight to their true desires.

Had not the "Songs of Sorrow" of the Aztecs mourned: "We are crushed to the ground," and the poet-priests intoned:

> Nothing but flowers and songs of
> sorrow
> are left in Mexico. We wander here
> and there
> in our desolate poverty.

The Aztecs had called their scared spectacles the "Wars of Flowers." When the *Huelga* began—the strike of the migrants in the vineyards of California—the first farm workers to strike were those in the flower fields; this was called the "Strike of the Roses."

The old trucks shivered down the dirt roads, bussing the "flower-children" to the vineyards. And the song they sang was Luis Valdez's "Los Ninos Campesinos"—"Song of the Farm Workers' Children"; a nursery rhyme of lament that the "People of the Sun" could have sung in the fields of their conquerors.

> One, two, three, four, five, six in
> the morning
> the sun warms wide ranches and
> bathes them in
> light, and to the camps go the
> children of the
> migrants, without a destination,
> without a destination.
> They are truly wanderers.

There are laws that frown upon child labour, keeping the children out of the fields most of the time. Except at harvest time. The growers will then welcome every helping hand, the hand of the smallest child; for when the grapes are heavy on the vines and the plums are purple ripe, if the fruit is not plucked it will rot prematurely, or dry to prunes and raisins in the sun. Children are then beckoned to the fields. The families of *campesinos*, too, need every hand that will help them pluck enough earnings to get through the winter. Laws of child labour are superseded by the higher laws of survival.

Once, in one of his lives, Luis Miguel Valdez was one of these children. A young man with grandiose Pancho Villa moustache, a Brechtian poet, a union organizer, a sometime college teacher, an alumnus of the San Francisco Mime Troupe, and the director of El Teatro Campesino, now renowned. ("A tough act to follow," wrote *The Wall Street Journal*.)

In November 1965, just two months after the *Huelga* in the San Joaquin Valley began, he established the Commedia dell' Arte of the farm workers—El Teatro Campesino. Established is too grandiose a word. In makeshift union halls and at roadside picket lines, with no scripts, no props, no stage, no experience, no actors, Luis Valdez created a theatre. Huzzahed from coast to coast, the troupe had engaged audiences from Stanford to Howard University, had starred at the Newport Folk Festival in Rhode Island and on television in New York City, had been awarded an "Obie" by the Off-Broadway critics, had performed before the U.S. Senate's Subcommittee of Migratory Labor and in the courtyard of the old Senate Office Building. It had performed at the invitation of the late Senator Robert F. Kennedy. Senator Edward Kennedy sang its strike songs.

Luis Miguel Valdez grew up in the fields, a child of *campesinos*. As soon as he was old enough, he picked grapes in Delano, California, where he was born. He heard the night wails in the migrant camps of those whose bone-bent hands were riven as claws by the picking, and he heard the sonorous songs of drunken joys of those who danced in the *cantinas* after work. He learned them as a poet will, and he remembers them as in a poet's dream.

"As a kid I can remember that Delano was a very different sort of town than it is now," he said. "There was a street several blocks long that had Mexican shops, a Mexican show, a Mexican dance hall. There were Mexican things for sale, Mexican candy, Mexican clothes, Mexican food. It was a place full of character—Mexican character.

"Little Mexico they called it. That's what it was. It resembled Mexico. It wasn't like we know California today.

"And then!" The young man shut his fist and jabbed the air with sudden anger, or was it despair? He squinted at his shattered memory. "Then! Six or seven years ago our whole section of town was ripped away. The freeway came through.

"You see, there were twenty-two whorehouses on one street to solace the single men who worked in the fields. Well, 'they' couldn't accept those whorehouses. They told us the freeway was urban renewal. It cleaned up our part of town. So the freeway came through like a surgical knife and cut out the very heart of our side of Delano. Urban renewal?" he laughed with a flicker of his teeth. "For whom?"

"A lot of people were upset," he said. "They had taken away our towns, our personality. It's not surprising that this town exploded and became the heart of the *Huelga*. They filled our hearts with emptiness. There is a contempt for Mexican things in the Valley.

"This is a society largely hostile to our cultural values," he said. "There is nothing poetic about the United States. No depth, no faith, no allowance for human contradictions, no soul, no mariachi, no chili sauce, no *pulque*, no mysticism, no *chingaderas*."

Luis Valdez had left the Valley when he was fourteen. Searching for what? He hardly knew. A freer life perhaps, or to flee the stigma of contempt for the "dumb Mex." He went to the cities. The young *chicanos*, the Mexican Americans, were leaving the little towns in the vineyards, hitchhiking out, joining the Army, looking for jobs in the cities, doing anything to get away, just wandering.

Education, everyone said, was salvation. His search led him, as it has so many bright, angered, restless young men, to the doors of a university.

Valdez suffered from "cultural schizophrenia," he said. And he described why he was forced to flee from the university: "I had an aunt who had worms crawling out of her stomach. We wrapped her in clothes, every day we wrapped her in clothes, but the worms kept crawling out of her stomach. I saw those worms. Then, when I went to college in San Jose, I was in a bio-chemistry course, and they showed us this film: I think it was an educational film about one disease or another. There was a boy with a bloated belly in the film, and there were worms crawling out of his stomach. I walked out of the class and I never went back."

Luis Valdez has a scathing laugh. It bursts from him unexpectedly, in a gust. It is ironic without being cynical, for he fiercely enjoys the irony. "That was no identity crisis. That was an identity catastrophe," he said. He wrote: "It is not enough to say we suffer an identity crisis, because that crisis has been our way of life for the last five centuries."

The odyssey of Luis Miguel Valdez led him back to the vineyards of Delano. He returned

to search for his origins. He brought home his suitcase full of the remnants of his education in the university and Haight-Ashbury and the unfinished play, *The Shrunken Head of Pancho Villa*, that he had written about his search.

"Life was absurd back then when I lived in San Francisco," he said. "Silly and tragic. I was trying to relate to the pre-hippie Haight-Ashbury, and I felt ridiculous. Moving back to Delano was a real, common sensical act for me. I can not begin to explain how much it was like 'coming home.' Without sentiment, you understand, only clear-headed *doing.*"

Huelga had come to the Valley. The upheaval in the lives of the farmers and migrants brought about by the *Huelga*, the strike of the grape pickers, had loosened a half-century of apathy that had hovered over the *barrios* in the immobile heat. Like a summer storm the *Huelga* struck. It was not merely a strike but a bolt of lightning that illuminated the Valley with an ugly, brutal, and naked truth, and every town looked strangely new born.

The prodigal was ecstatic. "*Huelga* means strike," Luis Valdez wrote, "with the poetic instinct of *La Raza* (The Race—the People) the Delano grape pickers have made it mean a dozen other things. It is a declaration, a challenge, a greeting, a feeling, a movement. It is the most significant word in our entire Mexican-American history. If *La Raza* in Mexico believe in *La Patria* (homeland) we believe in *La Huelga.*

"You can see a new spirit in the people," he said. "Where they were shy and retiring and frightened about American society, now they're expressive, courageous, and determined. The farm worker who has never said anything is now speaking."

Valdez heard singing in the vineyards. No wonder: The *campesinos* marched to the *Huelga* every dawn in song.

No one had sung in the vineyards when Luis Valdez was a boy. It was not because they knew no songs, or had no thoughts that sang. It is the heart that sings. Songs were for the churches and *cantinas*. Now the songs burst into the fields and unto the dirt roads with the coming of the *Huelga*—as in the fiestas of the Saints.

On the picket lines there were rude paintings of The Virgin, Biblical sayings, and Spanish songs. Choruses were organized by the union,

one for the men and women and one for the children. The union newspaper of the farm workers, *El Malcriado* (*The Mischievous One,* or *The Ill-Bred*) became an embryonic anthology of poems, stories, and essays. In the dull, dusty Valley there was a revival of *campesino* culture, said Valdez. He laughingly called it: "The cultural revolution of those who were too uneducated and too illiterate to know they were supposed to be culturally deprived."

Gusty, gregarious, and full of "genius and hot chili," Luis Miguel Valdez joined the *Huelga*. He was but one of hundreds of young *chicanos* who came to the vineyards of Delano that summer from the cities and universities. They came as if to Mecca.

The feeling of wholeness that comes of being one of a whole people overwhelmed Valdez. "I was stoned with emotion," he said. "No kidding, it was a wild feeling." Soon after the *Huelga* began he started El Teatro Campesino.

El Teatro's "actors" were farm workers, the vineyards the stage, the drama improvised by the *campesinos* themselves. Felipe Cantu became the star performer. An obscure grape picker who had worked, he said, at everything from "a policeman to a clown," he is a volatile man, the father of seven children. He "resembles a Mexican version of Ben Turpin," said Valdez: "He speaks no English, but his wild, extravagant Cantinflas-like comic style needs no words."

Yet another grape picker was Agustin Lira. Hardly twenty, an intense and sensitive young man, he became El Teatro's guitarist and poet. Lira's lyrics, "Yo No Le Tengo Miedo a Nada," (I Am Not Afraid of Anything"), and "Ser Como el Aire Libre" ("To Be Free as the Wind") are gentle and bitter evocations of the wandering migrants:

> When I was little,
> My mother said,
> Take care, my son,
> Don't get in trouble.
> Now that I am grown up,
> These words pain me,
> For life is long,
> And I go through it crying.

There was an Indian cowboy, Errol Franklin of Cheyenne, Wyoming. Lean and thin, he had been a horsebreaker, fisherman, apple picker, short-order cook, and longshoreman before coming to the Valley as a strikebreaker. He joined the *Huelga* and became the mask maker for El Teatro, doubling as the stage cop.

"The Teatro by its mere existence condemns the real loss of the human talent, the deadening of the human spirit, the brutalization of the mind and body caused by the callous feudal exploitation that is farm labour today; El Teatro is somewhere between Brecht and Cantinflas," Valdez wrote in *Ramparts*.

Using gargoyle masks and loud signs the company acts out the *actos*. This word is one El Teatro originated, as they did the theatrical form of quick, satiric, and baroque slapsticked-together morality plays of unionism. Each actor wears a sign of his character; ROTTEN GRAPE says the sign on the chest of one man who is picked from an imaginary vine and thrown into a garbage can by another man whose sign says, ESQUIREL (Squirrel, the *campesino* epithet for a strikebreaker). The lines are burlesqued. It is "proletarian pantomime," wrote the critic for *The Wall Street Journal*, but that is because he could not understand the Spanish. Neither could a Spaniard. It is the patois of the *campesino* world of jukeboxes, fiestas, and soap operas on Mexican television. It derives from the oldest theatrical tradition, the symbolism of Aztec rituals and of evil and good, the heaven and hell typecasting of the church plays of Spanish Catholicism.

Theatre has deep roots in the Southwestern deserts. On these ancient lands the earliest native plays and poems and books on American themes were written.

In the early 1500's the first formal theatre, in the European sense, was performed in Mexico. The *Conversion of the Four Kings of Tlaxcala* that was offered at that time to the remnants of the Aztec armies has been called "the first American play" by Dr. C. E. Castañeda of the Texas Catholic Historical Society.

"Theatrical performances began in Mexico shortly after the arrival of the Conquerors," says Riva Palacio, the Mexican scholar. "In all religious and political celebrations care was taken to include some sacred comedy or Corpus Christi Play, which was usually performed in the open air . . . In the famous festival of Corpus Christi at Tlaxcala in 1538, an elaborate *auto* was given, the subject being the sin of Adam and Eve." Indians were the actors, Palacio says, and they performed "in their own language."

And there were the fabulous horse-plays of the Southwestern settlers—*Los Moros y Los Cristianos* and *Los Comanches*. In these spectacles a poetic script of romantic oratory was wedded to the derring-do of a dramatic rodeo. They were performed in the fields, with armies of villagers in supporting rôles.

El Teatro Campesino did not spring innocent and ignorant out of the San Joaquin Valley, nor even out of the ingenious mind of Luis Miguel Valdez. The young poet of the *Huelga* knows this. He says of his theatrical origins:

"Once we had our own gods. We had Quetzalcoatl. Then Western civilization came with new gods: Well the Indian conversion is a matter of history. What did happen to those old gods? What happened to that ancient view of life? Does it influence us? I think it does. It is still there.

"The conquest of Mexico was no conquest at all. It shattered our ancient Indian universe, but more of it was left above ground than beans and tortillas. Below the foundations of our Spanish culture, we still sense the ruins of an entirely different civilization.

"Most of us know we are not Europeans simply by looking in a mirror—the shape of the eyes, the curve of the nose, the colour of the skin, the texture of the hair; these things belong to another time, another people. With a million little stubborn mannerisms, beliefs, myths, superstitions, words, thoughts—things not easily detected—they fill our Spanish life with Indian contradictions."

And Valdez added, "The old Aztec universe was a universe of contradictions." He gritted his teeth. And his grin became a grimace. The young man with the big cigar—he is a chain smoker, or chewer, of long Cuban-style cigars —took the cigar out of his mouth to think aloud.

"Somehow, away from this chaos, away from this American life, back in my memory, there's a different sort of life. There is a more stable life, full of traditions, of beauty, with a human view of people. And I sometimes look back at this with a great deal of nostalgia. It's kind of foolish. How can I have a memory of the Aztecs, of Mexico? It's impossible because I was born in Delano, California."

Where does his memory come from? "It's a feeling more than a memory," Valdez said, "though it feels like a memory.

"Culture? What about culture?" he continued. "It is akin to a political act, when a man stands up and takes his life in his hands and says, 'I am going to change my life.' That's what culture is all about. I feel that before you get any political act out of a man that man has to feel a certain pride in himself. He has to touch his own dignity, his own destiny.

"*La Raza* needs the arts to tell itself where it is," he said.

"The arts are largely prophetic. Even the Teatro. Many of the things we do on stage now prefigure the course of social action that *La Raza* will take in the future. We have been organizing the organizers. Let me explain that: The Blacks have a tradition in the arts that is as old as the country. Theatre, poetry, novels, essays, paintings, music; they have been expressing what they feel for a long time. Good and bad ideas, but articulated thoughts nonetheless. Ideas about the Black people's relation to the white society that oppresses them. Marcus Garvey, Booker T. Washington, W. E. B. Du Bois, Malcolm X, James Baldwin, Richard Wright. Some of their ideas have suggested integration, some segregation, some a complete return to Africa, but they have all suggested *something*. Black liberation is predicated on ideas that have gone before.

"We don't have that," Luis Valdez said. "There is no *chicano* leader who has put his finger on our problem because we have lacked the poets, novelists, and essayists that prefigure the appearance of such a leader of leaders."

Luis Valdez and his troupe have joined the migrations of the poor *campesinos*, going north to the village of Del Rey, the village of The King, near Fresno, California. It is a tiny village of one thousand. Poor and unknown, it lies hidden from the highway in the midst of the region where the grapes of the raisins grow. Some say it is the village of the Swineherd. That too is the meaning of Del Rey. Near the village there are two dozen more villages of migrants. Their names describe these dots on the map of California: Raisin, Malaga, Conejo (Rabbit Wire), Orange Cove, Naranjo (The Orange), El Nido (The Hen's Nest), and a place named Tranquility. In the harvest season the countryside is home to tens of thousands of migrants living in the camps, by the roadside, under the bridges.

Why bury his theatre in so godforsaken a rural ghetto?

The contempt is only in his eyes. His voice is weary with the reply he has so often given: "We are not aspiring to Broadway. We aspire to build a theatre among our people. That's the whole bit about the Teatro. We are not a theatre *for* farm workers, farm workers are our theatre," he says. "Besides, we are trying to build something bigger than a theatre."

In an old brick building on the corner of Wildwood and Morro Streets in the village of the King (of the migrants?) Luis Valdez is building the Centro Campesino Cultural. He added: "In English you could call it La Raza Folk Cultural Center. But it will be more than that. Someday it will be a centre for *chicanos* all through the Southwest."

The building is dilapidated and threadbare. In its inauspicious interior, hardly 50 feet by 50 feet, "We have our art classes—life drawing and children's art," Valdez said. "We have guitar lessons. We have our Teatro. We have 'history happenings,' every two or three weeks, dealing with the history of *La Raza*. *Actos* about La Conquista (The Conquest), the Alamo, Gold Rush, the Cisco Kid, and Pancho Villa."

Workshops for farm workers are envisioned; classes in the making of woodcuts, murals, and sculpture; photography and language classes; and the writing of a "primer and colouring book" to teach "the young Mexican American his twenty-thousand-year-old heritage." These workshops are to be free to the *campesinos* and their families.

"*Campesinos* are far from 'culturally deprived,'" says a brochure of the Centro Campesino Cultural; "They possess and live within a 'culture'—one that is, however, largely unfamiliar to the mass of English-speaking North Americans. It is a culture native to a great part of the United States and has been for the last four hundred years. It is an untapped resource of human experience . . . The Mexican-American farm worker in the Southwest has long been denied the tools of (his) cultural expression . . . El Centro Campesino Cultural is an attempt to hand over these tools—the tools of the arts—directly to the Spanish-speaking people of the Southwest . . ."

Poverty is what most people think of when they think of *campesinos*, if they think of them at all. The *campesinos* live in huts and makeshift trailers, in *colonias* without water, electric lights, or sewers. They are hungry for bread half the time, or meat, or a drink of wine. The children are poorly schooled and parents often illiterate, and the television sets broken. The *campesinos* cling to the edges of the rural towns.

Why talk of the poverty of the poor? Valdez said: "Everyone knows the poor are poor. That's no news. It's our way of life."

"*Chingaderas!*" he exclaimed. "Here in the United States, *La Raza* is confused by the bourgeois *chingaderas* all around. The car, the house, the furniture, the TV—all these things are *chingaderas*, because they are the second-hand, used objects handed down from the genuinely bourgeois life of your prosperous middle class. I am using Octavio Paz's definition of *chingada*, meaning not merely the 'Great Whore,' but a place of broken-down things faraway and distant. Look, we don't need your broken-down TV sets. We don't need the scraps of your culture.

"There are beautiful things in our lives," he said. "We have had them in our past and we will have them again. We will create own own 'flowers and songs.' "

But, the old building of the Centro Campesino Cultural is not yet blooming with "flowers and songs." Luis Miguel Valdez sat down to write a letter: "The roof is leaking again," he wrote. "I mean the ceiling. The neighbours upstairs pour water all over the floor in an effort to drown the cockroaches. The water is flooding part of my desk."

Saul Bellow: Master Writer

In one Nureyev leap, Saul Bellow suddenly, after twenty years and five novels, has become with his sixth, *Herzog*, the big American novelist, a disciplined craftsman, a creator of characters that stick in the mind as though written with ink and epoxy. Just after *Herzog* appeared, Bellow's first full-length play, *The Last Analysis*, showed up for a short time on Broadway. It swung surrealistically, witty, cracked, sometimes on target, sometimes far off, its central character, Bummidge, an aging actor who psychoanalyzed himself on a closed television circuit. Bummidge and Herzog are blood brothers and their second cousin is Bellow, a slight, greying University of Chicago professor. His talk is delightful, colloquial, forthright. His eyes, ringed like those of an eagle, are older than his handsome face—and his mind is far older than both, overflowing with a marvellous ranging erudition. In describing Moses Herzog, the slight greying professor, Bellow wrote that Herzog thought he was going out of his mind and began writing "endlessly, fanatically, to the newspapers, to people in public life, to friends and relatives, and at last to the dead, his own obscure dead, and finally the famous dead." In addition, Herzog "sometimes imagined he was an industry that manufactured personal history, and saw himself from birth to death." (So Bummidge saw himself.) In between, Herzog leads a full and often ridiculous life, set down with gusto, with massive and subtle invention, rounded and ripe. Bellow, after twenty years, has at last caught up with his own brilliance.

IRVING PENN

I Won't Pay for the Trip

No Chemical Routes to Paradise

BY JONATHAN MILLER, M.D.

EDITOR'S NOTE: *Although he is a doctor of medicine, Jonathan Miller is pinned to fame as a writer and director, working both in the United States and in England. Last summer he directed Robert Lowell's adaptation of* Prometheus Bound *at the Yale Drama School. This season some of the films he has made in England for British television will be seen on American television; among them, two films on Plato's Dialogues and an hour-and-a-half-long colour special, "From Chekhov with Love," with Sir John Gielgud, Dame Peggy Ashcroft, Dorothy Tutin, and Wendy Hiller. Dr. Miller's next case, possibly: directing a movie version of Dickens's* Bleak House.

The first time I ever took a drug was when I had my tonsils out. I was twelve at the time, but I can still remember the mortal chill of the gas, and the way the voices of the staff became very loud, over-meaningful and then vanished altogether. It's one of my strongest memories, but the wooziness and falling asleep seem now to be no more than corollaries of the main attraction. It's the *smell* of the ether which I recall more than anything else. Not that you could properly call it a smell—there's not enough body in it for that. That's why the name is so perfect—ether! The cold vapour has such an empty keenness that it rocks the mind long before it actually stuns the brain. It smells like nothing on earth, except a threat. It's a smell which glitters, like a blade perfectly sharpened to slit the throat of consciousness.

The actual process of going under has never appealed to me much. The singing in the ears, the loss of grip and so on are empty by comparison with the retrospective knowledge of the blackout which follows. It's only the oblivion, or rather the threat of it, which I find exciting. I am just the same with sleep. I am a sleep junkie, hopelessly addicted to long dreamless draughts of the stuff. It has nothing to do with dozing, or any of the hallucinating reveries that go before. The trip to unconsciousness can't be too short for me. I do not enjoy the deliquescent imagery you get halfway between full awareness and actual coma. I like oblivion, but I like to contemplate it with every faculty intact. The *thought* of unconsciousness, the view from the brink, is perhaps the most psychedelic experience there is. But it can only be got by paying minute attention to the details of what's involved. The kick comes from grasping the intellectual contradictions; from knowing that as you get snuffed, only a thin trickle of personal experience vanishes at that moment from the grand stream of the world's onward motion. It comes from knowing that for some time at least

40

your body stays just as it was, preserved in every detail, just as the owner left it.

I just love the way one leaves the body there, like a bag left on a seat, reserving a place in the world, awaiting the owner's return. It's one of the oddest experiences to watch one of these slow breathing proxies waiting for *its* owner to slip back into the place kept warm for him by that provisional presence, snoring away on the pillow. Just thinking about this can drive away sleep altogether, as one imagines one's forthcoming absence. After a while the mind reels with the metaphysical implications of it all.

I am not denying there are thrills to be had from alterations of consciousness a long way short of complete oblivion; it is nice to jar the appearance of things and feel for a moment the primaeval oddness of simply being-in-the-world. In the normal way, everything around us becomes more or less invisible through habit; but that is just as it should be, of course. We could never get on with life, if we were pulled up short by everything that touched our senses. We could never find our way about, if we had to attend to the tickle of the clothes on our back to listen to every one of the million sounds which did not have immediate importance. We seal ourselves off from most of what the world has to offer, in order to make the best of the few things we *can* set our minds to.

But every now and then, the mental insulation breaks down, and the world floods in to overwhelm us with its raw, complicated foreignness. In these rare flashes there is no focus and no perspective. Everything seems to bear down with equal importance, and the will is paralyzed with an *embarras de richesses*. Nothing seems quite as it should be; everything goes topsy-turvy. Familiar sights glow with unjustified novelty, and new experiences are greeted as *déjà vu*. Luckily for us, these episodes only last for a minute or two, but in that moment the world seems to gleam with high romantic value, and our spirit is renovated as it is brought face to face with the vast unmanned enormity of the physical creation.

Paralyzing and impractical though these moments are, they are so disturbing and so beautiful that it is not surprising if people seem to spend so much time trying to improvise the condition at will. At one time or another there is always a recipe going the rounds for a sure-fire milk-of-paradise: alcohol, laughing gas, breath-holding, mushroom juice, morning-glory seeds, or hard drugs. But I have always been completely cut off from any of the chemical routes to paradise. Alcohol gives me scalding heartburn, and "pot" gets me no further than vertigo followed by a fitful sleep. I daren't try any of the more powerful agents, as I know they would unhinge my mind forever, or hustle me into an eternity of hellish vomiting. It's no good saying that this is not what such drugs do—they would with me. I have never even got a glimpse of Xanadu through the thick poison clouds of nausea. There must be thousands of people like me, pharmacologically underprivileged, who will never know the delights of chemical psychedelia but all of us want a share of the transcendental cake. What hope is there for us?

Let me say for a start what I don't need. I am not really interested in hallucinations. Nor do I really want to see colours brighter than I do already. In fact, I can do without any of the optical displays. To judge from the reports, these retinal shows are as brilliantly monotonous as the best Op art, and they wouldn't hold me for more than a minute or two. In fact, I don't really want any improvement in my powers of peripheral sensation.

What I really want, if it can be arranged, is simply a sharper sense of how odd it is to be here at all. Therefore, I insist on preserving the full power of my critical and intellectual faculties. So far as I am concerned, there is no point in having one of the varieties of religious experience unless I am in a position to describe and amplify what I have known in words. Half the pleasure in any new or extravagant experience lies in being able to fix the whole thing. Most of the reports brought back from drug trips have a gaudy mediocrity. They are affirmative without being descriptive, and I am just not interested in an experience which slithers out of the bottom end of the mind, leaving nothing more than a sense of conviction behind.

There are said to be good substitutes for drugs. These usually take the form of violent assaults on the senses: flashing lights or unbearable noise. Well, that won't do either. I resent the idea that I can be raped into the higher sensitivity. Anyway, it doesn't work. Shows of this sort simply drum me into a state of mindless idiocy.

That leaves hard work as the only effective road to paradise. Not common-or-garden hard work but the sort of hard work which takes everyday experience and, by paying careful attention to it and rubbing its tarnished surfaces, brings the whole thing up with a supernatural glow. Chesterton says somewhere that it is only after seeing something for the thousandth time one can suddenly see it again for the first. But it doesn't come easy. One has to use all sorts of mental tricks in order to achieve this sense of freshly peeled newness. It's no good looking at the world straight on. You have to get at a peculiar angle to it before it will show its secret. It is rather like a gardener, who improves his sense of colour by occasionally looking at the landscape upside down between his legs.

One method, which I find works like a charm, is to take a trip to a foreign city. Any old city will do, since the actual scenery has nothing to do with the strange psychological effect of arriving. The place can be as dull as ditchwater and without a single tourist attraction. In fact, glamour of any sort would get in the way of what I am after. The dizzying, ecstatic mystery of the experience comes from simply dislocating one's self from the familiar stream of life and from arriving in a place which was there long before one arrived, unaware of one's existence. No drug on earth can produce such a cataclysmic heightening of consciousness; I got the feeling for the first time many years ago when I went to Paris. I arrived late one afternoon at the Gare du Nord. As I stepped out into the golden railway sunlight of that Parisian five o'clock, I was overwhelmed at once, not by the Gallic charm of it all, not by the boulevards, the smell of Gauloises, or any of the usual tourist clichés, but simply by the sense of civic otherness.

I had stepped out of the London time stream, where I had an unquestioned existence and some sort of quotidian pedigree, and had stepped into a Parisian sequence where I had no past whatsoever. All around, Parisians were scurrying backwards and forwards, trailing an invisible string of Parisian encounters and incidents. I, on the other hand, stood on the steps of the station without a single fragment of Parisian

past. I felt that it would be almost indecent to walk off into the hurrying crowds and join them without a past like theirs—I must have been as conspicuous as if I had had no clothes on. Free from the weight of shared memory, I felt as if the Parisian gravity just didn't apply to *my* body, and that if I took a single step, I would float off into the evening air like a whiff of transparent gas.

It was only years later that I realized how unnecessary it was to go so far as to cross the channel in order to get this feeling. Any city would do, so long as it was the same sort of size as London. So long as it was big, black, and busy. So long as it had rush-hour crowds hurrying to buses and subways, just as I would have been doing if I had been at home. The important thing was to arrive in a place similar in almost every respect to the city I had just left. In fact, the only feature it would *not* have to have was my previous presence in it. For against this plain backcloth of civic similarity, one's lack of past and future stands out in brilliant contrast. At one simple manoeuvre I am turned into a creature with instantaneous existence; a point in time whose feelings are therefore concentrated to infinity.

All this scores over drugs in achieving its effect by the unaided activity of the mind alone. There is no sharing the credit with chemicals, and since the intellect is intact, you get none of that blooming euphoric confidence which goes with drugs. The descriptions do not decay as normality returns and, unlike drugs, the dosage works in reverse. Simply with practice, you can get the same effects with smaller and smaller bits of travel. I don't even have to travel outside London now. I can get the effect by moving from one part of town to another, at an unusual time of day, or by taking a new bus route and by coming on familiar places from a strange new angle.

There is a weird railway line, for example, which runs around the back side of London, above ground and yet hidden from the streets by hoardings and factories. As soon as you move out of the station, you are knocked out by sense of *jamais vu*. Landmarks which seemed perfectly familiar now stand out as if seen for the first time, and with the train's eccentric course they change positions in all sorts of remarkable ways, and take up places that they couldn't possibly occupy according to the rules of common sense. And for some unaccountable reason, this backstage railway land is bathed in a sulphurous nineteenth-century light, so that nothing seems quite real; and as the train rattles on towards Kew and Richmond, you seem at last to be on a celestial railroad bound for Avalon.

The point is that ordinary reality is always on the edge of hatching apocalypses like this. The world is a miraculous chrysalis which cracks open under the heat of attention, yielding angels which whir about your head like dragonflies. It doesn't need any drugs to bring on the transformation—attention is enough.

You can sometimes get the effect in the middle of the English countryside, on a hot silent summer afternoon. Three o'clock seems about to go on forever, and the heat-stunned stillness seems like the edge of doomsday. All around the trees stand ankle-deep in the lifeblood of their own shadow, birdsong stops for a moment, the insect machinery switches off. The whole of creation sweats with expectation. There is no knowing what the scene is about to deliver. In one sense it is irrelevant. The expectation is all; fulfillment can only be an anticlimax.

And yet, these sacred instants can pass by without ever being felt. Drugs would simply blur the experience or reproduce it best in a chaotic form, so that its sacred precision would be lost.

All I want is some device which keeps me constantly in touch with the bizarre "there-ness" of the world in which I have been formed.

Fortunately, the world itself comes up with stimuli which jolt the mind in this direction. Once you are in practice, small changes of climate even will do the trick. There is nothing like a sudden wind, for example, to switch the mind into high gear. Or a sousing, catastrophic downpour of rain. Or a snowstorm when the whole city seems suddenly to have been seriously burned, then bandaged and consigned to a darkened invalid silence. The point is, once the muscles of the mind are in tune, very small changes of sensation, mood, climate, or interest can produce quite startling alterations in consciousness.

Barbra Streisand

suddenly looks so new she ought to be patented; what makes this invention is her hair, now a nimbus of champagne-coloured curls, corkscrewing in a froth which changes the shape of her face, the glow of her skin, the slant of her eyes. Not changed at all though is the energy, the voice, the headlong hurl of Streisand. She has finished filming *Funny Girl* and taping a television special, both scheduled for later this year, is about to start filming *Hello, Dolly!*, and has signed for the film *On a Clear Day You can See Forever*. Between times she stays home in her extraordinary Second Empire-rococo New York apartment to see the new world of her baby: "At the moment," she said, "I view the world through this curl in the middle of my forehead." Through a curl and a lorgnette. At a concert in New York with Leonard Bernstein she came onstage in a black dress made memorable by the yards and yards of black lace she had wound into a clown's ruff, and peered at Bernstein through her diamond lorgnette "like a diva soprano looking for her pianist." Barbra Streisand has always known how to use her accessories. Her inspiration is acute. "My personality changed my hair," she said, "not the other way around." But all the same there's not been a Streisand like this before, gentler, less armed. Apparently immutable are her ability to pounce on the inadvertent and the special, her impatience, and her humour. She does little pleasing parodies of herself, twitching her long gown into place with an exaggerated simper and rolling the whites of her eyes like a turn-of-the-century tragedienne. Long clothes are her everyday wear now, since she started to research into the feel and look of the period of *Hello, Dolly!*, research which also inspired her curls—they derive particularly from photographs of Sarah Bernhardt and Colette surrounded by clouds of crumply floating hair. "I loved the look. I secretly always wanted to have curls," she said, "but I didn't want to return to the Victorian era, I wanted the look in a modern way." As usual, she got it—with the help of her hairdresser Ara Gallant and curling tongs. There's never been a star like Streisand—a needling perfectionist who knows exactly what to choose from the stuff of the times to give herself the look of the times, while remaining absolutely herself. The only Streisand image she recognizes is the reflection in the looking glass, in other people's eyes, and she knows exactly what that reflection looks like. She's the original.

RICHARD AVEDON

Truman Capote

is an experimenter, an adventurer. His newest experiment is *In Cold Blood*, a unique, book, for it is the first non-fiction novel, a precise documentary, in many ways brilliantly composed, inventive in the telling, a mystery-detective story, true and factual. The facts are brutal, the detection intricate. On November 15, 1959, Richard Hickock and Perry Smith drove up in their black Chevrolet to River Valley Farm on the "high wheat fields of Western Kansas" where they murdered four of the members of the Clutter family, a crime for which they were hanged on April 14, 1965. The killers did not know the family. They came to rob the safe, but finding no safe, kept to Hickock's plan: no witnesses. After the pair had tied up Herbert Clutter, his wife Bonnie, his sixteen-year-old daughter Nancy, and fifteen-year-old son Kenyon, Smith shot them all. Just before the rope broke his neck, Smith said: "I apologize." A few days after the murders, but before the murderers were known, Capote, a small man with a gentle manner, a hard brain, and a remarkable stubbornness about his work, arrived at Holcomb, Kansas, picking up the details of the Clutter family's last day, learning about the shaken townsfolk and the detectives on the case. He stayed with the case for six years. In those years, he learned everything about everyone involved, knew that Smith on the morning of the murders had breakfasted on root beer, three aspirins, and a packet of Pall Malls. In a curious way Capote understood everyone, especially Smith, whom he called at times sensitive, but later described as "an uneducated, homicidal half-breed." By the end of those six years, *In Cold Blood*, then incomplete, had a significant, underground reputation that only increased Capote's enduring fame. A recognized writer since he was seventeen, Capote, now an easy forty-one, has written eight other books (and a play, a musical, and two movies) with none so wildly successful even before publication. The entire book has just been published in four big gulps by *The New Yorker* (the only important writing in those issues). Random House releases it in January, 1966. The Book-of-the-Month Club has it for its February choice. Columbia Pictures owns it. The Truman Capote literary adventure in crime has come off.

Two Faces and A Landscape

BY TRUMAN CAPOTE

The two faces belong to Perry Edward Smith and Richard Eugene Hickock. Smith, half Cherokee, half Irish, is the man with black hair, bangs, and a misty, brooding gaze. The other, the one with eyes of uneven size, he's Hickock. Together, they committed a quadruple murder on a lonely ranch in western Kansas: ended the lives, soon after midnight on a moonlit night in November, 1959, of a prosperous rancher, H. W. Clutter, his wife, and two of their children, a son and a daughter, aged fifteen and sixteen. Six weeks later, following a nationwide search, the pair was captured in Las Vegas and returned to the scene of the crime, a small prairie town named Garden City. These portraits, the work of a local photographer more accustomed to taking high school graduation pictures, were made in the Garden City jail-house the morning after their return and incarceration—a snowy morning in January, 1960.

The landscape, a desolate sand road winding across the western Kansas prairies, was photographed by me one afternoon last October, almost exactly six months after the two murderers were hanged for their crime in a cold warehouse at Kansas State Penitentiary in Lansing, Kansas.

During the more than five years separating those two dates, I wrote my book *In Cold Blood*, a true account of the case (and its manifold consequences), which attempts to explain the men behind these faces, to explore the contours and weathers of this landscape and the breed of Americans who inhabit it.

The first time I spoke to either Perry Smith or Richard Hickock was the day they posed for these pictures: the last was the night of their execution. In the half-decade interval, there developed between us an exceptional relationship, certainly the most intense I've ever had with anyone unrelated or with whom I was not in love. But the beginnings were difficult, the development a very gradual matter.

Well, no—not with Hickock. The basis of our relationship (mutual gain: he required certain kinds of assistance, I required his confidence) was quickly arrived at and, though it extended itself to an easy rapport, it never really altered, for Hickock, who had a mind that skated across surfaces with a cutting, chilling precision, could not adjust to any friendship with anyone of any depth or duration: he just liked to gab and entertain—amuse, as it were, a fellow passenger on a long train ride.

Perry Smith was another matter. At first nothing could win him; he wanted no part of me—or anyone else. He was like a broken-legged, ensnared animal. Yet, while he was awaiting trial, he over and again consented to my interviewing him—why not? He was bored and rather curious. He just didn't want me getting too close, that's all, and so was always suspicious, surly, and often asked, in a superior manner, my reason for wanting to write about him: "What is your *moral* justification?" My answer ("The only moral justification is the work itself") seemed to him, perhaps correctly, glib and evasive. More frequently than not our conversations ended with both of us feeling a high degree of frustration, even anger.

I don't know what caused him to change his mind and admit me to the lair where he had so long lain wounded and with rebuffing eyes. But I think it happened when one day he said, in tones of begrudging wonderment: "Maybe it's so. Maybe you don't think I'm just some monster. Maybe you even do like me a little." I told him I did, which was true, and he laughed and said then in that case I must be crazy. But from that moment, and though we were to have many disagreements, we became good friends and collaborators—I could not have written the book without his faithful co-operation. "The important thing is, it's got to be accurate," he never tired of reminding me. "You can write anything about me you want to. Provided it's the truth. But if you lie about me I'll kill you. I mean it. I will. I'll kill you."

He had every opportunity to enforce this threat, for I spent a lot of time alone with him in an unguarded visitor's room at the Kansas State Penitentiary. After he and Hickock had been sentenced to hang, and had begun their five-year stay on Death Row while appealing their convictions through the Federal courts, I visited them every few months, and we exchanged letters twice a week, which was the maximum amount of correspondence the prison allowed. Dick's letters were like himself: brisk, factual, organized, peppered with dubious jokes, self-pitying in a tough style. Perry, on the other hand, wrote like a primitive poet: all was dreams and searchings, emotions remembered, illusions gone wrong.

He once wrote: "I live for your visits." But in reality we both felt these visits were sad occasions. I remember, at the end of one visit, watching Perry as he was led by two guards across the prison yard toward the dark hostile little building that contained Death Row. It was winter, and it was raining, and I watched from a window as Perry and his companions receded into the rain, Perry, a small, handcuffed, child-man in drenched prison denims walking with bowed head. Then I returned to New York by train, and when I arrived, there was a letter for me: "I knew you were watching me from the window, I could feel it, and what I felt wasn't good. I don't want to be pitied. When you pity me I feel cheated. The one thing I know about life is that nobody can hurt you unless you expect more from them than they can give. And I want more than you can give. More than pity. That hurts. If I have to die, I guess it's better that I have nothing to look forward to or live for. So all in all I think it would be best if you never came here anymore. I say this for your sake also. Out of affection, if you want to call it that."

And the next time I saw him, six months later, was the last: 14 April 1965, the night Smith and Hickock were hanged. I said goodbye to them in the shadow of the gallows, first to Hickock, who grinned and shook hands as though we were standing on a station platform at the end of our long train ride, then to Perry, who kissed me and said: "Adiós, amigo."

And so, like their victims, they perished.

As for the landscape, the stark earth upon which this tragic design was inscribed, that endures.

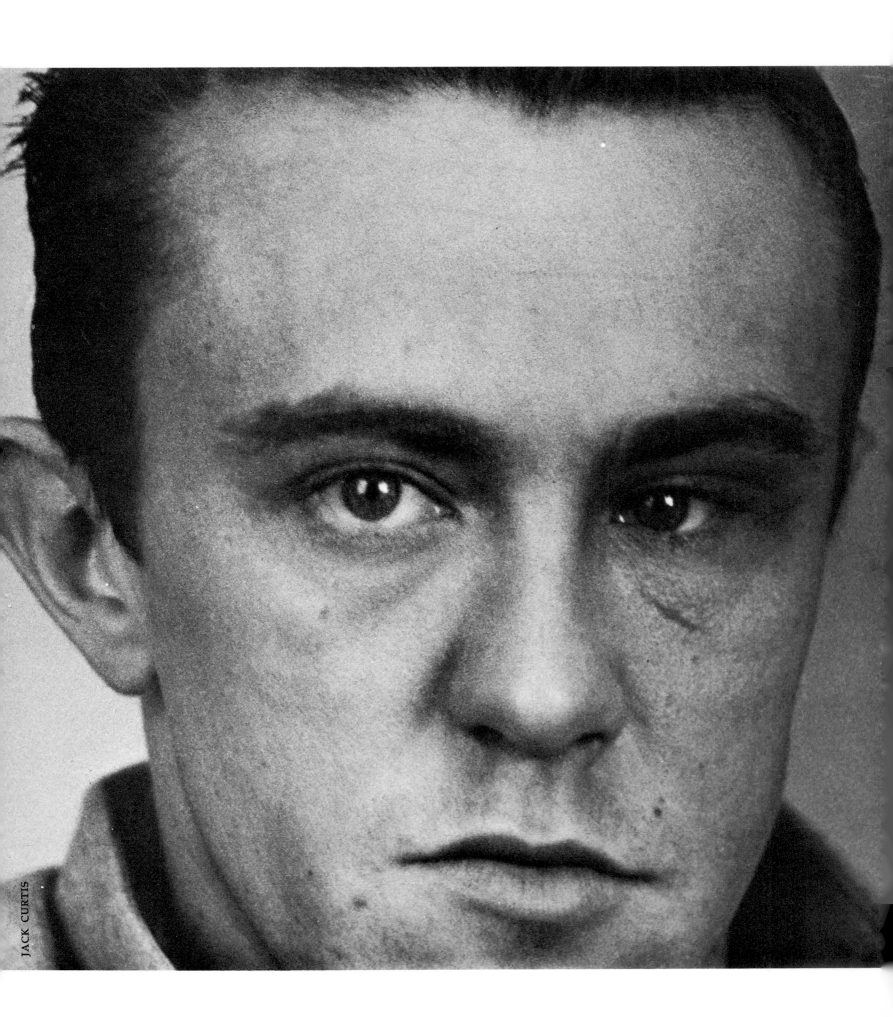

50

51

PHOTOGRAPH ON THE FOLLOWING PAGES BY TRUMAN CAPOTE

The Genius of Chaplin

"As Little as Possible Very Fast"

BY PENELOPE GILLIATT

Buster Keaton told me once that, when he and Chaplin first used the new sound cameras, what they most missed in them was the noise. The old silent-picture cameras made a rhythmic racket that both of them had unconsciously taken for a beat when they were acting. Perhaps this is why Chaplin now writes his own film music; knowing that he is going to be the composer, he can direct a scene with a tempo going on in his head.

To see him work on a scene in *A Countess from Hong Kong* is rather like watching a classical ballet master teaching behind glass. The beat that he can hear is out of one's own earshot, but it is holding the work together. Comedy for Chaplin is choreography, placing, movement, the intricate classical disciplining of vulgar energy. His urge to make his teaching concrete and physical is like the nostalgia of a great old dancer taking his thousandth *Swan Lake* class from a chair, unconsciously mimicking a pas de deux in a sort of muscular mumble, and exploding on to the set to dance the corps de ballet steps himself when some wretched cygnet misses a cue. The dancers in the pas de deux, whom he obviously greatly admires, are Sophia Loren and Marlon Brando. The cygnet one day was a ship's steward in the film who had to make an entrance during a scene with Brando and offer a double brandy. With so little to do he miffed it altogether; Chaplin catapulted on to the set and mimed it himself, and it was like Pavlova with a napkin over her arm.

A Countess from Hong Kong is being made at Pinewood Studios, near London, which have produced some of the most deathly conventional films ever made. To Chaplin, who is now seventy-seven and has made eighty-one films, this isn't of the faintest consequence. As with most of the great classicists of comedy, conventionalism is really just what his work springs from. Rules, propriety, order, loyalty, romanticism, and a sweet decorum are the elements of his style; anarchy suggests nothing to him. A studio that had been the home of other people's technical revolts would have little to offer Chaplin. His needs are simple, oddly formal, and entirely his own.

Buster Keaton told me that, to his mind, the most enviable place to work was a broom cupboard. Chaplin's broom cupboard is obviously a studio. I think he would be happy enough in any studio at all, provided it were professionally competent to do what he wants; and if it weren't, he could undoubtedly teach it to be, because he knows every trade of his craft backwards. The freedom that other directors find in working on location means nothing to him. The intrusions of commonplace life are not an inspiration to him but a distraction. He said once that if he works outside a studio, he finds his ideas and concentration blowing away on the wind.

The conditions at Pinewood are what he needs. They are a familiar focus for work, and everything extraneous to that seems to be invisible to him. The mock-Tudor front offices obviously don't jar on him, the friendly English crew has learned how to do what he wants, and the huge sound stages scattered with sets of a liner are a convention that only makes him imagine the reality of his film more fiercely,

Charlie Chaplin roars with laughter after most takes of "A Countess From Hong Kong."

like the genteel flower-curtained caravan on the set that is Brando's dressing room, and the tea stall where the technicians stand in line for currant buns and a black brew of tea that lays a coating of tannin inside the mouth like an animal's pelt.

Chaplin in his old age seems to feel physically forty-five. Anyone watching him at first is bound to have an undercurrent of worry at the sight of a man nearing eighty who not only keeps the ruthless hours of film making but also demonstrates practically every take himself; but after a while any concern seems a patronage. The outstripped crew has given it up long since. The only thing that bothers some of them is that they can't quite recognize him as the man in his films. I saw one of them holding up a finger against the sight of his distant face to blot out his upper lip and try to imagine him with the old Hitler moustache. With his present white hair he looks almost like the negative of his silent-film self. The wide mouth, stretched like a child's eating a slice of watermelon, isn't quite as one remembers it; perhaps it was always changed by the moustache.

He seems to feel the cold, but then he has lived out of England long enough to grow unused to the conditions that the locals dourly call livable. The studio is what the English think of as living-room temperature, which is like March out-of-doors. He wears a thick sweater under a thicker jacket. Usually he has a hat on against the glare of the lights. When he feels debonair he tips the hat over his eye; when he is growling at the stupidity of his extras, or at the unwieldiness of conventional modern-film fighting, he pushes it impatiently to the back of his head. During holdups he will often suddenly wheel away from the stage to find his wife Oona, a shy, beautiful woman who generally effaces herself behind a pillar. He seems to look to her not so much for advice as for some sort of confirmation. When he speaks to her about a scene between takes, he does it almost as if he were talking to himself. Her constant presence on the set, even and affectionate, seems to have some trick of pulling the knot of his mood.

He keeps the technicians at a distance. They call him "Sir," and if he jokes with them they watch carefully to make sure that they are right to joke back. "Okay, print that," he says once at the end of a take, and then he hears an aeroplane overhead that will probably have wrecked it. "Damn it," he says; not his furious version of the oath, which is an American-accented "God dammit," but an atavistic curse out of his English youth which is practically a pleasantry.

The crew members notice the inflection and deduce that they can freewheel with him for a minute. "There's a humming. Why didn't you tell me?" he goes on to the sound technician with the headphones, giving the start of his wide grin. "Because you were talking, sir," says the sound man daringly, because he is suddenly licensed to. The atmosphere on the set is at its warmest, sunny and trustful. But one take later Chaplin says "Oko" instead of "Okay"—he often pronounces words wrong when he is in a hurry, sometimes even trying to force them into other meanings—and when the crew tentatively kids him about it he ignores them, with an implied rebuke for diverting his attention.

The immediately endearing thing about watching Chaplin work on this picture is the way he goes on laughing at it. He doesn't laugh at the lines in themselves; he laughs at the way they are executed. One has the feeling that when he wrote them he probably wasn't even yet amused. The chuckles must have come later, when the actors had gone through the lines mechanically, over-emoted, lost their confidence, learned their moves backwards, broken through some sort of actors' sound barrier, and eventually found the work as easy as breathing.

It is ease that always makes him laugh. He keeps saying that this is a *romantic* film, not a comedy. He wants to make a film about love that simply happens to be funny, without anyone in the picture knowing it. "Play for absolute realism, not for comedy," he says again and again. One can see the details of Brando's performance becoming daily smaller and more meticulous, like the movement of a watch. His attention to Chaplin is total. I found it technically enthralling, and often moving.

Brando plays a stuffy American ambassador to Saudi Arabia, travelling from Hong Kong with Sophia Loren embarrassingly stowed away in his stateroom as a dispossessed Russian countess. The Ambassador's wife, played by Tippi Hedren, is an amused lounger who has been separated from him for two years. She discovers Sophia Loren's bra in his cabin with nothing more than elegant glee that he should have so undiplomatically boobed.

His Excellency is travelling with his valet, Hudson, played by a stone-faced English actor called Patrick Cargill; the valet has to be induced to marry Sophia Loren in order to give her his nationality as a way of getting her through American Immigration. The valet's resistance to marrying the most nubile woman imaginable is very funny. When the subject is broached he behaves as though he has been offered the wrong wine with the fish.

Most of the action happens on the ship. The sniffy valet is given his orders in the sun deck lounge. Before shooting, Chaplin sits on the edge of one of the chairs on the set and listens to Brando and Cargill running through their lines. He mouths most of the dialogue with them unconsciously and keeps making tiny replicas of their movements. When he is rehearsing actors, his muscles often seem to twitch like a dog having a dream. Eventually he nearly always gets up and skims through their moves himself.

"You are an American citizen, aren't you?" says the Ambassador to his valet.

"I've been an American citizen for the last sixteen years," says the valet stiffly, in the most English voice possible. Chaplin laughs at the way he does it. Then the valet is told that he is required to marry Sophia Loren.

"I'd like you to marry her," says the Ambassador.

"Make it very amiable," says Chaplin, sitting with his fingers pressed on to his knees and his palms bent upwards. His arms are very short. The elbows are straight and the position looks braced and ready for flight. When he is searching for a description of a scene, he always looks excited and physically rather as if he were trying to take off. "I'm looking for a word. Almost—quiet there—give them to me. . . ." He beckons to his producer, who prompts him with the lines, and runs through them under his breath to find out what he means. ". . . Disarmingly."

"I'd like you to marry her," says Brando again, so disarmingly that Cargill laughs, but also so lightly that he makes it seem like kidding.

"Don't denote anything on your face. Keep your voice up. Insist on the action." The Am-

bassador does the line again, bland and clear. It is very funny.

The valet pauses, and then replies: "If I may say so, sir, this is rather sudden."

Chaplin: "More polite. You're disguising feelings by being very polite."

Cargill says it again.

"But before you clamp down, just a shade of shock on that line of Marlon's, 'I'd like you to marry her.' It lays an egg a little bit." He laughs. "So long as you're not suave. A suavity here would kill the whole scene." This is real comic shrewdness: Most people directing these lines would have thought that unruffled suavity was their basis. Chaplin turns out to be quite right, of course.

It is like the funniness of P. G. Wodehouse's Jeeves. The comic point about the godly servant isn't that he is totally impassive, but that across the immortal calm there is an intermittent flicker of ordinary humanity. The crack in the Olympian surface has to be microscopic, but it can be gigantically expressive. It is a difficult thing for an actor to do without over-signalling. Lazy American comedians now would tend to make the crack a large crevasse: lazy English comedians would leave it out and settle for unbroken haughtiness. Chaplin is patiently insistent about the point. Finally the lines make him laugh.

"When does all this happen, sir?" says the valet to the Ambassador.

"Oh, in about ten minutes," says the Ambassador.

"From now on your mind is racing," says Chaplin to the valet. He says the line himself. "But not at all anxious on the face. Very pleasant." Then he says Brando's line. " 'Oh, in about ten minutes.' You put on great *magnananity* here." This is one of his out-of-focus pronunciations, but Brando sees what he means. Later Chaplin does a variant. "A little more *magnaminity*. 'Oh, in about ten minutes'—you get him married as though you're ordering breakfast."

The extras have to walk across in the background. They have been told exactly where to go and how fast, but everything is fumbled, and Chaplin watches in agony. Some of the extras are old trouts who habitually go to sleep in the armchairs on the set although one of the masters of the cinema is working under their noses. Some of them are bored young hacks who aren't even alert enough to be nervous. They import an atmosphere of crassness and laziness that is sniffed by the members of the crew with instant dislike.

The fact that they have turned up in the wrong clothes is one of the common absurdities of big-budget film making, but it is enough to upset a perfectionist like Chaplin for the morning. "They should be in lovely summery clothes —lovely pale shoes," I hear him saying to himself unhappily between takes. "They look as if they've just got off the 8:17 at Victoria Station," says the amiable cameraman with an edge of irritability.

"Remember your tempos," Chaplin calls out to the extras, who do their jobs again. One group has to saunter, the other to scurry. They manage it eventually, looking as awkward and unreal as any extras in any big studio in the world, which is one of the penalties that Chaplin pays for working under conventional conditions.

The rehearsals for this scene take a long time. Chaplin himself demonstrates a steward's entrance twice, arriving and pivoting exactly on cue, saying "So-so-so-so; so-so-so-so-so-so" as dummy dialogue. It is rather like Toscanini giving an entrance to the triangle player after a hundred and fifty bars of silence.

Eventually the moves harden and become mechanical, which is what he wants. Once the routine is fixed and has started to bore the actors, the comedy begins to emerge. He works from the outside inwards: First the mechanics, then familiarity and physical skill, and after that the right emotions will come. It is the diametric opposite of the Stanislavskian style that has become accepted modern dogma.

"Do that line again, Marlon. 'Oh, in about ten minutes.' Quickly. Take off the fat." The working atmosphere between them is relaxed and easy. Brando is one of the greatest screen actors in the world and he has been trained in exactly the opposite tradition, but he listens and absorbs with an attention that seems unflawed.

He is doing a close-up shot of the scene now, with the cues given to him by the producer, Jerome Epstein. Brando fluffs twice, saying "husband" instead of "Hudson" each time, and the producer starts to get the giggles. Epstein finds himself infected and starts saying words upside down. At the end of the final take Brando squints at Chaplin and laughs, and says to the producer: "Do you want to get some Scotch tape and sew yourself together?"

Epstein is an old associate of Chaplin, and an obvious contributor to the mood of fun that Brando and Loren both sense on the set. His way of giving Chaplin a prompt when the director is signalling for it looks like the result of years, rather like a theatre sister shoving the right instrument into a surgeon's hand. To an outsider Chaplin's "so-so-so" and grabbing fingers aren't at all explicit, but Epstein obviously feels that he should know by instinct the line that he wants, and when his concentration is absorbed enough he does.

The attention that Chaplin demands, and gets, is fierce and total. When other directors become most inventive by allowing energy to fly outwards, with Chaplin the pull is always towards the centre. He knows exactly what he is doing. When he is shooting a scene he seems to be gently chivying the actors towards something that is already complete in his head.

Like a tug edging a liner away from a quay, he has coaxed the incomparable Brando into a manner that is just faintly at odds with the one he is known by. The sumptuous, time-taking style, spaciously intelligent behind an opiate gaze, has become smaller, quicker, and sometimes comically testy, just as the histrionics of Sophia Loren's abundant comic temperament have been converted into a very funny stoicism.

In her work before *A Countess from Hong Kong*, she made people laugh by Latin fluster; in the scenes that I saw, she does it by phlegm. "He has made me quite different," she says. "When I see rushes I don't recognize myself. There are hardly any gestures. He doesn't like me to use my hands much, especially near my face. We're trying to do everything as naturally as possible."

Directors and actors always say now that they are working for realism, of course; it is one of the modern pieties of the profession, but in Chaplin's case it is precisely true. Again and again when he is directing a scene, he will cut out some gesture or response that reveals itself the moment it has gone as a hamstrung comic mannerism. His laughs in this picture nearly always come from doing apparently as little as possible very fast. "Lots of lift, lots of tempo," he says often. The takes that he decides to print are always the ones with the most dash and lightness; sometimes, when he is talking under pressure, he makes a bouncing movement upwards with his hand as though he were keeping a ball in the air.

"It wants a beat," he says to Tippi Hedren, after she has been working on a scene where she enters with the identifiably out-size bra that she has discovered in her husband's cabin. "This is all a great comedy to you. No malice. You haven't lived with your husband for two years. You come in with great gusto. You're kidding him." Through the next take he looks worried. "There was no tempo." He gets up from his chair by the camera, wrinkles his nose and prances through the moves himself, saying "so-so-so," like a groom sedating a horse. "So-so-so *Your Excellency*," he says, pivoting on the words. "You're mocking him. You're glib. That's it. Can we come in with a bigger spread? One—two—" he gives her the time, and catches his breath on the upbeat as she enters. "Can we keep that lovely movement?"

In a previous take she has turned on one of her lines and practically flowed onto a sofa; he does it himself to fix the move in his mind, looking comically grand in an imaginary tea gown, and makes sure that the camera movement fits it.

For Chaplin, the placing of a camera articulates a scene. On the whole he doesn't seem to like camera movement very much. ("The actors should be the performers, not the lens.") He doesn't care for trick angles and he hates the laziness of cryptically significant shots that show nothing but door-opening. "Orientation" is an important idea to him. He believes that an audience must always know where it is in a room, and that actors must know exactly where to stop, where to turn, where to stand, whether to talk directly or indirectly.

I had expected his physical business to be graphic and hilarious, but I hadn't been quite prepared for the precision of his sense of words. To talk about Chaplin's mime is rather like praising the height of Everest; it is his pin-fall ear for dialogue that is technically so absorbing to anyone fortunate enough to see him working. "There's something woolly in that word, Sophia," he says; the fuzz is there, an emphasis that is faintly implausible and faltering, but a lot of good directors would have let it go. "Most films are just in and out," said the chippie (the film carpenter). "Not this one. He's definitely got something on his mind."

When he is coming back from the lunch break or inspecting the sets in the early morning, he carries his script against his chest like a buckler. Like Keaton, he stands and walks with the arched back of a small boy, perhaps because of the ferocious physical training that both of them had as tiny children in vaudeville.

"He's a perfectionist," said the director of photography, Arthur Ibbetson. "Every little thing. You should have seen him showing Sophia how to read a book. Slowly coming to and realizing he's forgotten the paragraph he's just read, and turning backwards and forwards. When he did his own bit it was rather a day." (Chaplin appears in the film in a tiny part as a steward who gets seasick.) "All he really did was sweep the deck with his head down. Other people would have made a production out of it." Ibbetson does a mime of someone milking laughs. "There's one passenger asleep on the whole deck, and when he's finished, he sweeps the muck very neatly behind that passenger's feet. That's all he does, see?"

CABARET *with Joel Grey and the Girls*

Slinky, deliberately cheap, low-down, *Cabaret*, a hit musical of the New York season, is a marvellously naïve musical about Berlin in 1929-1930. Its essence of decadence lies in the convolutions of young Joel Grey, the only new star so far, as the master of ceremonies in the Kit Kat Klub, his slicked hair parted in the middle, his eye shadow blue, his cheeks bright with pink rouge, his lipsticked mouth agile and false. Gaiety is his front. His voice has the right buzz, his dancing is light and amusing. He grabs the stage and holds on, trying all his tricks and always winning what there is to win. (Off-stage, Joel Grey is an amusing man, charming and knowledgeable, the father of two young children.) Surrounding him at the Klub are the chorus girls in their glitter, their black stockings, their black garters, with their come-hither glances that lack desire, their sing-song voices that bleat, their sharp dances designed by Ronald Field, who catches the shod of their crazy lives in his frantic patterns.

BERT STERN

Lynn Fontanne

There is no one like her. In her seventies and in *The Visit*, which is just reopening. Miss Fontanne has a beauty that is neither young nor old, coupled with a mysterious force for horror as she unfolds the character of the rich, icy Madame Zachanassian, a terrible but attractive being with a knowledge of the turnpike way to corrupt even those apparently uncorruptible. She does it with the dignified assurance of someone dealing herself a fifth ace in a game with children. When Miss Fontanne first appears brilliantly gay in red, she starts on a key of comedy with her entourage and an empty coffin, but when she leaves the same dingy station platform she is all in black with her entourage and a filled coffin.

In this brutally unsentimental play by Friedrich Duerrenmatt, in which there are no good people at all, Miss Fontanne has a pretty charm, like a green glass of poison, inviting and fatal. She walks with an imperious grace, as though she thought she were the Emperor Caligula. Her famous voice is flexible, ensnaring, implacable. She never wavers, in spite of her gaiety, which in the circumstances is gallows humour. All that Madame wants of her pauperized native village is the communal murder of her girlhood seducer. Playing equally superbly as the seducer is Alfred Lunt, looking like a squashed brown paper bag, his neck skin swagged and drooping.

Part of the fascination is that Miss Fontanne looks so striking in her Castillo clothes and never more so than when she sits in a red velvet-lined sedan chair, wearing her wedding dress of white moire, a small pearl coronet on her orange-coloured hair, her veil floating as she smokes a mild Phillies Panatella. When a Vogue editor asked her to repeat the same small malicious smile that in the second act shows that she knows the town will eventually kill her victim for her, Miss Fontanne consented but said that Madame Zachanassian was not really malicious: "I have my own explanation for her—she's mad."

JOHN RAWLINGS

Andrew Wyeth

A study of the great American painter whose still paintings of remembered emotion are now on exhibition at the Albright-Knox Art Gallery. Photographed at his house at Chadds Ford, Pennsylvania, by Henri Cartier-Bresson.

BY ALLENE TALMEY

Andrew Wyeth, his November face tanned, weathered by the sun and winds of Maine and Pennsylvania, is the sunshine boy of museums this year. Right now the Dallas Museum has installed one of his quiet works, "That Gentleman," for which it paid $58,000. The Albright-Knox at Buffalo has installed a large show of his tempera paintings. On January 1, the Fogg Museum at Harvard will exhibit his watercolours, his studies, his drawings, among them "Young Bull" in dry brush, shown on the preceding page. That bull, painted just before Christmas, 1960, has much of the quality of any Wyeth. It has reality, but it is an abstraction from reality. The early morning light, the stone wall, the wire gate, the branches of a low tree, the sky, the hill are the hand prints of Wyeth. Even a fool who had seen enough Wyeths would recognize them, but fools invest them with peculiar notions. They think those paintings of a field of blowing grasses, of a barn with hooks, of a farm woman sitting down at last, of a boy standing in a barn door are excursions into nostalgia, that they stand for the apotheosis of adolescence, of country women. They do not. They are portraits of specific women, of definite boys, of a particular man. Karl is Karl, not a formless yearn for an old-timey farmer. "It's not the object," said Wyeth, wearing a sandy shirt, brown slacks, cut-down jodhpur boots, in his old stone house at Chadds Ford, "it's what you pour into it. It's what happens when the object brings back your

own thoughts. A hump in the earth. Hell—a nice shape, but it reminds you of your father. Where he's buried."

He added: "I try to put down as simply as possible my feelings towards places, objects, and the people that are part of my life. I hate formalized design. I like to catch things off balance, out of the corner of the eye. All past experiences are endless in their return to me. In my paintings there is a quiet, personal tie-up, an echo of the past. The past gets richer and richer as I paint. At first the picture is too thin but after six months I get to the bottom of realism." Wyeth probes into himself as though the canvas were an analyst's couch.

Wyeth, usually disliked by the abstract expressionists, the hard-edge boys, makes the same points that they do. He paints not exactly what is there but what he feels. It is his own emotion, coupled with painterly skill, that gives the further drive, the extension of dimension. It irritates him to see fuzzy writing about his work—coating the paintings with the slithery Nujol of sentimentalism. He dislikes the pathetic fallacy of investing objects with emotions. "Barrels," he said, "are not lonely." When he paints an ugly object, it is because he sees it in its ugliness and he wants the ugliness that way. The beauty is there because he sees beauty in his winter landscapes with the waters frozen in the meadows, with a stand of birch by the Brandywine River.

Andrew Wyeth was born at Chadds Ford, Pennsylvania, on July 12, 1917, at home on a hot day. His own stone house is now only about a mile or so from his parents' house. The yellow and white clapboard studio where he works is practically in that house's backyard. Unlike the order in his paintings, the studio is a clutter of rusty tools with an old-fashioned pier glass in a corner. His father, N. C. Wyeth, a famous illustrator of his day, was a big, vital, handsome man, six feet three, weighing two hundred pounds, with solid muscles. He looked rather like his own illustrations of Captain Bones in *Treasure Island*. In large blocks of paint—like a realistic Mark Rothko—N. C. Wyeth painted action, pirates with handspikes, cutlasses, spades, pistols, the details simplified.

The elder Wyeth settled down at Chadds Ford in 1903 because his teacher, Howard Pyle, lived there. (Pyle was a great man for pirates,

too.) While N. C. worked on murals in the studio, his son played around with paper and colours, like a mouse of an apprentice in the corner.

When young Wyeth reached fifteen, his father said: "Come into the studio and start to study." The boy began with cubes, spheres, and cones, with white objects on white paper to get the values. His father also said: "First live, then paint." After the white practice, Wyeth progressed to casts of Lafayette and Washington for about six months, and then took on life models, worked on still life, and persuaded his neighbours to pose for him. Between the casts and the neighbour period Doubleday asked him to illustrate a book, as one of the editors had seen some four or five juvenile books that young Andrew had illustrated with pen and ink studies for Little, Brown. He did not do the Doubleday book, although he had his father's permission.

Working away with his father, whom he always called Pa, Wyeth studied steadily. Once when he was painting watercolours in the orchard, his father watched, ready to criticize but never to touch, said: "Andy, free yourself." The kernel of N. C. Wyeth's teaching for his son lay in his advice: "Be like a sponge, Andy, soak up all experiences but be sure you squeeze them dry. Leave no water or everything becomes soggy."

A few years later the Macbeth Gallery in New York gave the new Wyeth, then twenty, a show of his watercolours of the Maine landscape at Cushing, where he still spends his summers. The Wyeth orbit in a space age revolves primarily around Maine and Chadds Ford; he has never gone to Europe. He believes in what Pyle once told N. C. Wyeth—"A week off sets you back two months." In his deliberately circumscribed life of family and the land, he lives deeply, has gone through most of the universal emotions of despair and happiness, has had setbacks, anxieties, misunderstandings and has come through to reasonable serenity, strong in his feeling for continuity. When the first John Chadd in the 1700's lived at Chadds Ford, a John Wyeth (no relation) lived there, too.

As a teacher for his son, N. C. Wyeth was a great disciplinarian but a man of humour, with great but frightening dignity. To the neighbours

Wyeth's "Roasted Chestnuts," tempera, 1956. This austere autumn repose on a country road has intensity of concentration on its objects, which gives to each detail—the glove, the pebbles, the twigs—a deep significance. A romantic, poetic painting with big scale, it has within its stillness the sense of motion about to happen, the mystery of the unexplained, the feel of greatness.   33″ x 48″

he was always Mr. Wyeth but Andrew is still Andy to them.

These days in his rather bare, deliberately severe house, there is the feeling of family. The June afternoon I spent there, his mother had come over from her house. A white-haired, delightful woman, she sat reading by a window in an upstairs bedroom. On the wall hung the "Young Bull," owned by Mrs. Andrew Wyeth. Mrs. Wyeth, called Betsy, has a pretty face, healthy, open, her hair cut short. She wore flat red slippers with a red-checked gingham dress that had a highly sophisticated look, that of Givenchy, not country store. The Wyeths admired the way Cartier-Bresson seemed to have his camera like a sixth finger. "A camera," said Mrs. Wyeth, "can be as annoying as an ill-fitting pair of fake teeth." While we talked, two dogs wandered around; Rattler, an American hound with some golden retriever in his heritage, and Amy, a miniature poodle that belongs to their younger son, Jamie. A tall, good-looking boy of fifteen, the original of the famous Wyeth portrait of a boy in a coonskin cap,

Jamie works now in his father's studio doing charcoal studies.

Outside the living room that day men were busy with the restoration of an old mill. The mill race comes down through the property, fed by the brown-green water of the Brandywine River. At Wyeth's mill George Washington had flour ground for his army. There are three buildings on the place, the 1711 mill, the granary, and the miller's house, all of field stones, browns, greys, washed-out whites. On one of the buildings a huge black and white quill, a weather vane, turns showing its holes from autumn hunters.

It is old country there, beautiful, quiet in any season. The historian of those seasons, of that life there, is Andrew Wyeth, who has a quiet personal tie with the land which reminds him of experiences. A boy near a barn reminds him of himself years ago. He knows the shanties, the old barrels, the gasoline cans, with which he refreshes his memories. He never dreams. He sees, has a warm, healthy reaction, then builds deeply, slowly. That is what he paints.

Intimate Letters of Pasternak

INTRODUCTION TO THE PASTERNAK LETTERS BY DAVID MAGARSHACK

Boris Pasternak's letters to his Georgian friends cover a period of twenty-eight years, from 1931 to 1959, years in which he had to battle against ever growing official hostility to his poetry which took the form of a ban on his books and forced him to take up translations as a way of earning a living. It was by sheer chance that he became a translator of Georgian poetry and it was this accident that, according to his fellow poet, Nikolai Tikhonov, was to be "a turning point in his work" and, one might add, in his life. It was his newly-found friends, especially the poets Titian Tabidze and Paolo Yashvili, both of them victims of the purges of 1936-7, who, to quote Tikhonov again, "surrounded him with such warm friendship and friendly sympathy that this first indelible impression remained with him throughout his life." Pasternak himself was to describe Georgia [in southern Russia] as a country "which has become my second motherland" and his Georgian friends as "people whom I love like brothers."

It is this deeply emotional attitude towards his friendship with some of the most prominent Georgian poets that immediately strikes the reader of these letters. But it is also this aspect of his ties with Georgia that lays bare not only the personal feelings of a poet who was one of the most reserved and reticent of men imaginable, but also his views on the grimmest period of suppression and persecution which the liberal arts in Russia ever experienced. . . . It is these letters [to Nina Tabidze] that plumb the depths of Pasternak's emotional life and reveal his character as perhaps none of his autobiographical sketches does. . . .

Born in Moscow in 1890, the son of Leonid Pasternak, a fashionable painter, and Rosa Pasternak, née Kaufmann, a concert pianist, Pasternak received the usual education of a son of a well-to-do professional family. He was educated at a Moscow secondary school and, after meeting Alexander Scriabin at the age of twelve in the spring of 1903, was so carried away by Scriabin's "freshness of spirit" that he decided to become a musician and devoted the next six years of his life to a thorough study of the theory of composition. . . . He soon realized that he could never be a success as a composer. . . . He was then and till much later convinced that everything in art must be a miracle and nothing must be deliberately designed or planned. Inclined to mysticism and superstition from early childhood, he believed that everything must be predestined from above. . . .

Pasternak's first met the Georgian poet Paolo Yashvili, one of the founders of the symbolist movement in Georgia, in Moscow in 1930, the year in which *Safe Conduct*, Pasternak's first autobiography, was being serialized in a Moscow literaray magazine. . . . Pasternak was afterwards to describe Yashvili as a brilliant man of the world, a cultured and entertaining conversationalist and a "European" in every sense of the word. Soon after his visit, Yashvili was to become one of his closest friends. In his moving letter to Yashvili's wife after Yashvili's suicide in 1937 during the terrible year of the Stalin purges, Pasternak recalls Yashvili's "striking face with its high, inspired forehead and laughing eyes" and the sound of his voice "that was so fascinating from its overflow of ideas." Yashvili was to come to his rescue at a critical period of his life. For in 1930 his first marriage foundered and in the changes that took place in his family and in the family of the woman he had fallen in love with, the two of them for some time had, as Pasternak expressed it, "no roof over our heads." They took refuge in Yashvili's house in Tiflis. . . . Pasternak had never been to Georgia before and the Caucasus and the life of the Georgian people were a complete revelation to him. He admired the dark overhanging cliffs towering all the streets of the city. He found the life of the ordinary, and particularly the poorest, inhabitants much brighter, more candid, and much less inhibited than in the north. The educated classes of the population showed, in his view, a higher level of intellectual life than he was used to in Moscow. The fine buildings in certain quarters of Tiflis reminded him of Petersburg. The city was full of picturesque lanes. There was the continuous sound of popular Georgian folk music: tambourines, bagpipes, and other national instruments. He was fascinated by the brightness of the stars in the sky at night and the scent of the flowers from innumerable gardens mingling with the smells issuing from coffeehouses and confectioners' shops. But the spell the southern city cast on him was nothing compared to the spell of the two poets who became his closest friends and whose lives were to end so tragically six years later—Paolo Yashvili and Titian Tabidze. . . .

Pasternak himself had only just returned from a journey to Paris where he had attended the first anti-Fascist congress and where he had met Marina Tsvetaeva, the poet he so greatly admired. On his return to Russia he fell seriously ill after a heart attack. . . . How little he realized the danger threatening Tabidze and numerous other writers and poets can be gathered from the letter he wrote on 8 April 1936 to Tabidze at the time of the most acrimonious debate in the general and literary press about "formalism." . . .

In March 1959 Pasternak and his wife paid a last visit to Georgia. They spent three weeks as guests of Nina Tibidze who, Pasternak wrote on 17 March 1959, to one of his Georgian friends, "showered love, care, comfort, and repose upon us." . . . On his return "portents of dangers and sufferings" awaited him, but, he added with his usual stoic acceptance of whatever misfortune befell him throughout his life, "everywhere in the world one has to pay for the right to live on one's own naked spiritual reserves." It was his last letter to his Georgian friends. He died on 30 May 1960.

THE LETTERS—SELF-REVELATIONS BY THE GREAT RUSSIAN AUTHOR OF "DOCTOR ZHIVAGO"

To Titian and Nina Tabidze

8 April 1936

My dear friends Titian and Nina,

. . . What is keeping you, Titian? Why are you not coming? I did not want to telegraph you about my love and loyalty. You know that already and must have been bored with it for a long time. I wanted to tell you not to lose heart, to believe in yourself and stand firm in spite of temporary misunderstandings. I was so delighted by your telephone call! Even Nina came to the phone—thank you! But it was difficult to talk. You did not hear me, but I heard you excellently.

There is a great deal that is deceptive and indefinite in the painful discords of the recent past. I felt it at once. [A reference to the articles published in connection with the debate about formalism in 1936.]

If there is a particle of truth in anything that has been published and discussed, it is only that it coincides with the overall plan of the times, with its historic infinity. But how can infinity be a particle, and of such a worthless whole as the critical semolina porridge which people have been so touchingly gulping down for over a month? Here is the answer: this truth was ladled out in a dismally weak solution. . . .

Don't believe in solutions, Titian! Believe precisely in that line, precisely out of loyalty to the revolution believe rather in yourself, Titian Tabidze, for, say what you like, the chemistry of your way of thinking dissolves everything in the world, whatever you may call it, at a higher temperature than is acceptable to the "Literaries" or the "Evenings." [A veiled reference to *The Literary Gazette*, the official organ of the Union of Soviet Writers, and the evening *Izvestia*.] And even if you did not want it, the revolution has been dissolved by us more strongly, and more strikingly than you could decant it from the debating tap. Do not turn to public charity, my friend. Rely only on yourself. Dig more deeply with your drill without fear or favour, but inside yourself, inside yourself. If you do not find the people, the earth and the heaven there, then give up your search, for then there is nowhere else to search. That would be clear even if we did not know anyone searching in a different way. Are there so few of them? The fruits of their labour are here for all to see.

You need not worry. I am not the only one who appreciates you and believes in you. Don't believe in solutions. Believe in revolution as a whole, believe in the future, the new promptings of your heart, the spectacle of life, and not the construction put on things by the Union of Soviet Writers, which will be changed all of a sudden before you have had time to sneeze—believe in the Age and not in the week of the formalist. . . .

Come as soon as possible. I have rarely been as composed as I am now. I have not changed a bit. It was only in the idiotic verses written before Minsk and which will be published soon in *Znamya* that I removed the dedication to Leonidze for fear that he might get into trouble because of a certain independence of its content. . . .

To T. G. Yashvili

                                28 August 1937
My dear, poor Tamara Georgiyevna,

. . . When I was told about it [the poet Yashvili's suicide] the first time, I did not believe it. It was confirmed to me in town on the seventeenth. The shades and half-shades fell away. The news grasped me by the throat, I was in its power and still am. Not everything that I experienced under the impact of that terrible fact is irremediable and death-dealing—not everything.

When again and again I come to the realization that never again shall I see the wonderful face with its high, inspired forehead and laughing eyes and never hear the voice whose very sound was fascinating from its overflow of ideas, I burst into tears, I toss about in anguish and can find no place for myself. With thousands of well-remembered details my memory shows him to me in all the changes of the situations we have been through together: in the streets of several towns, at excursions to the sea and the mountains, at your home and at my home, on our latest journeys, when presiding at conferences and on rostrums. The memory wounds and drives the pain of bereavement to a point of insanity, flies in my face with reproach: what have I done to be punished by an eternity of this parting?

But it happened on the very first day, the seventeenth, that its irreversibility cleansed me and brought me down to elementary facts which can not be disputed, as in childhood, when after crying youself into a state of torpor you suddenly want to eat and sleep from sheer fatigue. That blow was so powerful that it flung me far away from everything urban, from everything that is loud, not by right, not from necessity complicated, hysterically indifferent, eloquently empty. "What nonsense," I said to myself again and again, "Paolo? The Paolo I knew so well that I did not even care to analyze how I loved him, Paolo—the name of my delight, and everything that an average man A or an average man B might communicate to me with a serious air, men who will be forgotten in a moment. This," I thought, "is for the future." Everyone has to die anyway, and, moreover, in some kind of definite surroundings. So they will say: this life, preserved by posterity, came to an end in the summer of 1937, and they will add the authentic facts of the time in question: the topics that occupied the minds of the public, the names of the papers, the names of acquaintances. In exactly the same way as in reference to some other age one would talk of wigs and jabots or, further back in time, of hunts with falcons. . . .

I would have liked to have a bathe. The day was drawing to a close. On the bank, in the shady ravine, when, after lying down comfortably, I gradually recovered from the agitations of my journey, I suddenly began to catch, here and there, the features of some kind of marvellous likeness to the deceased. It was all inexpressibly wonderful and terribly reminiscent of him. I saw bits and pieces of his spirit and style: his grass and water, his autumnal, setting sun, his stillness, rawness and secretiveness. So, indeed, might he have said, how they were burning and hiding, winking at each other and dying out. The sunset seemed to imitate him or reproduce him in memory.

I began thinking of him somehow in a new way. I always admired his talent, his unsurpassable flair for the picturesque, rare not only in Georgian literature, not only in the whole of our modern literature, but precious at any and every time. He always astonished me. People have letters which show how highly I thought of him. But it was for the first time that I began thinking of him quite apart from what I felt for him. Just as one moves away from something very, very big, his absolute outlines began to take shape only at the fateful distance of his loss: what he was away from us, away from me, Titian and Gogla, what he was not only apart from our admiration of him and our desire to see him victorious, but, on the contrary, in defiance of our love: what he was himself with the water and the woods, and God and the future. . . .

What surprises me is something else, however difficult it may be to express it: how much of him there remains in what he touched and what he named: in the hours of the day, in the flowers and animals, in the verdure of the woods, in the autumn sky. We lived and did not know the power he wielded among us, the authority that he still remains. . . .

. . . However difficult my existence has become of late, nothing will be impossible for me so far as you are concerned. . . .

To Nina Tabidze

6 April 1950

. . . I have been feeling very well lately, I have been working a lot and easily, and there have been no more changes. . . .

I am very satisfied with my life, with the chance of earning an honest living, and with the serenity of my state of mind. I have never considered myself in any way offended or passed over. If anyone thinks that to a detached observer I may appear to be a "martyr," then let me say that, first, I am not responsible for anyone's crazy ideas or ridiculous fancies and, secondly, it is sufficient that they who may be interested in such a theory should lift the ban on my books and let me mount the rostrum and this "semblance of martyrdom," which does *not exist* as far as I am concerned, will disappear by itself. An announcement over the air that I am not a martyr I regard as utterly unthinkable and as sheer idiocy. I am a very proud man, but I should have been a petty and envious person, a bragging nonentity, and a young commercial traveller to believe, like any journalist, in the air itself, and in its knowledge of me and its existence for me, when, to be quite frank, I sometimes find it difficult to believe that I interest you or Zina. Besides, if a person suspected of martyrdom declares that he has never had it so good, a suspicion may arise that this declaration has been wrung from him by his sufferings.

All this is an extremely stupid vicious circle. What sort of person must one be to worry one's head about such things?

It seems to me that all a man's efforts must be concentrated on his activity—successful, bold, and productive—and that life should be allowed to do the rest. Happiness in all sorts of higher spheres of existence, such as love (not only love of a woman, but love of one's country or love of one's contemporaries), creative work, and so on, is either given or not given at all, in which case there is nothing to worry about, because one could do nothing about it however hard one tried. Or else it will be a fake. To me, unfaked failure is still more acceptable than faked success. I am sorry, Nina, to have written you such paltry rubbish, but I did it to set your mind at rest if you should be made nervous by some literary gossip.

To Nina Tabidze

15 April 1951

. . . Nina, my best friend, my joy, I am ready for anything at any moment. But if I were no more, my life would be left behind, such a happy life, for which I am so grateful to heaven, a life which, like a book, was full of such quiet, concentrated meaning. What was the chief and fundamental thing about it? The example of my father's work, love of music and Scriabin, two or three chords in my own writings, a night in the Russian countryside, the revolution, Georgia. . . .

To Nina Tabidze

30 September 1953

. . . Ever since my childhood I have nourished a timid feeling of adoration for woman, all my life I have remained stunned and stupefied by her beauty, by her place in life, and by my pity of her and fear for her. I am a realist who has a thorough knowledge of the earth not because, like Don Juan, I have frequently had a lot of fun with woman on earth, but because since childhood I have gathered pebbles from under her feet on the path she has trodden.

The few women who have had an affair with me were magnanimous martyrs, so unbearable and uninteresting am I "as a man," so often am I incorrigibly and inexplicably weak, so much do I not know myself even now and know nothing of this aspect of life. They are perhaps touched by the fact that some poor human being has in spite of everything dragged himself to them from far, far away, a being devoted to them since childhood and since childhood shaken and racked with pain for them, and also shattered on the way by the high-minded war he has fought for them. Perhaps, too, they are touched by the strange purity, always familiar to women from memories of their own childhood, which has encompassed so many things in life, and still remains to this day. . . .

Now, secondly—art. In *Resurrection* and *Anna Karenina* Tolstoy shows how Nekhlydov and, in the second case, Vronsky, who had gone to Italy with Anna, buy all the necessary art accessories—canvases, pencils, brushes, paints, in order to paint pictures, but somehow nothing seems to come right, either the mood is wrong or the weather is not good enough, and beside them is shown a man who is mad about painting and who contracts tuberculosis because of his dedication to art, a poor, simple man. . . . It is this gentlemanly, amateurish, idle attitude towards the whole world of self-sacrifice and hard work, which I know so well and to the service of which I am devoted, that surprises and repels me. I saw something in life that had some connection with great men. It must be remembered that this kind of upper-class idea of art, an art for young ladies and the cinema—does not belong to my repertoire. I do not say that one ought to hang anyone who is not a genius, but in that case one's approach and one's standards must be quite different. . . .

ELLIOT ERWITT

See Them Now

Ed Murrow and the Man Behind Him, Fred Friendly

BY PETER REED

Among the more fascinating unfilmed views of the television program, "See It Now," are those of Edward R. Murrow and Fred W. Friendly during the telecast. It is like a scene in a submarine movie at the moment of attack; everyone knows what to do and does it. There is no excitement. The public fails to see the cramped oblong studio, too small for the machinery, the cameras, the monitors, the intercoms, and the twelve men in attendance. The oddity in the scene lies in six-foot-four Friendly sitting on the floor, with his pencil in hand, whispering to Murrow during the middle commercial. "Do you want to be punched at twenty seconds or thirty?" The public sees only Murrow, poised, elegant, notably handsome.

Although practically everyone in the country recognizes the Murrow face and the Murrow voice which comes through exactly accented as though beating out the regular feet in a stanza of poetry, practically no one knows the face or the voice or even the name of Murrow's co-producer and co-writer on this famous program. Yet on every telecast of the program Murrow mentions the name of his partner, Friendly, and the credit line carries the name. Even the television critics in praising the program rarely mention him. For spotting Friendly is like that childhood game in which the problem is to guess an object plainly in view.

The team of Murrow and Friendly are a proper mixture, equal in physical size but with completely different qualities. Where Murrow is slim, with a suspicion of gauntness, Friendly is hulking, somewhat too fat. Where Murrow is low-pressure, pessimistic, silent, tense, and controlled as though he worked himself by levers and gauges like the dashboard of a plane, Friendly is high-pressure, optimistic, enthusiastic, talkative, given to "reasonably magnificent gestures," and as relaxed as an open valise. Perversely, Murrow, whose business is words, is highly photographic with his three deep forehead wrinkles, his trade-mark mole, the cluster of crow's-feet at the corners of his dark blue eyes; on the screen he often holds his head down, with chin tucked in and eyes forward, before he smiles a sudden sweet gentle smile at millions unseen in living rooms. But Friendly, whose business is pictures, is highly unphotogenic, with his large kind slab of face, his tortoise-shell glasses which fail to be a trade-mark like those of Steve Allen and Robert Q. Lewis.

Although Murrow says that his own horizon never extends beyond ninety days, Friendly has visions to spare of where the program will go two years from now. Sometimes he can't wait; then he telephones Murrow in the middle of the night, selling an idea with boundless verse. The bulk of the work, however, all the nasty planning, gets done in Friendly's office with the two of them gossiping over the germinating notions that usually start in Friendly's fecund mind. The pair spend most of the time deciding what to cover, occasionally stepping boldly into controversial matters. Last November they did the case of 1st Lieutenant Milo J. Radulovich (whom Air Secretary Talbott later retained in the Air Force Reserve) after an Air Force board had found the young man a security risk, because his father had subscribed to a pro-Communist newspaper and his sister had marched as a picket in a Communist demonstration. On the same program, Murrow and Friendly also presented the case of the American Civil Liberties Union fight to hire a hall in Indianapolis, a procedure blocked by the American Legion. A Catholic church took the Civil Liberties Union in, then "See It Now" showed both the Civil Liberties meeting and the Legion meeting. For this, John Crosby called Murrow the St. George of television. He might have called St. George twins.

Once the film is in, the pair spend the rest of their time writing what they have covered, with Friendly doing three-fourths of the writing, but both rewriting each other. When Murrow goes on the air, it is almost impossible to decide who wrote what. But in the main, Friendly is an adjective man. Murrow a verb man. Lately Friendly has swung over, relying properly on verbs for the bone of the script.

To get that script, Murrow will go anywhere, fly exhaustedly to interview someone inconveniently. He is a highly intellectual counterpart of Joe Friday, the cop in "Dragnet," with his "All we want are the facts, Ma'am." For those facts Murrow has flown to Berlin, to Korea, and he can't keep away from floods. When the Missouri overflowed, Murrow rushed out. Formal, unshaved, with stick microphone in hand at four A.M., he tapped strangers (who immediately called him Ed) to ask his questions. The resulting script is full of Friendly-Murrowisms: "A sandbag makes all men equal. Sometimes a sandbag is thrown at the river and the river throws it right back." No adjectives. The script is also full of the unfaked eloquence of tired men.

Such a tired man was the helicopter pilot in Korea in the blood plasma story on "See It Now." It was quick and brutal. The film showed a donor giving blood, the blood taken to Korea and dripped into "a kid's shoulder after the bullet was removed and spattered into a white basin." Then the pilot said: "See them hills? All cost blood."

Although practically everybody knows the story of Murrow, practically no one knows the story of Friendly. The son of a manufacturing jeweller, he was born in Providence, Rhode Island, went to business college, did a little documentary radio writing, and then went into the Army. There his mild Providence personality underwent a curious forced growth in the Orient. By the end of the war Master Sergeant Friendly, on the staff of the *CBI Roundup* (the Far East equivalent of *The Stars and Stripes*) was a fairly flamboyant, unorthodox character, called "The Man," had four battle stars, the Soldier's Medal, and the Legion of Merit. (A minute after the Merit award, he rightly was chewed out for not wearing the proper uniform.) Friendly, as a correspondent, went on two B-29 missions at a time "when even the [airplane] designers were quivering. . . . He rode the Stilwell Road with the first convoy, being injured so badly that he almost lost a hand. He flew night missions with the first P-61 Black Widows." Then the war was over, and Friendly was back where he started—documentaries. He has made a good thing of it, always trying to cut back the blubber of radio writing, then of TV. "Got to be lean," said Friendly. Murrow was lean. They are both Jack Spratt.

Pinter

"Funny and Moving and Frightening"

BY KATHLEEN HALTON

No living British playwright is more influential than Harold Pinter, and none has a more unsettling effect on drama critics. They persist in finding him devious. In some circles he has even acquired a reputation as master of the put-on (the "if he's fooling us, then he can't be a fool" principle). When tackling the work of writers like John Osborne or Arnold Wesker, the critics happily explain it as tabloid slogans and social messages. Faced with Pinter, they frequently wander off into quagmires of confusion. Nihilist, symbolist of suburbia, metaphysician, gamesman, hoaxer: You name the cap, and they'll make him wear it.

Bewildered and surprised, Pinter has on several occasions denied these accusations: *The Birthday Party* could not have been influenced by Ionesco or Pirandello since he hadn't read either. The woman in *The Homecoming* is not a nymphomaniac, and if she is playing some kind of game, she's doing it for a very practical reason. Despite suggestions to the contrary Pinter is not concerned with using the theatre to express philosophical concepts or solutions: He would consider that an impertinence.

Pinter has said: "I've never started a play from any kind of abstract idea or theory. . . . You arrange *and* you listen, following the clues you leave for yourself, through the characters."

As one of the large public who admires Pinter more than any other living dramatist, and finds him funny and moving and frightening in the way he drills to the core of somebody's private being, I decided to follow the clues.

All I had to start with was the memory of a very curious first meeting in which the conversation with Pinter, his wife, Vivien Merchant, and my companion could only be described by the fearful word "Pinteresque." The scene was a theatre bar, the crucial prop, my friend's elaborately latticed black shoes. And this is how it went:

FRIEND: What did you think of the play?
PINTER (eyes fixed on friend's shoes): Vivien and I have been looking at your shoes and we think they are the sexiest shoes we have seen.
FRIEND: My shoes?
PINTER: Yes, your shoes. Can you tell us where you got them?
FRIEND (Pause): I don't know whether I've forgotten or whether I don't want you to know.
PINTER (Pause): I didn't see the play.
At this point, as Pinter whipped off heavy spectacles and stared with a fierce smile before him, I was convinced my friend would fall—like Bill in Pinter's play *The Collection*—pole-axed to the ground without a blow's being struck.

I was the more bemused in New York recently when that most candid and reliable judge, the English playwright Peter Shaffer, explained: "Harold's reputation for being oblique is the result of his being so straight. He's not withholding anything, and the implications people see in his work genuinely baffle him."

Shaffer and Pinter had built a close friendship during the spring months of this year while Pinter was in New York with *The Homecoming*. Pinter had disliked New York and what he described as "All that endless smiling." Bored by being lionized and by most of the people he met, he managed to remain elusive. His haunt was a theatre bar on West Forty-fifth Street, where he fancied the liver and onions and the good wood on the bar.

On my return to England, Pinter was in Nottingham directing Robert Shaw's *The Man in the Glass Booth*, his first production outside his own work. While I waited his return south, I filled in some of the basic clues.

Harold Pinter, British man of all theatre, wrote "The Birthday Party," opening this month on Broadway, and directed "The Man in the Glass Booth," now a hit in England.

He was born in Hackney in 1930 in the East End of London, an area where the dingier belt of suburbia meets what is optimistically called "country." (Pinter has described it as "weasel-under-the-cocktail-cabinet land.") The only son of a hardworking Jewish tailor, he won a scholarship to the local Hackney grammar school, and got into fights with the Fascists who were menacing the East End at that time.

Pinter refused military service as a conscientious objector and after a period at drama school became a repertory actor, touring Ireland for eighteen months with the late Anew McMaster and later England, with that rumbustious tyrant of English classical theatre, Sir Donald Wolfit. Pinter read modern novels; wrote poems and prose pieces, some of which appeared in small magazines; and introduced his friends to Samuel Beckett. (A friend recalls, "He was the earliest Beckett fellow I ever heard of.")

In 1956 Pinter married the actress Vivien Merchant whom he'd met on tour. When she became pregnant in 1958, they found a basement room in London's Notting Hill Gate where Pinter worked as a caretaker to pay the rent. (He worked at other times as a street salesman, doorman at a dancehall, and snow shoveller.)

Pinter's first play, a one-acter called *The Room*, was written in 1957 on commission from a friend at the University of Bristol drama department. He managed to complete it in four days. Close on its heels followed *The Birthday Party*, Pinter's first full-length play and a total flop when it was first performed in London. The critics soon changed tack, and *The Caretaker*, first done in 1960, assured the Pinters some financial security. It was followed by a number of television and radio plays and in 1965 by a third full-length play, *The Homecoming*, which later won the Critics' award for the best Broadway play of its season. In the later plays Pinter has extended his obsession with a couple of men confronting each other in a confined space by adding a woman and even stronger sexual overtones.

The Pinters moved eventually to a bow-fronted house in the seaside town of Worthing; and, recently, on the strength of his vastly successful film scripts—among them *The Servant*, *The Pumpkin Eater*, and *Accident*—they bought a five-storey period house overlooking London's Regent's Park. It is comfortably and elegantly decorated by the Pinters. They have one son, Daniel, who is nine.

My researches had brought me not much closer to Pinter. The next step seemed more auspicious. It was a conversation with the loquacious Liverpool playwright Alun Owen, who shared a dressing room and acted with Pinter in London.

"Harold is the most honest man I know and the most scrupulous observer of the truth. But things do happen strangely to Harold. He's a very emotional writer, with a very private vision.

"We were both acting and writing verse when we first met, though we were mainly concerned with the price of a pint. I remember that ferocious old autocrat Donald Wolfit, in whose company we were, casting Harold as the tailor in *The Taming of the Shrew*. 'Of course, Pinter,' he said, 'the tailor stammers.'

PINTER: I don't stammer, Mr. Wolfit.

WOLFIT: Nonsense, the tailor always stammers, it's traditional.

PINTER: I'm sorry, I don't see it that way.

WOLFIT: You stammer Pinter, or you lose the part!

"Harold lost the part, but for days after Wolfit could be heard mumbling to himself in the wings, 'Pinter won't stammer!' Harold launched a war of nerves on poor Wolfit, and at the end of the season, Wolfit complained: 'Only one member of the company didn't say goodbye to me, the boy Pinter. But *he* writes poetry.'

"Harold was very popular with the girls. When he met Vivien he had to get rid of a number of ladies. He's not a puritan, but he's not licentious. I saw him recently wearing a black silk shirt. It was elaborately camp without being homosexual. He's very socially assured. He'd never pick up the wrong knife, and if he did he'd make you feel *you* were using the wrong one.

"Harold can be very violent. Once, in a Sloane Square bar a bowler-hatted chap was saying something about Hitler being right. This man turned to Harold and said 'I suppose you're a filthy yid yourself.' Harold took off his glasses and said, 'You shouldn't say that.' The man said it again, and Harold hit him, gashed his face. Then he hit Harold, whereupon Harold went for him and knocked him all over the bar. The police came. When things calmed down, this bloke said to Harold, 'Are you a Jew?' He said yes, and the other fellow said curiously, 'In that case I can understand why you hit me. But why did you go *on* hitting me?'

"Harold is straight down the line. You could argue that his work was up a dead end with *The Homecoming*, although I don't feel that myself—but you couldn't say it was phony."

I had felt some of the same doubt about *The Homecoming*, as if it were so perfect an example of the sum of Pinter's work that it had died the death, so compressed and elliptical at times that one lost the sense. The thing to do might be to recap, to isolate some of the ingredients of the other plays.

These ingredients are nearly always a struggle for territory or conversational ascendancy. His first plays all take place in confined and seedy environments. In the first play, *The Room*, the security is shattered by a violent intrusion that ends in death. Stanley in *The Birthday Party*, the mild self-styled concert pianist who finds a retreat under his landlady's roof, is menaced by two sinister outsiders, who come to humiliate and finally take him away. In neither case is the intrusion fully explained. A room is still the pivot of *The Caretaker*, but there is no outside menace, only a clash of personalities within. An old tramp thinks he's found a safe place to hole up, plays off his hosts against each other, and is finally thrown out. Here the characters—especially Mick, the younger brother, whom Pinter once played himself—are totally and uncompromisingly themselves, creating their own circumstances.

Pinter has said of his preoccupation with a confined space, "Before you manage to adjust yourself to living alone in your room, you're not really terribly fit and equipped to go out to fight battles." I add that Pinter spent his early years as a travelling actor for whom finding a place to bed down was a weekly, sometimes a nightly, hazard. (An actor friend recalls overhearing him—out of work and penniless—confidently explaining how to set about buying a house.)

A room is also a useful dramatic prop. Pinter has admitted that he's not very good at com-plicated theatrical devices: "I find myself stuck with these characters who are either sitting or standing, and they've either got to walk out of a door, or come in through a door, and that's about all they can do."

In the later plays the setting becomes decidedly smarter: offices and upper-middle-class apartments of the kind in which he set *The Collection*, a perfect example of a play based on suspense and manoeuvring for position. Did or did not Stella, a dress designer, commit adultery? The answer is maddeningly unrevealed.

With this change of background, Pinter introduces a new emphasis on sex. *The Lover* is an erotic charade. *Tea Party* (another television play) is a study of an industrialist disintegrating under the pressures of self-deception. In both, sexual games and fetishistic objects like high heels, leather, and special costumes spice the confrontation (and nearly always the woman has been played by Vivien Merchant, a hypnotically sensual actress).

But the effects are sometimes overexposed. What sticks in the memory are his meaty, very vocalized, often very funny, and beautifully loquacious characters. Between what they are and what they aspire to is a world of wishful thinking. Stan in *The Birthday Party* imagines a world concert tour. Goldberg, in the same play, a boastful predator, sentimentalizes his childhood. Funniest of all, the crass and domineering Max in *The Homecoming*, who is all that's wrong with the patriarch: "I respected my father not only as a man but as a number-one butcher! And to prove it I followed him into the shop. I learned to carve a carcass at his knee. I commemorated his name in blood. I gave birth to three grown men! All on my own bat."

Not since Eliot's "Sweeney Agonistes" has anyone picked up the nuances of English suburban speech so accurately.

Pinter's characters repeat themselves, go round in circles, and at all costs avoid direct communication. They say anything but what they mean, in order to avoid the danger of being found out. So sparse is communication in Pinter's movie script for *Accident* and in much of *The Homecoming* that the audience is in danger of losing touch. He is excessively fond of long pauses. (Peter Cook of *Beyond the*

Fringe recalls a revue, *Pieces of Eight*, for which he and Pinter wrote sketches. The writers were paid according to the length of their contributions, and Cook would sit in the stalls listening enviously as Pinter's pauses ticked by —"Every second was money in the bank for Harold.")

The day before I met Pinter I came across the following in a British weekly: ". . . he's not leading me up any garden, he's not slipping me any wink, he's not flogging me a remedy or a path or a revelation or a basinful of breadcrumbs, he's not selling me anything I don't want to buy, he doesn't give a bollock whether I buy or not, he hasn't got his hand over his heart. Well, I'll buy his goods, hook, line, and sinker, because he leaves no stone unturned and no maggot lonely. He brings forth a body of beauty. His work is beautiful." A total commitment to Samuel Beckett by Harold Pinter.

When we met in Brighton, I showed Pinter the quotation. "I couldn't write that now," he said regretfully, "because I distrust words. What I feel about them is almost a kind of nausea. But that is everything I feel about Beckett. When I was young, I wrote long poems in the style of Dylan Thomas. I used words with considerable freedom. I came across one or two poems the other day and felt a profound nostalgia for the way I could let words rip."

I had gone to Brighton on one of those bright seaside days that smell of oysters and ozone. Earlier that morning I'd watched Pinter rehearsing Robert Shaw's *The Man in the Glass Booth*, standing in the front row of the stalls, very cool and meticulous in a silk jersey rolltop sweater pushed back over thick forearms, a Scotch-on-the-rocks in hand.

At lunch in a nearby fish restaurant where we'd gone to talk, Pinter continued: "I edit myself so much I can't write anything. My only fixed plans are to go over to New York for the production of *The Birthday Party* and to write the screenplay which a young American wants to direct. Otherwise I've called a halt on films, though I've been offered at least a dozen. Both Antonioni and Godard were trying to persuade me to work for them. But I just want to clear the air. There is one film I'd do like a shot, only there are problems over the rights. It's L. P. Hartley's *The Go-Between*. I loved that bloody book."

We walked to Pinter's hotel suite in a crenellated English seaside palace called The Metropole. From the windows, as we talked, came sounds of squealing bathers and the glare of early afternoon sun. "I was a morbid youth," Pinter said smiling broadly. "But I had a remarkably enjoyable association with five other boys. It was a great relief, I remember, that they knew what I was on about. Ruthless mutual confrontations. Out of that group two have remained my closest friends.

"Other friends are theatre people like Robert Shaw and Donald Pleasence. But I live a pretty closed life. I sit and talk to my wife a great deal in the kitchen. We're pretty tight as a family. People don't come round except by specific invitation. Nobody just rings the door and comes in. There's a secretary in the morning and two dailies, but no living-in staff. (He snaps his fingers and rips off his glasses): At one o'clock —that's the point—we're alone.

"Daniel, my son, is a very intelligent fellow. I like him very much. What can I say about him? He's himself. He's a great joy." (Nobody I have met before can say, "He's a great joy," with such convincing and innocent candour.)

We drink a lot of coffee and Pinter paces up and down. I return to Beckett: "The finest prose writer living." And who else does he admire? "Albee, and young English playwrights like Edward Bond and the late Joe Orton. I like the Beatles, I'm very fond of them. And cricket. That obsesses me. I like Yeats, and Larkin, and Hardy—I read them aloud. (He demonstrates this by reading a poem of Thomas Hardy's.)

"I'll tell you what I've just done. I've got this book on Francis Bacon, a big bloody book with a lot of paintings, and since I don't know where to look for the originals, and I couldn't afford them, I've cut out and framed about sixteen reproductions. I'm going to stick them all over the house."

And health and happiness? "I'm very rarely ill. I use a stationary bicycle, which is useful because you can read at the same time. Happy? I am happy. But at once sad. At—you know the passing."

I asked him what he wanted to write next. "I hate to be categorical especially about my own work because I know very little about it. But I've got a feeling that I can never again deal with a room and people who come into it, not in the same way as I did in *The Homecoming*, though I'm very fond of that play."

What about the accusation that it is full of gamesmanship? "The game is the least of it. What takes place is a mode of expression, a chosen device. It's the way the characters face each other under the game that interests me. The woman is not a nymphomaniac as some critics claimed. In fact she's not very sexy. She's in a kind of despair which gives her a kind of freedom. Certain facts like marriage and the family for this woman have clearly ceased to have any meaning.

"But I only formulate conclusions after I've written the plays. I've no idea what I'm obsessed with—just so pleased to see the words on paper! Wolf Mankowitz suggested I look at the Greeks for a subject. So I've been meaning to look at the Greeks. But I'm just not capable of it. I can only proceed through my own curious funnel. I'm not politically committed though I've recently associated myself publicly with

two causes: I'm categorically anti the Americans in Viet Nam. And I feel strongly in favour of Israel.

"As for the work, I started something last year in Boston, but that was no bloody good. I'd done it before. Now I've started a couple of pages of something quite different. A new form, and I'm diving. It's simply, as it stands, about a woman around fifty. And she's talking. That's all I bloody well know. I don't know where she is. Certainly it's not a room. So the characters can't open a door and come in, but I think they're there.

"I'm very excited by the stage, and I still want to write for it. It's physically restricted and very naked; and whatever the next thing is I write, it's got to be even more naked than the last.

"I'm very irritated by the assumption that the theatre is finished," said Harold Pinter snapping his fingers, and whipping off his glasses. "It is *not* finished while *I* am alive."

The Quest for Beauty in Dahomey

BY JACQUES MAQUET

A PHOTOGRAPHIC ESSAY BY
IRVING PENN

EDITOR'S NOTE: *Dr. Jacques Maquet, a dark-eyed, bearded French anthropologist, is director of anthropological studies at L'École Pratique des Hautes Études at the University of Paris. The author of seven books, mostly on the civilizations and anthropology of Africa, he holds degrees as a Doctor of Law, of Philosophy, and of Social Anthropology. He is working now on the sociology of primitive art. Based in Paris, where he lives with his wife and two sons, Dr. Maquet often goes to Africa, often to America, where he has been visiting professor of anthropology for part of this year at the University of Pittsburgh.*

African art calls to our minds the graceful antelope headpieces of the Bambara, the baroque bronze queens of Benin, the mysterious masks of the Dogon. African art evokes the creative discovery of tribal sculpture, during the first decade of this century, by Picasso, Matisse, Derain, Vlaminck who found in the powerful styles of Black Africa a confirmation of their passionate aesthetic researches which eventually led to Cubism. But the urge for beauty, the pursuit of form as an aim in itself, is not restricted in Africa to statues, engravings, and paintings: It is to be found also in the adornments of the body.

Of the Dahomean girls photographed on these pages, some belong to the Tofinu and Aïzo groups who live along the lagoons which line the Atlantic shores of Dahomey; other ones are members of the Pilapila tribe who dwell in a completely different environment, the open grasslands of the north; a few are Fulani, the proud pastoral nomads of unknown origin who wander throughout the savannahs from Sénégal in the west to Cameroon in the east. Differences in their clothes, maquillage, jewellery, scarifications, hair-dressing reflect the different values and patterns of life of their peoples but, under this variety, we find a common aesthetic orientation: We are in the world of art. In their recent monumental survey of African art, *Afrique Noire: la Création Plastique*, Michel Leiris and Jacqueline Delange are right to be provocative innovators by devoting the first part of their work to "the arts of the body."

Rarely in Africa is the body left in its natural condition. Modifications such as the cicatricial patterns on the torsos of the girls from Ganvié are not purely ornamental; they indicate that the person belongs to a certain tribe, to a certain clan, or has undergone rites of initiation. Yet,

IRVING PENN

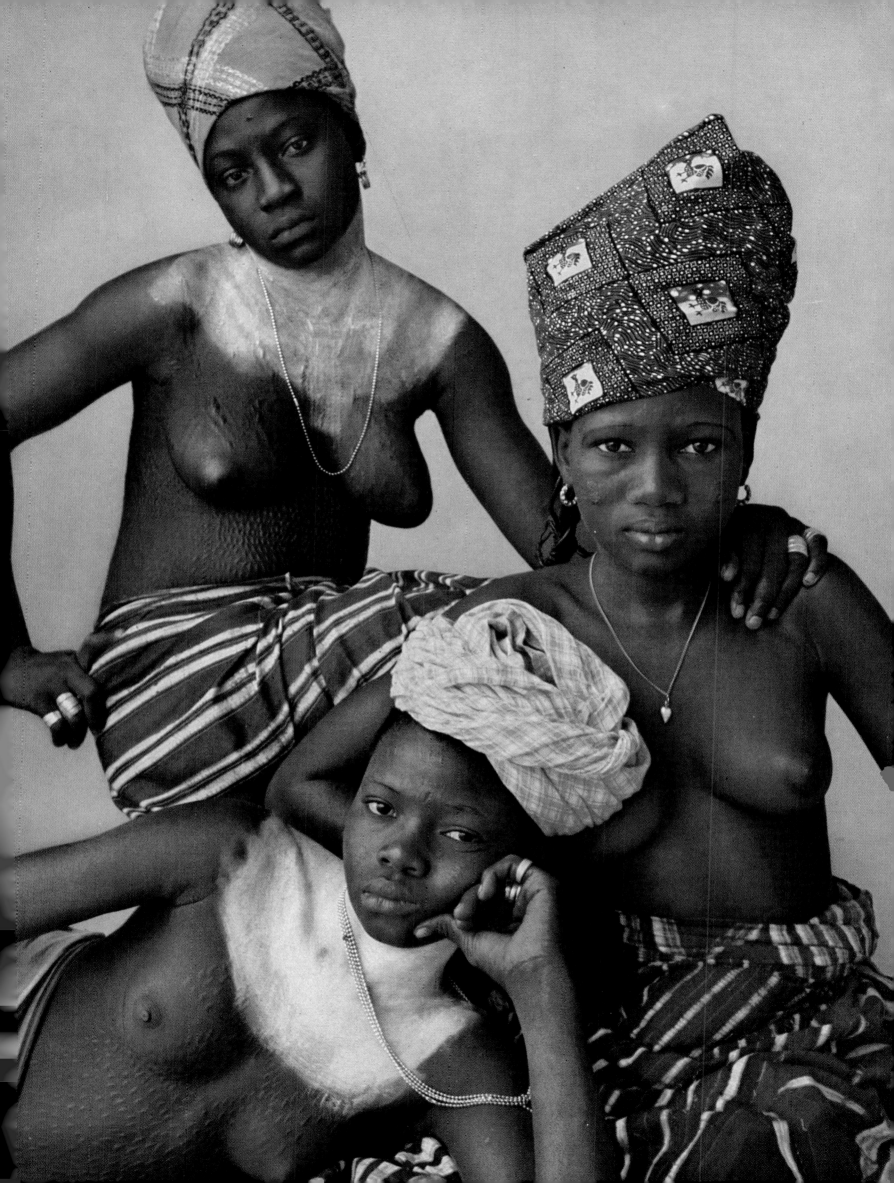

at the same time, the regularity of the markings, the intricate patterns they draw on the smooth skins shining in the sun, the emphasis on the harmony of the shoulders, on the delicate roundness of the breasts reveal the search for beauty.

This is not an interpretation by scholars of foreign cultures. Dahomean peoples of the lagoon villages, men as well as women, say explicitly that scarifications enhance the handsomeness of the bodies. Aesthetic concern in Africa pervades the whole range of individual and collective activities: Political assemblies, religious rituals, family ceremonials are all conducted with formality and etiquette, the ornaments of social relations. Villages and family compounds are laid out with a sense of order and balance.

Yet aesthetic concern rarely conduces to art-for-art's-sake production. Senufo masterpieces were religious; Kuba royal statues were dynastic. So were our mediaeval cathedrals and our Renaissance palaces. It is only in contemporary industrial societies that art tends to be a separate and marginal activity. In traditional Africa the quest for formal beauty was diffused but ever-present.

The colourful striped cotton *bouba*, the elegantly wrapped kerchiefs, the necklaces and earrings, the expertly done maquillage of the coastal Dahomean young women express more than refinement and sense of beauty; they indicate joie de vivre, fulfillment, freedom. These gay, proud, and resourceful women are not simply servants of the men, objects for the males, an image of the female condition in Black Africa. This stereotype is not valid for Dahomey—and I do not mean only present day Dahomey, independent since 1960, nor colonial Dahomey, under French rule from 1892 up to 1960, but I mean the traditional kingdom of Dahomey which in the eighteenth and nineteenth centuries was a prosperous, powerful, and turbulent state.

The story of that kingdom—its territory, centred around its capital city of Abomey, never covered more than the southern part of the present Republic of Dahomey—reads like the semi-legendary tales of the origins of kingdoms and principalities of European Middle Ages. In the early seventeenth century, when the King of Allada died, his sons disputed his succession;

one was able to keep Allada, and the others, obliged to leave, founded each a kingdom: Abomey, Whydah, and Porto-Novo, as that place became known later on. Of course, they struggled for supremacy among themselves and with their neighbours.

Feats of arms, military glories, gallant conquests lost their chivalrous pageantry when, in 1672, the Guinea Coast slave trade began. The profitable sugar-cane plantations of the West Indies needed labour, and for two centuries the Dahomean population was, like other West African peoples, heavily taxed. The population, but not the rulers. European slave traders bought their black cargoes from African kings for firearms, fabrics, alcohol.

Wars became more frequent. Dahomey annually attacked its neighbours, just to make prisoners and sell them. It was violent, cruel, merciless. The outcome of a battle was no longer for the vanquished to pass under the authority of another ruler, which is not for the common man a terrible fate. It was to be severed from one's family, from one's community, and to be shipped to the faraway land of no return. Fighting became fierce and bloody, which is not in the African tradition.

The sweet, elegant, and poised Aïzo girls are descendants of the people who lived in and around Whydah, the main port of slave trade for the control of which Britain, France, and other European powers played the diplomatic game for two centuries. How did Dahomean women succeed in keeping through generations their high human qualities on the background of violence, cruelty, injustice?

A part of the answer is certainly to be found in the ancient Fon world views, expressed in traditions before the beginning of the slave trade. The Fon people constituted the nucleus of the Dahomean kingdom. Their philosophy, underlying their religious beliefs and cults, is still a living force in Dahomey today. There is a profound conviction in the minds of the Dahomeans of the essential equality of men and women. Of course, it is not expressed in the dry and abstract language of jurists and philosophers but in the rich and vivid idiom of myth and religion.

The creating deity is designated by a double name, Mawu-Lisa, and it is understood as a pair of beings, one female, Mawu, and one male,

Lisa. They are regarded as twins and united they organize the world. The late Melville J. Herskovits, the American scholar who had the deepest knowledge of the Dahomean culture, wrote that the high god "is envisaged as a Janus-like figure, one side of its body being female, with eyes forming the moon, and bearing the name of Mawu; the other portion is male, whose eyes are the sun, and whose name is Lisa."

The dual nature of Mawu-Lisa expresses, even before the world of men was ordered, the complementary forces which were to be active in it. As another specialist of Dahomey, Paul Mercier, wrote: "Mawu, the female principle, is fertility, motherhood, gentleness, forgiveness; while Lisa is power, warlike or otherwise, strength, and toughness. Moreover, they assure the rhythm of day and night. Mawu is the night, the moon, freshness, rest, joy; Lisa is the day, the sun, heat, labour, all hard things."

These complementary beings are seen as equal: There is no priority of Adam over Eve. It is not only a principle, asserted in myths about the origin of the world, it is lived in everyday human relations, even the most intimate ones.

There is a charming tale in which the girl acts as an equal of man: She feels the urge of desire, she expresses it, she takes the initiative. Finally the brief encounter ends up in a tragic romantic love. In both stages of the story, the sensual and the romantic, the girl has the leading part. This tale was collected in Dahomey by Melville J. and Frances S. Herskovits and published in their book *Dahomean Narrative*. The following summarized version is mine:

Long ago, when a child, boy or girl, was vowed to a god, to a *vodun*, by its parents, he or she had to enter in a convent at the age of twenty and stay there in celibacy for eight years. Ahwala, a girl selling cakes in the market, saw a young man in a convent. She entered the house, although it was forbidden, and said to him, "You are a fine fellow; I never saw you before, yet I want to lie with you." The man, whose name was Hundjo, answered that to touch a woman had been prohibited to him by the priest. Ahwala then threw off her cloth and stood there wearing only beads. After some resistance, Hundjo gave up and they had intercourse. When it was over, Hundjo died. The

priest ordered that the girl should be bound, but it was not necessary, as she remained beside the dead body, keeping off the flies. . . .

Of course, this is a tale. In real life, things do not occur in such a straightforward manner. Yet for Dahomean listeners the girl's uninhibited behaviour was acceptable and was not mistaken for a prostitute's approach. Like men, women could feel a sexual inclination and say so. Equality of the sexes was more than a mythical idea; it was deeply ingrained in minds and mores.

Before going back to the lovers for the end of their story, I should like to stress the importance of religious practices in daily life. Under the supreme deity, Mawu-Lisa, gods were numerous in the Dahomean pantheon. They were called *vodun*. Each of them was honoured in a cult centre ministered by a priest. Some of these centres were also institutions for religious training. They are usually described as "convents" for reasons made clear by the story: Young men and women, who as children had been dedicated to a certain god because their parents were devotees of that *vodun* or because the diviner had said that it was necessary in order to recover from an illness, were obliged to serve the priest for a certain number of years before getting married.

Their initiation into the esoteric knowledge of a particular cult was indicated to everybody by bodily markings such as the beautifully patterned scarifications on the back of the Ganvié girl vowed to a local *vodun*. Some of the Dahomean gods came to the Americas with the slaves: In Haiti, Legba the trickster-god, became Papa Lébat the Dahomean name *vodun* was changed to *vaudou* in Haiti, and to *voodoo* in Louisiana.

Now the *vodun* who had been offended by the lovers and who had sent death to his disobedient initiate spoke through the medium of another worshipper of his. He said to bring firewood, to pour jars of oil on it, to light it, and to put Hundjo's body in the flames. "If," added the god, "someone has the courage to enter the fire, the young man will be restored to life." Hundjo's mother, his brother, his best friend approached but, afraid of being burned, stepped back.

Then Ahwala rose, sang, "If I do not go into the fire, I will not be able to live with my soul,"

FISHING PEOPLE OF LAKE NOKOUÉ,
as carved as Fon sculptures against a silver sky,
poling their pirogue to watery villages
of stilted pavilions, roofed in palm fronds.

and threw herself on the fire. In a few minutes, the two came out alive. The people were joyous, beat the drums, and danced. The king decided to reduce the seclusion period in a convent from eight to three years.

Here are the themes of our romantic literature, love and death. We are not far from Tristan and Isolde, although the Dahomean tale is definitely more optimistic: Love defeats death. A love transcending social rules and human condition was probably as rare among Dahomeans as among ourselves, but the audience understood it, and the beautiful young women certainly dreamed about it. I stress this as it is often repeated that the notion of romantic love does not exist in a society which considers polygamy as the ideal type of marriage, with the élite, at least, practising it. Such was Dahomey, polygamous yet open to delusions of absolute love.

The marvellous freedom and unself-consciousness of Ahwala assuming her desire and her love, weighing the importance of "living with one's soul" bear witness to the mature and independent position of the Dahomean women. But we have more concrete proofs of that than the tale of Ahwala and Hundjo. The rôle women had in the public life of the kingdom of Dahomey was immense, and this has startled anthropologists.

The administrative structure of the kingdom was double, masculine and feminine. Every office was conferred simultaneously on a woman and on a man. The woman official lived within the palace and her male opposite number outside it. The Dahomean administration was elaborate and fulfilled many tasks which are not usually carried on by non-literate societies, such as to keep a record of each birth and each death, to organize a comprehensive system of taxation, levies, and contributions, and to check its operation in order to avoid tax evasion.

In any pair of officials the rôles of the man and the woman were different but complementary. The man acted in the field, for instance, supervising the production of salt, counting the sacks, and establishing on that basis the taxation to be paid later on. The female counterpart would keep the pebbles representing the sacks of salt, compare independent reports on that matter, and remember the figures of the previous years (when records are kept without the help of writing, memory becomes the most precious tool). The female half of the pair did not have a subordinate function; on the contrary, she checked the activities of the male official.

Still more striking was the place of the women in the army. The standing army of Dahomey was composed entirely of women, the famous Amazons, whom the nineteenth-century travellers have found so puzzling. When each year after the harvest the king went to war, female troops constituted the core of the army. Male soldiers, more numerous, only supplement the permanent corps of Amazons.

Amazons have fired the imagination of Europeans who saw them or heard about them, and it is difficult to get a true picture of these she-warriors. For some, they seemed a volunteer élite force of virgins submitted to a monastic discipline; for Sir Richard Burton, British consul in Fernando Po, off West Africa, who saw the Amazons in 1863, "they were manoeuvring with the precision of a flock of sheep," and they displayed "harshness of feature and robustness of form rivalling the masculine." Whatever the reality, probably somewhere between idealization and debasement, the Amazon army is another proof of the egalitarian premise of the Dahomean culture.

In the grassland dotted with scattered trees, north of the traditional kingdom of Dahomey with its male-and-female creator, its *vodun*, and its Amazons, is another African civilization, the one of the Sudanese savannah. There live peasants, such as the Somba, the Bariba, and the Pilapila, in clusters of huts built under the protective shadow of the giant baobabs. There live the Fulani herdsmen, sometimes readily accommodating to their agricultural neighbours, sometimes aggressively fanatic Moslems. There, also, the aesthetic interests find an outlet in the adorning of the body, male as well as female. The peasant girls' makeup has not the sophistication of the maquillage displayed by city women of the coastal area but it has the impromptu quality and the colour boldness of psychedelic decoration.

In African aesthetics, the Fulani challenge the usual ideas and categories of art historians. They do not carve masks and statues as do most of the African villagers. They do not smelt bronze or brass into figurines and pendants as do Fon and Yoruba craftsmen. They do not chisel golden jewels as do Ashanti and Baule. Yet, they have an exacerbated sensibility for beauty, to use the words of Jacqueline Delange who has recently given a brilliant analysis of the strange position of the Fulani in the arts of Africa.

Fulani aesthetic feelings are expressed in non-figurative arts such as poetry, music, song. The Fulani appreciate the refined use of language. Their short, vivid verbal images have the haunting quality of the Homeric poetic comparisons in the *Odyssey*; their songs, accompanied by stringed instruments, are delicate and nostalgic.

The sensibility of the Fulani is visual, too. They neglect the permanent objects in which other societies embody their artistic strivings but they care for the ephemeral achievements of fashion. In one group of Fulani, the Bororo, there is an annual beauty contest for young men, the *gerewol*. In the competition, an elaborate makeup (cheeks tinted red, lips underlined in black, white triangles drawn on mahogany skin), original headgears with ostrich feathers, new arrangements of beaded bands, metal disks, and rings are as important as the perfection of physical features, of which the main ones are considered to be eyes and teeth. As much as a beauty contest, it is a fashion show.

Intense interest for corporal adornment, care to innovate and not to lag behind what is in fashion permeate the culture, technically poor but aesthetically rich, of the Fulani. The elaborate and imaginative hairdos of some Fulani women are daring, aerial, butterfly-like constructions that have been compared to Calder mobiles. The hair of other Fulanis, such as the one photographed, is more simply dressed: This style is suitable to young girls who recently came of age.

Societies of traditional Black Africa were not affluent. To satisfy the elementary needs of food and shelter, Africans had to struggle against a difficult environment, and their crops were rarely much above subsistence level. Yet they did not devote all their creative activities to material pursuits, they needed beauty, too. Through their sculpture, they reached one of the summits of world's art. Through their concern for form in the ornament of their bodies, they have introduced art to the ephemeral aspects of daily life; and this makes them close to us.

Markings

BY DAG HAMMARSKJÖLD

The late Secretary-General to the United Nations, Dag Hammarskjöld, whose unshaken courage, monumental sense of duty, and intellectual brilliance were respected universally, left a manuscript—part diary, part poetry, part musings—the "markings" of his life, including the excerpts above, written from 1925 until shortly before his death in 1961 in a plane crash in Northern Rhodesia. In his extraordinary career as a scholar, a Swedish economist, and an international diplomat, he touched, on all sides, the events of world history, but he included no names, no specifics in his book. At times an almost unbearably intimate disclosure of one man's spiritual labour, Markings was translated from the Swedish by Leif Sjöberg and the distinguished poet, W. H. Auden, and will be published by Alfred A. Knopf on October 19. Although the book's contents often take the formal shapes of literature (as in the case of the fourteen haiku opposite), they were not intended as literature for its own sake: as Dag Hammarskjöld explained, the manuscript was to be understood "as a sort of white book *concerning my negotiations with myself—and with God."*

Hunger is my native place in the land of the passions. Hunger for fellowship, hunger for righteousness—for a fellowship founded on righteousness, and a righteousness attained in fellowship.

Only life can satisfy the demands of life. And this hunger of mine can be satisfied for the simple reason that the nature of life is such that I can realize my individuality by becoming a bridge for others, a stone in the temple of righteousness.

Don't be afraid of yourself, live your individuality to the full—but for the good of others. Don't copy others in order to buy fellowship, or make convention your law instead of living the righteousness.

What is one to do on a bleak day but drift for a while through the streets—drift with the stream?

Slowly, with the gravity of an inanimate object, now coming to a standstill, now turning, where currents meet, in listless leisurely gyrations. Slow—and grey. The November day has reached the hour when the light is dying behind a low cold bank of cloud, but the twilight brings no promise of mitigation or peace.

Slow and grey—He searches every face. But the people aimlessly streaming along the grey ditches of the streets are all like himself—atoms in whom the radioactivity is extinct, and force has tied its endless chain around nothing. "That one may be translated into light and song." *(Erik Blomberg)* To let go of the image which, in the eyes of this world, bears your name, the image fashioned in your consciousness by social ambition and sheer force of will. To let go and fall, fall—in trust and blind devotion. Towards another, another. . . .
To take the risk—

In the dim light he searches every face, but sees only endless variations on his own meanness. So might Dante have imagined the punishment of those who had never taken the risk. —To reach perfection, we must all pass, one by one, through the death of self-effacement. And, on this side of it, he will never find the way to anyone who has passed through it.

To become free and responsible. For this alone was man created, and he who fails to take the Way which could have been his shall be lost eternally.

Do not look back. And do not dream about the future, either. It will neither give you back the past, nor satisfy your other daydreams. Your duty, your reward—your destiny—are *here* and *now.*

Congenial to other people?
It is with yourself
That you must live.

Denied any outlet,
The heat transmuted
The coal into diamonds.

Not knowing the question,
It was easy for him
To give the answer.

Do you create?
Or destroy? *That's*
For your ordeal-by-fire to answer.

I ask: what am I doing here?
And, at once, this *I*
Becomes unreal.

He fell from the rock ledge
When, too scared to walk upright,
He tried to crawl.

Be pure and dare—
In this fight with the mountain,
With myself against me.

He gave his life
For the happiness of others,
But wished them evil.

What the shaving satyr
In the mirror mocked at,
He bought with his life.

Let them keep
All the petty secrets
They have guarded so anxiously.

This accidental
Meeting of possibilities
Calls itself *I*.

When the gods play,
They look for a string
That has never been touched by men.

That chapter is closed.
Nothing binds me:
All is made ready, all waiting.

For him who has faith,
The last miracle
Shall be greater than the first.

Hans Hofmann

*At eighty-five Hofmann is a vanguardist
built to last—the world's oldest.*

BY HAROLD ROSENBERG

*"Being incomplete in concept,
the creation will be inadequate."*

HOFMANN

Hofmann could be billed as the world's oldest vanguardist painter—he shades Picasso by more than a year. Though his career spans the entire development of twentieth-century art, his canvases of the last twenty years have the look of the middle 1960's, of today. Those astonishing panels of light—broad, open "landscapes" sprung from a festival of colour and movement, and ranging from sombre chocolate to piping yellows and reds and from slaps and swirls of the brush to smooth placid rectangles—seem to grow fresher every season. When a retrospective of Hofmann's paintings opened at The Museum of Modern Art in 1963, a band of young artists demonstrated at the entrance in favour of Hofmann as the artist who stood for the direction in which they wanted art to go.

There is something paradoxical about being eighty-five and of the vanguard. Shouldn't the row up front be reserved for the newest generation? Hofmann worked in Paris from 1904 to 1914, in the discovery period of Matisse,

Braque, Delaunay; he was an adult at the time of the Armory Show; it is exactly half a century since he opened his famous art school in Munich. Yet this veteran German immigrant was among the "young" artists who created the new American painting in the years following the Second World War.

To stretch so far, Hofmann's up-to-dateness had to be anchored in a principle different from that of the calendar. In art, 1965 is not necessarily ahead of 1925, any more than James Baldwin is ahead of James Joyce. While still working in Paris, Hofmann concluded that all paintings of this century, regardless of the mode in which they were executed (Cubist, Fauvist, Futurist), belong to the same aesthetic moment so long as their creation embodies the new plastic insight developed since Cézanne and Van Gogh. The key word is "creation," the quality of which, rather than the date of performance, determines how far "advanced" the work of art is. To put the idea in another way: There is modern art but no such thing as most modern.

Thus Hofmann has sought an approach to creation that would draw upon all the resources —technical, intellectual, psychic—developed by

IRVING PENN

painting since Impressionism. His vanguardism is a formal position fortified by conservative concepts. Or, to be more precise, by concepts that have been applied for decades, though not necessarily understood. It is a vanguardism built to last. Through half a century of search he has uncovered the core of a new tradition in painting, "the underlying aesthetic principles," as he calls them, of the modern masters.

A permanent outpost on the frontier of the new, Hofmann appears, in the expansiveness of his temperament, his moral and intellectual solidity, even his massive Bavarian physique, more of the nineteenth century than of this one. The broad, colour-saturated continent evoked by his paintings is a resurrection on the plane of inwardness of the American West brought into art by the painter-explorers of a hundred years ago. To the pioneer heritage belongs also Hofmann's faith in the creative possibilities of all individuals (a faith which has survived in spite of data to the contrary supplied by his years as a teacher). For Hofmann creation is the normal daily business of the human being; it has nothing in common with that induced confusion, egotism, and anti-intellectual pretentiousness that causes the ideal of creativity to amount (in Jacques Barzun's opinion) to a national malady. In painting, Hofmann has insisted, creation depends on mastering certain fundamental concepts, plus long term exercises in "learning to see" and a still longer—a lifetime—training in learning to feel and respond.

Nothing nervously all-out here. Stability was built into the "plan" of his personality—his robust humour and eroticism, his ignoring of offense, and his inability to hold a grudge, his liking for food, swimming, gadgets, animals, lively company. In a room with Hofmann one is aware of him laughing, a laugh that jogs his whole body and reddens his face. Before the evening has fatigued him, he is on the alert to give a comical twist to what he hears—or mishears when he's forgotten his hearing aid. His wit, sometimes bawdy but never lewd or malicious, shows a shrewd, detached familiarity with the people and goings-on in his neighbourhood, a form of perception that surprises admirers who expect the stereotype of the exalted artist and theoretician. Hofmann's stories, going back to his Paris Left Bank days, the Munich school, summer sessions in Capri, the

passage to Berkeley under escort by a University of California professor, artists and students in Provincetown and Greenwich Village, are always funny stories and some of them are hilarious. Serious incidents in Hofmann's life, miseries of individual artists, the bankruptcies brought by currency inflation in Germany during the twenties, the abduction of friends by the Nazis, used to be recounted by his wife, Miz (she had to stay in Germany for several years under the Hitler regime while Hans was establishing himself in the United States).

In telling his tales Hofmann plays with his thick accent as a means of achieving dramatic contrast and suspense. Sometimes a phrase fails him and he asks for translation of an expression in German or French. But a moment later he draws out an uncommon English word, apt and precise. Throughout, his talk is spotted with interjections of "nikke," his private version of "nicht wahr?" which has become famous as his conversational trademark.

"Yes, art, nikke, is cray-ah-teef not decorateef." Somewhere near the close of the evening Hofmann is sure to deliver a brief and utterly grave lecture on how only the creative, as manifested in the proper practice and appreciation of art, can in this mechanical age save man from turning into a robot.

Hofmann's development has been cautious and persevering. He and Miz managed for the most part to live comfortably in the spare, economical style of Left Bank artists and intellectuals. The Hofmann house in Provincetown has the proportions of a mansion but it was acquired to provide room for The Hans Hofmann School of Fine Arts. The School continued until 1958 when Hofmann's income from painting gave him security without it. Since then he has complained about spending so much on a house too big for his needs.

To his situation—whether involving income, reputation, or old age—Hofmann has always responded with an amused matter-of-factness. Having become in the past few years a near millionaire (the tax laws do not permit an artist to become the real thing), he remains in every respect exactly as he was during the period in the thirties when he had to subsist on fish obtained free on the Provincetown docks. He has

"'. . . and out of the caves, the night threw a handful of pale, tumbling pigeons into the light. . . .' Rainer Maria Rilke": A 1964 Hofmann.

the indifference to public opinion of the old-fashioned Bohemian. He prefers an argument about painting to adulation of his work. The celebrity game into which American artists have recently been drawn does not arouse him, though he seems to find it fun to appear on TV or have his picture taken for the press. He has never expressed any longing for success nor any disdain for it; in his scheme what success has to offer is extremely limited. In becoming an artist he chose, he is convinced, the most rewarding life available to man.

What could be more novel among the gallery displays of the 1960's, with their refurbished art packages and imitation lab charts, than an exhibition of Hofmanns founded upon an aesthetic synthesis of the spatial concepts of Cézanne and the Cubists, the colour dynamics of Matisse, the Fauves, and Delaunay, the animism of Kandinsky and Klee, the geometrics of Mondrian? The school which Hofmann opened in Munich in 1915 had as its aim "to clarify the then entirely new pictorial approach" of modern painting. The greatness of this approach, as Hofmann set out to demonstrate, lay in binding together art, the artist, and the visible world in a deeper union than had been achieved in the past—though Hofmann conceded later that Michelangelo and Rembrandt had brought forms to life by the same principle.

Technically, the new aesthetic begins by addressing itself to the problem of space. Before Cézanne the canvas was a "window" opened on the scene. The sensation of depth was produced through the illusory device of perspective. Discarding perspective, modern painting sought more candid means for representing the depth of nature on a flat surface. In the art of our time, Hofmann has written, "depth is created on a flat surface not as an illusion but as a plastic reality." What "plastic reality" signifies and how it is achieved is not easy to grasp—all through his years of teaching Hofmann had to keep reiterating to students that doing away with perspective did not mean that painting had turned into the two-dimensional patterns of linoleum design. On the contrary, depth had become all-important. Instead of being poured into the funnel of a vanishing point as in Renaissance compositions, it was now to be brought into being everywhere on the canvas. As conceived by Hofmann, depth is a dimension

introduced into a painting not by aligning forms one behind the other, or through tonal gradations ("another doctrine of the academician"), but by means of the backward and forward animation of the whole picture surface through colour, shapes, rhythm. No longer is there depth but depths. They result not from tricking the eye but through "the creation of forces." (Ironists, from Magritte to Johns, have played with this problem of depth by inserting a strip of painted or photographed sky into a realistically painted landscape or by modelling a "0" or a "5" as if it were an object in a realistic painting.)

From depth as a technical problem of painting Hofmann proceeds in a straight line to his metaphysics of an ever-active nature, of the artist as a creator, and of the work of art as a magical effigy pulsing with captured energies. Make a line, he suggests, and after a few additions "your empty paper has been transformed by the simplest graphic means into a universe in action. This is real magic." In the last analysis, depth means to him feeling into and identifying with the inner life of things. In the modern conception of pictorial space Hofmann has found a technical equivalent for his pantheism, a Whitmanesque nature-feeling that places him in the mainstream of New World sentiment. "The experience of space," he wrote thirty years ago, "depends upon the spiritual understanding of the 'living' coherence of things." The artist enters into this coherence and recomposes it, thus bringing nature to human fulfillment in the work of art.

Painters and critics still speak of "space" as if it were the inside of a box, a curtain, or a dish rack, that is, as a passive receptacle of objects or signs. With Hofmann, in contrast, space implies action—"where there is matter and action, there is space." "In nature," he wrote, "space is charged with a whirlwind of inner disturbance and so it shall be with the picture."

Space is active, and so also is colour, line, the surface on which the painter works. Hofmann could see in a spot of paint or the random mark of the crayon the start of a creative transformation. Thus he was the first to produce "drip paintings"—the 1939 "Red Trickle," and the 1940 "Spring." For the painter, action is already present in nature as a form-giving potential; it is not a mere "happening" instigated by the will. About painting, Hofmann could say with Rimbaud: "A touch of your finger on the drum lets loose all sound and commences the new harmony."

Intuitions of invisible acts have inspired scores of Hofmann canvases since 1940 when his paintings began to abandon, though not altogether, recognizable motifs. The part played in his imagination by the natural shocks and vibrations evoked by the act of painting is suggested by such characteristic titles of the past twenty-five years as "Effervescence," "Cataclysm," "Storm," "Radiant Space," "Scintillating Space," "Fortissimo," "Undulating Expanse," and "In the Wake of the Hurricane."

These abstract Action Paintings are the dominant mode of Hofmann's later years. As counterpoint, however, he also employs smoothly brushed rectangles of pure colour either as balances within his shaken-up depths (as in "Sun in the Foliage," shown in his February, 1965, exhibition) or as blocks in compositions conceived on a structural hypothesis. The 1960 "String Quartet" expresses the musicality of Hofmann's equilibriums of colour and size in the simplest of mathematical shapes, as does "To Miz—Pax Vobiscum."

Of all the Action Painters, with the possible exception of De Kooning, Hofmann avails himself of the widest repertory of gestures: furious strokes, rubbings, jets of pigment out of the tube, subtle feathers of tint, sprays, bricks and slabs of raw colour, exposed stretches of canvas or board, transparent washes, serpentine dribbles. A single painting, like the 1961 "Wild Vine," may use a majority of these. Others, like "Serenade," done in the same year, is constructed almost entirely of wide brush strokes like receding panels. Rare in the late Hofmanns, but still occasionally manifest, is the interlocking of sharply contoured curved and rectilinear shapes, as in the 1944 "Seated Woman" or the 1947 "Delight," with which he converted figures and still lifes into clashes of energy.

For half a century Hofmann has laboured to reconstitute the vocabulary of art by infusing into it his activist vision. This effort has been only partially successful. Art thinking still takes place largely in static nouns: Colour, for instance, is described as an area of hue adjacent to other areas rather than as an "interval" in a

total creative process. The greatest obstacle to a wider apprehension of "the new pictorial approach" has been the dogged conservatism of self-styled modernists, including admirers of Hofmann, who can recognize in his teachings, as in his paintings, only the weary tale of post-Cubist technical evolution. Yet the chief virtue of Hofmann's animism is that it has lent to the craft problems of the contemporary artist the scope of a philosophical adventure. At the same time, his generalizations, often so difficult to grasp in themselves, are rescued from vagueness by the way he has pinned them down to studio practice. Whatever "the spiritual understanding of the living coherence of things" may mean as a verbal formula, in the workshop it requires studying the model not as a composite of separate forms but as an organic entity enmeshed in moving planes and volumes.

In America, no one is regarded with more suspicion than an artist who thinks. It is common to criticize in Hofmann the clash between rule and impulse, concept and spontaneity. It requires no rare expertness to identify as weak those Hofmann canvases in which the ebbing of the artist's élan forced him to resort to his space and colour formulas. Or, at the opposite extreme, those which, carried by too swift an impulse, were finished before the artist could encounter the resistance necessary for a genuine act. The great Hofmanns are those composed of acts protracted in the vibrant centre between theory and the unexpected. These masterpieces would not have been possible without Hofmann's long striving to get his concepts straight.

Although Hofmann's career spans the history of twentieth-century art, one element is missing in it: the anti-art impulse so prevalent in all the arts since World War I. To this rebellious inclination, which makes modern art perennially young—and old before its time—Hofmann is a stranger. "Painting," he has said, "puts me in a positive mood." He has passed untouched by the general crisis of belief. For Hofmann art is never in question. Nor is nature, beauty, truth, affection. Each evening he and Miz liked to go to some favourite point on the shore of Cape Cod to watch the sun go down. Now he makes the journey alone up the side of a hill, with a distant view of the sea, to water the flowers he has planted on her grave.

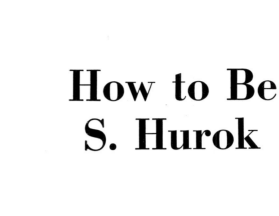

How to Be S. Hurok

BY ALLENE TALMEY

To be S. Hurok is a trick that sometimes even S. Hurok has not mastered. Most of the time, however, he is the supreme performer of this extraordinary rôle that might have been written by Alexandre Dumas to be acted in French and Russian. Hurok has added the English translation and a charming one, too. Although there are a few men in this country who juggle in the culture field, none has the dash, the confidence to book on long tours so diversified a cultural menagerie as pianists, violinists, the Edinburgh Tattoo, the Bolshoi Ballet and the Royal Ballet, the Old Vic and the Comédie Francaise; to keep the publicity bubbling, the mail orders coming in; to soothe the stars, meet the planes, give opening-night parties, kiss the hands of the ladies, and to make money.

To be S. Hurok one ought to look as impressive as S. Hurok, who dominates his oval size as would an Amazonian wife a mild husband. On winter nights his seventy-four-year-old round pink face, partly hidden by heavy black-rimmed glasses, shows above this superb costume: a Persian lamb-collared overcoat, long and European, a soft black fedora pulled down over his sparse white hair, a silver-headed cane held at an angle as though Otis Skinner, acting as an adventurer, were holding it. No young actor now has the panache for this part. Not since Sergei Diaghilev brought his Ballet Russe to Paris in 1913 has an impresario looked so much like an impresario as S. Hurok looks—nor for so long. Ever since 1921, when he took Anna Pavlova, one of the greatest prima ballerinas ever, on her tours, Hurok has been The Impresario. Now almost the whole dance world calls him boss—and so at times do many others, including Artur Rubinstein, Isaac Stern, Lorin Maazel, Maya Plisetskaya, Margot Fonteyn, Uday Shankar, Roberta Peters, Nathan Milstein, Andrés Segovia, Victoria de los Angeles, Jerome Hines, Byron Janis, Jean-Louis Barrault, Emlyn Williams, the bandsmen of the Black Watch and the Grenadier Guards.

To understand the power and the influence of S. Hurok one must realize that at bottom this short, but outsize man is a gambler intent on culture, knowing and loving the whole serious world of entertainment, but one who sometimes takes years for his curious speculations to pay off. When, about thirty years ago, he brought the first Ballet Russe to New York on December 21, 1933, he induced Otto H. Kahn to give an opening-night champagne party, and managed shortly to lose $88,000 on the troupe. Many troupes have come between. Now, he will bring the Bolshoi Ballet to the Metropolitan Opera House on September 6 with not only a sold-out three weeks there, but with the whole thirteen weeks in the country sold out—and this for its second tour in two years. Like England's Royal Ballet, the Bolshoi will take in some two million dollars to cover an expense of some one and a half millions. The important difference in these figures lies not in finances but in S. Hurok's effect on this country. For the country now spends about five million dollars a year to see performances by the New York City Ballet, the San Francisco Ballet, by other companies not managed by Hurok. It sends its children to some five thousand or more classical ballet schools. The change between 1933 and 1962 is mainly S. Hurok.

There is a change in S. Hurok, too—and not just age. In 1906, he left Pogar, a village in the Ukraine where his father had a hardware store, to learn more about the hardware business in the nearby city of Kharkov. On the way there, he detoured to New York, arriving here with just about enough money to get him into the country after a long steerage voyage, plus enough to take him to Philadelphia. At eighteen he put on a pack filled with needles and notions to sell at back doors. Later, by a few months, he put down the pack and sold bed springs from a shop. He has been selling ever since, but these days when he returns to Russia this American capitalist lives in the suite used by Lenin in a Moscow hotel.

In the early days he left Philadelphia for New York to organize musical programs for labour clubs in Queens and Brooklyn. That enterprise led him directly to his first famous musical outburst. He took over Charles Dillingham's enormous Hippodrome Theatre only on Sunday nights for concerts starring Mischa Elman, Efrem Zimbalist, Alma Gluck, Eugène Ysaye. Every Sunday he sold out, the tickets ranging from fifty cents to $2.50 for 5,980 seats, one thousand on the stage, plus four hundred standees. It was 1910 and he was twenty-two.

A few years later came one of his few non-entertainment investments. To him it is better to lose money on dancers than on products. After his joust with an embroidery factory in West Hoboken, New Jersey, he went back to music, his only consolation. In his young enthusiasm he hit on a formula for himself that has never failed him. "If you love what you do," he said, "you will have no trouble with your stomach, no ulcers, no headaches that need pills. Money, perhaps." He chose the long road, knowing early that it would not be easy. In fact, ease still makes him feel nervous. He likes the complications of involved transactions with the Soviet Culture people, with our own State Department, with theatre owners. He even likes the first disappointments over the public's reluctance to accept the domination of his artistic will. Then he bends the public will like a New England cruller.

For successful cruller-bending, he always needs an extraordinary performer—a dancer, a musician, an actor. He needs someone who can set afire a middle-aged cynic in the thirtieth row, a sourpuss dragged in protesting. Such performers do not come often in a generation. Of all those that he managed, the apple of his heart is still Anna Pavlova, ballerina. "An-na Pav-lova was the greatest personality I ever knew," he announced in his deep voice with its still foreign emphasis. "She had fire. She was a great actress. A Great Dancer. An-na Pav-lova gathered in the whole audience into a magic circle." Even these days, S. Hurok keeps in the top drawer of his desk in his old and comfortable office at the corner of Fifth Avenue and Fifty-seventh Street a file of her photographs. On one wall hangs a frame of some twenty photographs of her, balancing a frame with an equal number of photographs of the basso profundo. Feodor Chaliapin. On another long wall hang some sixty photographs, a mixed batch of some of his other stars. In a corner stands a new chartreuse refrigerator and the photographs of his family, his wife, his daughter, his grandchildren.

When he reminisces, he always starts off with An-na Pav-lova, whose name is never shortened, and then unwinds a long rope of the names of Russian dancers plaided with the names of great Russian composers, great Russian soloists, with a long fringe of Spanish, French, Italian, and American names. Hurok feels deeply their link to each other and to him. He understands the passion, the suffering that mortises these creators. Now it is part of his unconscious power, a spine of idealism that keeps him upright in this curious, backbiting, temperamental, financially unnerving, personal service business.

So personal is this business in Hurok's unique, strong hands that when one of his dance troupes—the Bolshoi, the Moiseyev, the Ukrainian Dancers—is at the Metropolitan Opera House, S. Hurok leaves his seat each evening just before the dancers applaud the audience, to stand like a short idol hunched into a corridor doorway, watching people leave, listening, listening. . . . It is an old habit. On a good night, this travelling man, who watches his diet when in New York at Henri Soulé's Pavillon, somehow looks a little fatter.

But he was thin in 1923 when a friend introduced him in London to the master Diaghilev, saying, "This is your young man." The last contract Diaghilev signed was one with Hurok for an American tour of the Ballet Russe. The six-foot Impresario and the about-to-be-impresario disagreed on the ballets for New York; Diaghilev thinking "Scheherazade," "Prince Igor," and "Petrouchka" too advanced for the opening night. Before the Ballet could come, Diaghilev died in Venice. These days, Hurok

is an anthology of death notices—"An-na Pav-lova died of double pneumonia at The Hague. Isadora Duncan from a scarf-auto accident on the Riviera."

Isadora, one of his managerial planets, "gave me a lot of trouble, but she was a great personality. There should be a monument to her," he added. "She popularized interpretive dancing, gave women freedom from tight corsets, she bobbed the hair of the girls in her troupe, let them dance barefoot on lawns. Interpretive dancing. She revolutionized it. She was a sensation in Paris, in Moscow, in St. Petersburg. A great philosopher, but she had a dishevelled personal life." When An-na Pav-lova lay sick at The Hague, she told Hurok to take on the imposing Mary Wigman, a notable German modern dancer—"a fine, intelligent woman." Hurok went on, "An-na Pav-lova had an open mind."

When he sits behind his enormous cluttered desk, he seems perhaps a trifle lost. His natural habitat is the fine restaurant, the concert hall, the theatre, the opera house. Then, wearing his fur-collared long coat, with his black hat and his cane in his hands, he looks like the humanization of his personal understanding about life. "Be happy. Enjoy while you can. Don't postpone. Give joy and pleasure to the world."

He likes to tell a corny little fable that is not corny to him at all. "Back at the time of the Hippodrome concerts, I used to stand in the lobby, a young man, poor, watching the people come in. Sometimes there would be a young couple, a little cross with each other. They walked side by side but separate. What would happen to them inside the theatre? When they came out for the first intermission, they were excited. They discussed the music. They smiled. They walked back, their arms linked. I had helped."

Philip Johnson is that rarity, an architect who designs his buildings like a sculptor, who uses sculpture as part of his buildings, who starts off each venture—art gallery, house, theatre, synagogue, church, office building—with a soaring theorem, its principles not new, but it conclusions daring. Born fifty-seven years ago in Cleveland, he started architecture late, but has bloomed profusely around the country in the last fifteen years. He is a quick-minded, clipped talker, a dasher rather than a contemplative when the work is rushing along. An architect who does some of his most courageous efforts for private clients, he prefers to work with scale models; *opposite*, he is shown with the model of the David Lloyd Kreeger house in Washington, D.C. That house, deliberately built for a great art collection, has three main characteristics: it is of travertine, it has cross-vaulted domes, and it has the proper vistas.

Philip Johnson

An architect who lives in a glass house and throws stones, too—a man of charm and controversy with three monumental buildings just opened, four new private houses in process.

BY CLEVELAND AMORY

Philip Johnson, who lives in a glass house, eats in a glass restaurant, and works in a glass office (all of which are, of course, his own design) knows he shouldn't throw stones, but the most controversial architect of our times likes nothing better than to do so. Once the Peck's Bad Boy of the business—"Now, dammit," he snaps, "the kids call me the Grand Old Man"—he thinks nothing of snapping off opinions on everything from picture windows ("the greatest prejudice arousers in the world") to the American automobile ("It should be technical perfection and instead it's the greatest example of planned obsolescence since old age"), from Washington ("It is an ugly city—very ugly. I would call it strangulation by spaghetti") to the World's Fair ("Do you know what imposed the whole new plan out there? Sewer lines—thirty-year-old sewer lines!").

On the subject of Robert Moses he is more gentle. "He has," Mr. Johnson says, "a good, clean, honest—and totally false—conception of architecture." And, when other whipping boys fail him, he turns on himself. "I confess," he declares, "to the same blind arrogance that all artists and even would-be artists are afflicted with. I tend to dislike, or envy, or be jealous, of all work but my own."

One thing is certain. Opinionated or not—and it should be noted that the majority of his opinions are delivered with a devastating grin—Mr. Johnson is in a position of eminence few architects in history have ever attained. He has recently seen open within a few days of each other, no less than three of his monumental new public buildings—the New York State Pavilion at the World's Fair, the New York State Theater at Lincoln Center and the new wings of the Museum of Modern Art on Fifty-third Street.

When I talked with Mr. Johnson in the last frantic throes before these openings, however, he was still in high throwing form. "I visited two of the jobs this morning," he told me, "and picked up two horrors. Pure Hell.

"Those exit lights at the State Theater—honestly, god-*awful*. And that spandrel glass at the Museum. God, I *still* can't make up my mind about that!"

One thing Mr. Johnson had no difficulty making up his mind about was me. "I am sick and tired," he said, "of all the word-minded people in this world. It's my great fight on this earth—that the word-minded people are the ones who set the standards. What they say about everything counts. An artist or an architect conceives and creates—but then in the final analysis he's at the mercy of some *writer*—a man who knows absolutely nothing about what the artist has spent his life trying to do—a man who uses up hours and days of his time asking his childish, idiotic, asinine questions and then, as a final irony, assesses him for all time. Why I'm submitting to it I don't know. In Gothic times the word-minded people didn't count. The architect of Chartres cathedral isn't known. He had no P.R. man. Well, neither have I. But I'm submitting to it because nowadays you have to. The first mistake in this whole world was the invention of printing. And the second was the invention of the automobile.

"The values of our culture," Mr. Johnson continued, warming to his task-taking, "are all based on the word-minded. The visual arts are simply unable to rise above our communicative publicity media—all of which are, by definition, words. An architect, on the rare occasion when he is allowed to come in by the front door, still ranks somewhere between the accountant, who is, of course, vastly more important, and the Fuller Brush man, who is only slightly less. After all, *they* are utilitarian. Architects are actually so non-utilitarian we're almost extinct. Do you know that ninety percent of the cubic feet built in this country are built without any architect at all?"

Rather timorously, in view of not only Mr. Johnson's distinguished distinction, but also his attitude toward words of any kind, I asked him whom he considered the greatest architect of all time. "Imhotep," he said quickly. "You remember him, of course," he smiled cynically. "I-M-H-O-T-E-P. He did the tombs of Saqqara, about 3000 B.C. No," he added irritatedly, "no 'U' at all. S-A-Q-Q-A-R-A. I forgot the word-minded people always have such trouble spelling."

I managed a smile. But I was relieved when Mr. Johnson passed on to his second greatest. "The architect of Teotihuacán," he said. "One of the largest pyramids in the world—probably the finest example of the relationship of urban space in the whole world—far better than the Egyptian, of course. And yet there is not one single written report of anything about the Teotihuacán culture It's fascinating, you know, what we *don't* know from words."

By now even my nods were wan ones. I asked Mr. Johnson if he had spent much time there. "I was there last week," he said, surprisingly patiently. "I worked on four of my new buildings there."

Mr. Johnson's third, most famous architect of all time is also unknown—the architect of the Ryoanji Gardens at Kyoto, Japan. "It's my favourite building in the world," he told me, "or at least it was until I'd seen Saqqara and Teotihuacán. Favourite buildings change around, you know. Consistency, your word-minded Emerson said—surely you remember *him*—is the hobgoblin of little minds."

The irony of Mr. Johnson's anti-word-mindedness is that he himself first entered architecture by the humble word route. Not until he was ten years out of college did he even enter architectural school, and, before that, at Harvard or his previous schools, he had never even taken a single course in architecture or, for that matter, in art history. By that time, however, he had already published, in 1932, with Henry-Russell Hitchcock, his landmark book, *The International Style—Architecture Since 1922*, and had already established himself as one of the world's leading critics in a field in which he, personally and technically, had no training at all. To this day he is known in his profession as a miserable draftsman. "Why are your drawings," Paul Rudolph once asked him, "so ugly and your final buildings so beautiful?"

Johnson was born in Cleveland in 1906, the only son—he has one older sister and one younger—of a successful corporation lawyer and a mother who had taught the history of art in school. "Father was very successful, but he didn't like high living. He was a Puritan. He didn't touch liquor or smoke but there was a bit of the village atheist in him, too—he was basically a nice man, extroverted, with an easy smile. He was the sort of person people invited because they liked him. Mother was very different.

"She had been in love with father for years and years before they married, but he had married two other women first. He was forty-five when I was born, she was thirty-eight. She was the country-club set, but she was an intellectual, more or less—in any case she got a master's at Wellesley back in the nineties—this, in those days, was very odd."

From seven to fourteen, young Johnson went to school at Pinehurst, N.C., where his family also had a house. "It was so small it was almost a tutoring school. I was always second at school, never top—a good position, it gives you ambition. I liked to read books but I hated mechanical things, anything with my hands. Sports were awful—I can still remember the agony of having to play baseball."

At the age of thirteen, he went with his mother abroad and had what he realizes now was the great "architectural experience" of his life—he visited Chartres. "Catholicism was a mystery to a young Puritan from the Midwest," he recalls. "There was a funeral going on. I was so moved I don't know why *I* wasn't dead. The idea of people building something so extravagant—so beautiful—to a *God!* For twenty-five years they built—the whole population—the whole population from *all around!* Can you imagine the people of, say, Birmingham, then, or now, or *ever*, importing the whole population of Alabama and for twenty-five years, building *anything?*"

The second great architectural experience came ten years later when, at twenty-two, he stood below the Parthenon. "I never saw it in ruins at all," he says. "I saw it then and I still see it now just the way it was originally." To this day Mr. Johnson sees the buildings he has conceived as completed before they have even been begun. "I can stand in my house," he says, "and talk about the gallery I am going to build up on my hill for my pictures. I stand and look at it and point out things about it to people, and of course they don't see it, because it isn't there yet."

A man who can stand with you and look out at one of the most beautiful vistas in Connecticut and point out the details of a building that isn't there is also, of course, a man who is bound, on occasion, to run afoul of reality. And Mr. Johnson has done so in spades. First, though, came Harvard. He went there in 1923

but he did not graduate, because of several breakdowns, until 1930. "My first ambition at Harvard," he recalls, "was to be a piano player. My next passion was Greek and Greek philosophy. I was pretty nearly friendless—the closest to a friend I had was my tutor, Raphael Demos."

Before his graduation, in 1929, Johnson read an article by Henry-Russell Hitchcock in *The Arts* about the work of the brilliant Dutch designer, J.J.P. Oud. "The minute I read that article I knew what I wanted to do with my life. It was Saul and Paul." From college he came to New York, met Hitchcock and almost at once began the collaboration which resulted in *The International Style.*

At the same time, with another friend, curator Alfred Barr, Johnson, the young architect who was not yet even an architectural student, founded the Department of Architecture at the Museum of Modern Art.

Then, still before he entered architectural school, came eight long years when reality really overwhelmed him. During this period he ran the gamut of the "causes" of the thirties. "I think the only one I didn't get mixed up with was Communism—Communists weren't very amusing even then. It seems hard to remember the thirties now. I wanted to *do* something. I was for anyone who was trying to do anything about poverty in the midst of plenty. It seems even more incredible now—how *could* this country have been so stupid? Anyway, museum work seemed pretty illogical in that sociological hour."

Together with another friend, Alan Blackburn, who had been in charge of the business and of the Museum, Mr. Johnson, the nonathlete, mounted his white charger and rode off to do battle with The Depression. His first charge led him to perhaps the wildest of all the wild men who were trying to "do something"— the late Mr. Huey Long. "When we descended upon Huey," Mr. Johnson recalls, "he was amazed. After all, here we were, two Harvard intellectuals in a sea of practical politicians. Neither Huey nor any of the rest of them knew what the devil we were all about. I think we got to see him all of four times."

Meanwhile, back at the farm—his father's— in Cleveland, there was, if not mortgage trouble, at least a milk strike. Once again, Johnson

Philip Johnson explains his re-markable underground museum. "The gallery is underground for four reasons. First, I did not want another building on the property to spoil the view from my glass house in Connecticut. Second, an underground building has a feel-ing of cosiness and tomb-like separation from the world, con-ducive to concentrating on art. Third, I do not like daylight on pictures; it is too hard to control. Fourth, the heating and air con-ditioning are much simpler with-out glass, since earth is a won-derful insulating material. The gallery consists of three tangent circular rooms with twenty-eight moving walls that rotate on ceil-ing tracks. The walls that are stacked behind the visible walls are storage panels. Shows can be changed with this system in three minutes. The contents of the gallery are questionable. I have yet few great works, but I am assured at least that all I can afford to buy will be well housed."

Photograph shows Philip John-son in one of the galleries, stand-ing next to the Craig Kauffman, "Chartreuse-Red," 1965. The sculpture is John Chamberlain's "Tomahawk Nolan"; welded and painted auto metal, 1965. On the wall at the far right is the Roy Lichtenstein "Girl with Beach Ball," 1961.

HORST

mounted his charger and rode into the fray. "I made inflammatory speeches," he says. "The only trouble was they didn't inflame other people as much as they did me. Often I got so tongue-tied in the middle of my speech I had to leave the platform. But I did get that grass-roots feeling—you know, the pee-pul—and my speeches convinced me that I was the man to run for the State Legislature."

Johnson resigned before the election ("I learned the State Legislature is the *last* place you can really have fun"), but his successor, carrying on his campaign, actually won. Then, in 1937, he made the first of two trips to Germany. In this period, too, he considered buying the *American Mercury*. "I was mixed up with all the right-wing fringes," he admits, "meanwhile all the time I was steadily voting for Norman Thomas. Those were my thirties. By 1938 I was so sick of myself I was going to shoot myself. I was so worried about what I was going to do with my life and the irony is I didn't have to do anything. I could just have lived on my inheritance. And, if I had been a European, I would have done that. But Americans always say, 'What do you do?' It's a terrible country, really."

Then, at the age of thirty-four, at long last, he entered Harvard's School of Architecture. "That first day I will never forget. I was older than some of my professors and my fellow students were little children. I knew I couldn't draw and I didn't see how I could keep up. But that feeling only lasted three days. Then I realized maturity had certain advantages."

Mr. Johnson puts it modestly. Actually, from the very beginning he led his class—despite the fact he was in total disagreement with the leadership of the school under Walter Gropius. "By the second year I was doing two designs for every problem—one for myself and one for the school. I still recommend that procedure today to all students."

His doctrinal differences with Dr. Gropius, however, did not in the least affect his enthusiasm for what he calls the "whole forward thrust" of modern architecture. "Of course," he says, "to talk of 'modern architecture' today is meaningless. Everybody is modern. But, in the twenties and thirties, it was definitely something. People were still doing revivalist architecture. It's perhaps an over-simplification to say

so but so-called 'modern architecture' is really the first architectural movement in history to derive from painting. Usually it's the other way around—baroque architecture bred baroque painting But, over-simplification or not, modern architecture derives from Cubism."

As a student he had designed and built his own house in Cambridge—his "Court House" with its glass exterior—one which shows, from the road, nothing but a wall. The wall was promptly called a "spite wall," and Johnson had his first battle with public opinion. Then, in the most unlikely spot imaginable—when he was in the Army serving as a latrine orderly—he designed his first building for somebody else—a barn and tool house for, of course, his family.

Years later, in 1949, but out of his Miesian conception in Cambridge, came his epochal "Glass House"—still his present-day New Canaan, Connecticut, house. When it was finished, once again Mr. Johnson found it necessary to put up a wall—this time a six-foot one to keep out the crowds of curious who would gather on the road up above, and especially on Sundays, peer down at him. "If Mr. Johnson wants to make a fool of himself," said a letter in the local paper, "why doesn't he do it in some other town?" Mr. Johnson himself added to the consternation by his cryptic comments to those to whom he did show his house. "This is the library, Ma'am," he would say, showing an area of empty space. "You see it's an *American* library—no books." And when he received, from another lady, the inevitable, "It's a nice place but *I* could never live here," he replied firmly, "Madam, *i* haven't asked you to."

Even today, asked how many people have said, "I want one just like it," Mr. Johnson answers simply, "No one." "You see," he explains, "it's not a house. It's just where I live."

At first he had only a tiny kitchen in the middle of the room and no storage closets— "All the things," he says, "that bore me. I just thought we'd have delicious little omelets which I'd be brewing while I talked to my guests." Nonetheless, after one "half weekend," Mr. Johnson repented and hired servants who now do most of the cooking in another house nearby —and then bring the food over.

But to this day one feature of his mono-roomed house, a large statue of two indefinable, mono-bosomed women, is inclined to test the small talk of even people of the best of will. He recalls particularly the visit of a Congregational Minister. "Ah," the minister said, trying not to be too worried about the couple, "Mr. Johnson's parents, I presume."

When he first moved in, Mr. Johnson had no outside lights—and he soon found that darkness gave him the very same closed-in feeling he had built his "house" to avoid. Immediately he set to work conquering the problem. Soon he had both indoor and outdoor lights, both of which can be regulated from a central switch, so that he can sit, of a twilight, continually bringing up the outer lights and dimming the inside ones to give, from sunset to pitch dark, an effect so extraordinarily beautiful it must be seen to be believed—and not, of course, just written about. "The same critics who thought my house was a joke," he said, smiling, "now think it's the only good thing I've ever done."

In the fifteen years which have passed since his "Glass House" until the three new public buildings this spring, Mr. Johnson has been very busy indeed—in every possible architectural direction, from the Kneses Tifereth Israel Synagogue in Port Chester, New York, to the Four Seasons Restaurant on Park Avenue. ("The only person who can't stand it is Clare Boothe Luce," he says. "She won't eat in it because she says the curtain ripples make her nervous.") And not the least extraordinary thing about his triple-header openings in April is the fact that there is no similarity whatever between his three buildings. "If there were a common theme," he says, "like buildings of a University, that would be different. But like all 'modern' architecture—'modern' since the classic modern, in other words, since Mies van der Rohe—I don't think you could tell they were by the same architect. Which could not have been true, incidentally, in any other time."

To ask Mr. Johnson to name his favourite building is perilous indeed. "The one I'm working on," he will say quickly. But three of his buildings which have won awards are the Roofless Church, at New Harmony, Indiana, the Nuclear Reactor at Rehovoth, Israel, and the Kline Science Tower at Yale. And one with which even he refuses to find much fault—"It came out just *about* right," he says doubtfully

—is the jewel-like Dumbarton Oaks Museum built to house the pre-Columbian art collection of the late Robert Woods Bliss.

In recent years, it has become increasingly difficult to persuade Mr. Johnson back to domesticity. ("Architects," Erich Mendelsohn once said, "are remembered by their one-room buildings—temples, churches, theatres.") And only one family in the whole country can today talk of a two-Johnson-house family. They are the Robert Leonhardts, who now own not only the former, famous Manhattan "Guest House" of Mrs. John D. Rockefeller III (where the roofless outdoor part separates the two indoor parts by a pool) but also a cantilevered house on Lloyd's Neck in Long Island where the living room is breathtakingly suspended over a one-hundred-foot cliff. Four of the houses, however, on which he is now working are the Eric Boissonnas house at Cap Bénat, which hangs over a one-hundred-foot drop down to the Mediterranean, the James Geier house in Cincinnati, which was excavated into the slope of a hill so that the grass of the hill goes over the roof of the house and yet the house itself overlooks a lake, the Henry Beck, Jr. "Dallas Palace," which is some two-hundred-thirty-five feet in length ("I let *them*," Mr. Johnson says sternly, "do the upstairs"), and the David Lloyd Kreeger house in Washington, built, again, to house an art collection. ("It's not one of those passports to posterity deals," Mr. Johnson said. "He's got a real eye for art.")

Mr. Johnson, who has no hobbies ("Architecture is my hobby") himself, started buying pictures at an early age, and his office is now crowded with everything from a wild Rauschenberg combine, complete with a real automobile tire, in the outer reception room, to a curious poster painting by Robert Indiana in the inner office that bears the huge inscription, "A DIVORCED MAN HAS NEVER BEEN THE PRESIDENT." Ironically, the painting dates to Stevenson days, but Mr. Johnson is nowadays continually embarrassed by friends who wonder how he can "do that to Nelson." As for the clients who may be put off by his more far-out art ("You're not going to hang something like *that* in *my* house, are you?"), they have been considerably relieved to know that Mr. Johnson is now building his own art gallery—with four

tangential cylinders in the centre of each of which will be a column holding a revolving screen by which he can regulate his pictures at will. He is, however, highly doubtful whether it will appeal to the public. "Remember what Breuer said," he told me. "All the public ever sees is the landscaping and the details."

"I am much more successful than I ever dreamed—in money," Mr. Johnson concluded.

"But I don't give any more of a damn about money than I do about words. The only real urge is immortality—not sex. Plato had it right —and Freud and Horace had it all wrong. What did Horace say, by the way? Well, it doesn't matter. Monuments last much longer than words. Civilizations are remembered by buildings. There's nothing more important than architecture."

Known as the "Roofless Church" at New Harmony, Indiana, *left*, this shingled dome with its sacred wall enclosing a Jacques Lipchitz sculpture, "Holy Spirit Descending," with its Lipchitz gates, is in effect a magnificent piece of sculpture. Its major Johnson point, the peace of its holy courtyard.

Marianne Moore Speaks

Her wisdom, with side comments,
collected by
HENRIETTA FORT HOLLAND

"I have read that several people think So-and-so is the greatest living woman poet; anyone would dislike applying so clumsy a phrase to Miss Marianne Moore—but surely she is," said poet Randall Jarrell.

So, too, says a chorus of critics of Miss Moore, who has won every poetry prize available in this country.

Yet there are many readers who accuse her of obscurity—who say that they simply can not understand her writing. To them Miss Moore has plaintively said that she is as clear as her natural reticence allows her to be.

It is to further this qualified clarification that the following categories are offered:

OF COURAGE

Victory won't come to me unless I go to it. What is there like fortitude—what sap went through that little thread to make the cherry red?

Again the sun, anew each day, and new and new and new, that comes into and steadies my soul.

OF THINKING

The malcontent attacks greatness by disparaging it . . . interpreting needful silence as lack of initiative . . . by distortion, by ridicule.

An architect of justice, determined and destined to win his "case," Lincoln did not cease until he had demonstrated the mightiness of his "proposition." . . . It is a Euclid of the heart.

Don't relive bad moments or revive them for others—or expect more of them.

I would, like Sir Winston Churchill, refuse to let a betrayal rob me of my trust in my fellow man.

One is not rich but poor
when one can always seem so right.

Patience—that is action.

Snobbishness is a stupidity.

Sophistication is, as it has always been, at the antipodes from the initial great truths.

A love of order, ardour, uncircuitous simplicity, with an expression of inquiry, are all one needs to be.

Words are constructive when they are true.

The passion for setting people right is an afflictive disease.

We do not admire what we can not understand.

One would not be he who has nothing but plenty.

OF READING, WRITING, AND WRITERS

The adjective "damn," the earmark of incompetence as an emphatic, operates in reverse—is equivalent to: "Spare diagnosis, this is no writer."

The accuracy of the vernacular: That's what I'm interested in—am always taking down little local expressions or accents. I think I should be in some linguistic operation or enterprise—am really much more interested in dialect and intonations. I scarcely think any of that comes into my so-called poems at all.

Spontaneous initial originality—says impetus—seems difficult to reproduce consciously later. As Stravinsky said about pitch, "If I transpose it for some reason, I am in danger of losing the freshness of first contact and will have difficulty in capturing its attractiveness."

I dislike the term "poetry" for any but Chaucer's or Shakespeare's or Dante's. . . . What I write can only be termed poetry because there is no other category in which to put it.

I may start a piece, find it obstructive, lack a way out, and not complete the thing for a year or years—am thrifty (though), I salvage everything promising and set it down in a small notebook.

Mr. Eliot's aptitude for mythology and theology sometimes pays us the compliment of expecting our reading to be more intent than it is; but correspondences of allusion provide an unmistakable logic of preference: for stillness, intellectual beauty, spiritual exaltation, the white dress, "the glory of the humming bird," childhood, and wholeness of personality. (Essay on T. S. Eliot)

The effect of Mr. Eliot's confidences, elucidations, and precepts, I would say, is to disgust us with affectation, to encourage respect for spiritual humility; and to encourage us to do our ardent best with the medium in which we work.

An author, that is to say, a fashioner of words, stamps them with his own personality, and wears the raiment he has made in his own way.

We fail in some degree—and know that we do if we are competent; but can prevail . . . we can in the end prevail, if our attachment to art is sufficiently deep.

One who attains equilibrium in spite of opposition to himself from within, is stronger than if there had been no opposition to overcome; and in art, freedom evolving from a liberated constraint is more significant than if it had not by nature been cramped.

The thing is to see the vision and not deny it, to care and admit that we do.

Originality is . . . a by-product of sincerity.

There is a language of sensibility of which words can be the portrait—a magnetism, an ardour, a refusal to be false.

Any writer overwhelmingly honest about pleasing himself is almost sure to please others.

We must not be sensitive about not being liked or not being printed.

WITH HUMOUR

Brooklyn has . . . helped to educate me, has afforded me, in fact, the kind of tame excitement on which I thrive.

I am such a cow
if I had a sorrow
I would feel it a long time.

Humour saves a few steps—it saves years.

. . . and lenient, looking
upon a fellow creature's error with the
feelings of a mother—a
woman or a cat.

Ireland—a place as kind as it is green—every name is a tune.

The French are a cruel race: they squeeze the diner's cucumber and broil a meal on vine shoots.

When one is frank one's very presence is a compliment.

The dutiful, the firemen of Hartford
are not without a reward,
a temple of Apollo, on a velvet sward.

He loves himself so much
he can permit himself
no rival in that love.

The Irish say your trouble is their
Trouble and your joy their joy. I wish
I could believe it;
I am troubled, I'm dissatisfied, I'm Irish.

OF RELIGION

You're not free until you've been made captive by supreme belief.

Clouds are to the child—an intimation of what glory is.

OF LOVE

Where the ground is sour—love won't grow.

Love is the only fortress strong enough to trust to.

There's hate's crown beneath which all is death. There's love's without which none is King.

One may be pardoned, yes I know one may, for love undying.

Don't smother the fire in my heart; which makes life dear; do not snuff me out yet. I'm not laid on my bier.

OF WAR

There never was a war that was not inward: I must fight till I have conquered in myself what causes war.

If all these great patient dyings
—all these agonies
and wound bearings and bloodshed—
can teach us how to live, these
dyings were not wasted.

Hate-hardened heart, O heart of iron,
iron is iron till it is rust. . . .
Beauty is everlasting
and dust is for a time.

FROM LETTERS

I was glad the Christmas bed jacket was only challis, and not Kashimiri-cashmere. How I suffer if miscast!

The more that happens that we stand up to, the more morally tough we become.

"May the Lord have his eye on you, and never take it off—"
Inconvenient if I did wrong? But I'd better not.

The mind plays us tricks—we can not trust its honesty—can not make it quite honest.

It is only in Andrew Lang (storybooks) that people like to be told that the hills are glass; and that the fairies' child is, and looks like, a fairy.

Do be happy—advice I dazzle myself with constantly—I could be a disillusioned orangutan if I permitted myself to be.

We should really know better than to magnify uncertainties and deficits.

Superiority to self-support is one of the signs of decay in this country.

My blunders would contradict both black and white magic. But God seems to safeguard me.

I feel with all my heart that aliveness and un-embitterment are what matters.

What I do with confidence usually fails—what I do intuitively seems better.

As I tell people who say, "How did you get so many prizes?"—I never won anything in a competition. I toiled at something and someone much later saw some point to it, and risked some kind of accolade.

We can't be happy unless we let ourselves be—quite a serious thought.

OF DRESS

Fashion subdues our resistance when it embodies style, but that is not very often.

(Kathleen Cannell said: One is not surprised to find that this poet has strong views on dress, though it is surprising to find how often they coincide with those of the fashion experts.

Her hats, like her prose, are controlled and definite. They may be "shiny Victrola record sailors," or cartwheels, or the renowned tricorne.)

Last Easter at a party, Miss Holland said, Miss Moore was wearing a cerulean blue suit by Ben Zuckerman. Someone praised it intensively.

"He's perfection," Miss Moore said. "His workmanship — the buttonholes — needlework on linings—makes me think of some of the masterpieces in the Worth collection at the Brooklyn Museum."

That Miss Moore has an eye for a silhouette or a nuance is brilliantly evidenced throughout her collected poems. Take, for instance, such descriptions as:

> The
> Kiwi's rain shawl
>   of haired feathers . . .

or

> The cardinal
> bird
>   looks somewhat odd,
> like the ambassadorial
>   Inverness
>   worn by one who dresses
> in New York but dreams of
> London.

Appropriately, Miss Holland added, for a poet who has written so intriguingly about dragons, alligators, lizards—one of Marianne Moore's earliest observations of fashion concerned a chameleon. When she was a small child, a touring actress got off the train at Carlisle, Pennsylvania, where Marianne was brought up, wearing a chameleon as a boutonnière, attached to her lapel by a tiny gold collar and hair-fine chain. It was mimetically at the instant a dusty jade, to match the star's tweed costume; and its eyes were turquoise. The little girl was entranced by this "automatic living ornament," its "incredible neatness," minuscule "hands."

* * *

Acknowledgments: "COLLECTED POEMS," MACMILLAN   "PREDILECTIONS," VIKING "LA FONTAINE," VIKING   "MARIANNE MOORE READER," VIKING   "CHRISTIAN SCIENCE MONITOR"

Mastroianni

BY LUIGI BARZINI

The case of Marcello Mastroianni which looks as if it were deceptively simple to dissect, is especially rich with the kind of information that helps illuminate the contemporary scene. Why should this actor of all actors, unmistakably Italian, with an Italian blend of qualities and limitations, have become, at this particular moment in history and not another, the idol of the multitudes everywhere? You are tempted to think that if you gathered all the necessary data (which data are necessary is, of course, difficult to ascertain beforehand, but that happens in all research work), avoided the facile clichés, disregarded the conventional marionettes invented by flacks and journalists, if you forgot a few of the things Mastroianni believes of himself or believes he believes (you must consider them mere psychological indications), if you did all this and you were brave enough to accept, in the end, the deductions, whichever they may be, dictated by impassive logic, after much washing of insignificant sand in your pan, you should find the gold dust of a few precious conclusions, valid for a revelatory understanding of the contemporary moral scene, the *Zeitgeist*, so to speak, and of the anxious, frightened, drifting, resigned mood of modern man.

It is elementary to see why (and of what) Marilyn Monroe, Sophia Loren, and Brigitte Bardot became symbols. But why Mastroianni should have become one, leaving so many seemingly better equipped rivals so far behind, is more difficult to determine. In fact, his success appears at times disturbingly unjustified. How much simpler it would be to analyze the various reasons for his failure, if he had failed! A shrewd Italian show-business expert who seldom makes mistakes, told him, years ago, when he was still a struggling young stage actor: "Marcello, stick to the theatre. You need footlights and distance between you and your public. You're not handsome and stupid enough for the movies. You'll never survive close-ups." It is obvious that in the cinema of the thirties and forties he would have been reduced to a few frustrating rôles, mostly dialect caricatures, the weak soldier, the betrayed husband, the timid lover, the bungling amateur. Those were, in fact, the small parts that came his way in the early fifties. Movie stars were supposed to be manly, muscular, well tailored, and self-possessed heroes: Clark Gable, Gary Cooper, and Cary Grant.

For one thing, he does not look and behave like a celebrity. He is approximately six feet tall, a little stoop-shouldered, with one foot usually turned slightly inward, as if he were on the point of starting a perennial slalom. He moves gracefully but always a bit uncertainly, as if he were an idle man vacantly drifting while making up his mind. He is forty-one years old and looks his age, with bags under his eyes like Jeanne Moreau's. His eyes are witty, mischievous, inquisitive, sometimes tender and vulnerable. His teeth are short and turn inward. He parts his hair on one side, like a school-boy, or as President John F. Kennedy did. The general expression of his face is incredulous and ironical, the expression of a man who does not want to get hurt. He pays little attention to his appearance: his shirts look ready-made for somebody else, his neckties won in a raffle; his coats have a tendency to stick out and not to hug the

ENZO SELLERIO

back of his neck in the approved manner; the creases of his trousers are seldom parallel and do not always point straight forward. He does not make himself scarce: anybody can see him dining out with a few friends, always the same, and his wife, at Il Bolognese in Piazza del Popolo, or at any other good *trattoria*, never in chic and expensive restaurants or in the dingy *osterie* the snobbish few discover every month and abandon hurriedly as soon as they are also discovered by others. He is so inconspicuous that American tourists often sit at the next table without realizing it. He owns an apartment in town and a villa on the Appia Antica. He also owns an estate in Tuscany near Lucca. This last sounds awe-inspiring until you see it: a small, bourgeois, nineteenth-century house with a garden and a few vineyards around it, which he could easily have inherited from an uncle.

There are many reasons why he appears stubbornly determined not to allow mere colossal success, world-wide fame, and immense wealth

ABOVE:

120

Mastroianni with Ursula Andress on a set of their new film, "The Tenth Victim." The kind of man Mastroianni is, "(shaped by blood, Italy, experience, wife, family, love, and fear of life), has somehow become a symbol of sorts."

to change his modest life, habits, and beliefs. To begin with, there are his few old friends, his relatives, his brother Ruggero, one of the best cutters in movies, who could cut him down to size if he tried to. Then there is his wife, Flora Carabella ("the beautiful and the dear" is the translation of her name), whom he married in 1950, the mother of his teen-aged daughter. Flora is the daughter of a musician and is inured to the makeshift papier-mâché triumphs of show business; she fears that Marcello's fortune may one day vanish as mysteriously as it came; she is as frightened as all Italian wives and mothers of successful men are, as Maria Letizia Buonaparte née Ramolino was, who always expected to see her son Napoleon's luck collapse one day without warning. Flora is more frightened than most, because she has a high idea of her husband and she knows that success seldom comes to the people who deserve it, and when it does, does not last long. She has a strong character. Her husband loves, respects, and trusts her.

Finally there is Mastroianni himself, his incredulous and skeptical turn of mind. He fears the revenge of the gods. In the old days he used to laugh at those who, to use a favourite expression of Roman cinéastes, were "overwhelmed by sudden fortune," not only those who bought the outlandish cars and the villas with swimming pools but also those who gave philosophical interviews attributing deep abstract reasons for their rise to fame. He is now naturally afraid to be laughed at: he sees the ghost of young Mastroianni mocking mature Mastroianni. Then there is a final motive. Some of the things successful actors do, as if compelled by biological laws, repel him because they are also those done by the unsuccessful who want to be thought successful. Many look like cheap flacks' gimmicks, signs of insecurity. Mastroianni shrinks from them because he wants to prove that his incredible luck is really due to his genuine talent, and to little else.

That his talent is great nobody denies. His mere presence somehow transforms a provincial pochade into a universal fable. All the directors he has worked for know this. They feel elated when they have him on the set. He is pliant, intuitive, resourceful, amiable, intelligent, inventive, and patient, above all patient. He makes himself putty in the hands of the men he especially values when shooting a story he is fond of. He respects Luchino Visconti (he still addresses him with the "Lei," the formal approach) who discovered him. He likes to work for Pietro Germi and for Mario Monicelli. But the man he really trusts is Federico Fellini. He seems to trust him as a baby trusts his nurse, and does the impossible for him. "It is easy for me to work with Federico," he explains. "It's like playing games. I amuse myself all the time. Never a dull moment." This is perhaps because there is an uncanny understanding between them: both are actor and director at the same time, each one electrifying the other and his possibilities. The movie he believed in with his whole being, and that fitted him like a second skin, was *8½*. In it he even managed to look and act like Fellini, a person entirely different from him. Fellini said: "Marcello gives me a frightening feeling of omnipotence. You can do anything, anything at all with him."

Mastroianni transforms himself into each new character with the thoroughness and the perfection of Alec Guinness. Like the great actor-managers of the nineteenth century, he still invents his own costume and makeup. In *The Organizer* he even stuck a green contact lens on one eye, to make it larger and glassy and to give himself a slightly insane appearance. "Such primitive people as the Italian socialist workers of seventy years ago," he said, "would never have risked their lives for a sober and rational gentleman. He had to be a nut." The technique of his trade fascinates him endlessly, although he is afraid to speak of it in the bated-breath jargon of the initiate of a religious mystery. He confesses he learned all he knows from veteran actors, working in stock companies. That the world should admire his capacity to impersonate a different person in each film irritates him slightly. "Why, that's what an actor is supposed to do, is it not?" he says. He contends it is not a difficult feat in the movies. A movie, he points out, takes months to make; a man has the time to invent a character, to ease himself into it, and can stick to it for a long time, perfecting it as he goes along.

The real tour de force to be admired is that of the leading men in the repertory companies who toured Italy until the last war. They stopped one day, one week, or a fortnight in provincial towns, and to keep the theatre filled, had to put on a new show practically every evening. They changed voice, face, bodily appearance, mood, century, and nationality every time, and kept all these different persons in their heads. "Critics," Mastroianni bemoaned, "also praise the little mannerisms I invent for each impersonation, like Baron Cefalù's nervous tick of sucking his teeth with the left side of the face in *Divorce —Italian Style*. Such expedients have been known for ages by all good character actors. Some are cheap, like stuttering, speaking without the 'r,' or lisping. Some are a little more ingenious, like one Lucien Guitry employed, who always turned a blank letter upside down before reciting its contents to show it was a real letter and that he was really reading it."

Talent, Mastroianni firmly believes, is not the only explanation of his rocket-like rise to fame. "Talent is not enough," he said firmly. He is a talented actor, he admits, but there are several in Italy and many in the world as good as he, few of whom have reached his popularity with the public. He likes to point out that, of course, talent is never enough without technique, but even great talent supported by the shrewdest technique can not go far, except with the intellectual critics. "There have been great actors in the movies at all times," he said. "Fredric March and Marlon Brando are the first names that come to my mind, but they seldom achieved the success of a few lesser men who imperturbably impersonated themselves movie after movie. Those possessed a particular personal quality." Talking about these matters recently, he picked up a pencil from the table to illustrate his views: "Talent is a pencil, see? Technique is the art of sharpening it. Choose the best pencil, choose the most modern electric sharpener . . . you still have nothing, because what counts is what comes next, what you do with the well sharpened pencil, the things you draw or the things you write."

Mastroianni is forty-one years old, born in Fontana Liri, in the province of Frosinone, September 28, 1924. He was brought to Rome at the age of three. He studied to become a *perito edile*, a noncommissioned officer of the construction engineering trade. He is a good mathematician, a capable surveyor, a skilled designer, and paints better than the Sunday amateur, almost as well as a professional. The feeling for form runs in the family: his father was a cabinetmaker who invented and designed most of his own models; Uncle Umberto is a well known sculptor.

At the end of the war Giulietta Masina, Fellini's wife, who had acted with Mastroianni in amateur theatricals, got him a small job in a stock company. From there he was plucked by Luchino Visconti, who gave him a few good parts in the great plays he produced and directed in the late forties and early fifties. Mastroianni was Cavalier di Ripafratta in Goldoni's *La Locandiera*, one of the sons in *Death of a Salesman*; he was, at one time or another, both men in *A Streetcar Named Desire*, and the little doctor in *Uncle Vanya*, all Visconti productions which are considered landmarks in Italian theatrical history. At the same time, to make a little extra money, he got small jobs in the movies. He was perennially cast as the loafer, the good-for-nothing, the idler, and always asked to speak in *romanesco*, the heavy Roman dialect of the people.

The break came in 1957, and he consciously engineered it. "I cheated"; he smiles when he remembers what he did. "I deceived my best friends. I had to do it to get my big chance." He was in Turin with the company of *Uncle Vanya* in 1957. Uncle Umberto, like a good uncle, was struck by his nephew's unique talent and told him he was wasted in a stock company travelling from place to place, even in plays written by great writers and directed by Visconti. He told his nephew to try the movies. Mastroianni pointed out he had tried the movies with little success. "I have rich friends in Turin," said the uncle, "I will get one hundred million together and you can then star in a movie of your own." One hundred million lire do not flutter in the air like butterflies, to be bagged by sculptors and unknown actors. Uncle Umberto was obviously dreaming out loud.

Back in Rome, Mastroianni told Visconti: "I have one hundred million to be invested in a movie. Have you an idea?" There weren't many movies being made at that time. Visconti was idle. He turned to Suso Cecchi d'Amico, one of the best writers in the business, who always wrote his screenplays, and asked her if she had an idea. She, being the daughter of Italy's most revered literary critic, Emilio Cecchi, asked papa. Papa thoughtfully sucked his pipe and said: "There is a small thing by Dostoevski, *White Nights*, which could be turned into a modern movie, if you had the right actors." Visconti, Suso, and a couple of collaborators got down to work, fell in love with the story. At the end of some months they had a complete script. At this point Mastroianni confessed that he did not have the one hundred million necessary. Nobody minded. They had a wonderful story, written exactly for him and for nobody else, to be directed by Visconti. Any producer would have grabbed the chance. One did. Mastroianni proved himself a superb moving-picture actor, even better than he had been on the stage. His next good film was *La Dolce Vita*. *8½* followed. Mastroianni was in orbit, a worldwide celebrity and, within a few years, a multimillionaire.

Journalists, of course, have no doubts. They list a certain number of conventional explanations for his rise to fame, none of them blatantly false but all of them absolutely worthless when examined closely. Many say he is a Sex Symbol. He is, according to popular magazines, today's version of Rudolph Valentino, Charles Boyer, Rossano Brazzi, the eternal Casanova every woman wants to be seduced by. Is he? The characters he portrays seldom have the enamelled perfection required. Only Baron Cefalú had the shiny brilliantined hair, the mousetail moustache, the sharp clothes, the long cigarette holder, and the dreamy eyes of the seducer, but he was a funny parody of one. His other characters usually lack the *aisance*, the self-possession, the male brutality, all the qualities necessary to silence a quivering woman's doubts and to make her wish to annul herself in a man's muscular embrace. This, some journalists point out, is true but does not diminish his fatal charm: if he had Valentino's qualities, he would get nowhere with modern women. Women no longer want to be smothered with charm and forced against their wish. The world has changed. His success with them is due to the fact that he looks tired, with bags under his eyes, uncertain, perplexed, a man in need of guidance and protection. It is all this that women now find irresistible.

Obviously there is some truth in this, but probably not enough to be the principal justification of his fame. He does not think of himself as a Latin Lover. "There are better Latin Lovers than I in the movies and in the waiting rooms of agents and producers," he says. His success with women is far from phenomenal. "I thought that when one became a famous star, one had women at one's feet all the time, one found them hidden in one's closet or under one's bed, eager victims. Nothing like that ever happens to me," he complains. "School girls want my autograph, that's all." Probably some women are kept away by his prejudices. He does not like them famous, well dressed, well made-up, well *coiffées*. "I like them to smell a little," he confessed. "Italian women have a body fragrance I could recognize in the dark. It is a sort of homely odour. I love it." He does not like them to be anonymously pretty, without character. "When I have been with too many beautiful women of that kind," he joked, "I long for a girl with buck teeth, crossed eyes, and bandy legs." He also wants women to make him feel like a man. The ease with which many contemporary ones can be pushed over shocks his old-fashioned prejudices. He loves the way his widowed mother still looks upon him with the traditional awe and respect of Italian women for the head of the family and is inordinately proud of the fact that women admire him all over the world.

He hates parties, film festivals, noisy press conferences, rowdy personal appearances. He loves obscurity, silence, the well-known friends with whom he talks in verbal shorthand, people he can trust. He loves his houses, especially his farm in Tuscany, filled with old furniture, where he wears old clothes and goes snooping in the kitchen to uncover simmering pots and find out what he's going to eat. He loves family life. He quarrels with his wife, of course, because she has a strong character and firm ideas, but "that's one of the ways of love." He loves his teenaged daughter. "Everything in the world is uncertain, ephemeral, deceitful, here today and gone tomorrow," he said. "Only the family is stable, something that will always be there. Only family sentiments are durable." All this does not add up to the conventional image of Casanova. In fact, his private life is practically blameless. No gossip has touched him.

Many European critics have another explanation. According to them, the character he interprets is that of befuddled man in a world in which all firm values have vanished, who tries to discover new rules with which to resume playing the game of life, but is perennially defeated by the mass industrial civilization; a lone individual vainly trying to follow his own private path to happiness, only to find it blocked at all turns. He has been compared to a modern Charlie Chaplin, without the clown makeup and the funny clothes, but just as pathetic. In other words, as one Italian writer expressed it, "perhaps he is still the character actor of his first secondary rôles in movies, the drifter, the failure, the anti-hero, the idler who could not make up his mind, too frightened of deluding himself. Only now such a man has become the protagonist, a meaningful symbol of our times. People recognize themselves in him. This is perhaps a revealing sign of the era we live in." This interpretation of Mastroianni, he admits, is a good enough description of him. He is a Roman who loves, understands, and fears life as good sailors love, understand, and fear the sea; skeptical and ironic because he knows one can easily get hurt if one does not protect oneself; a Roman, furthermore, of this generation, whose diffidence and mental defenses have been strengthened by all the false hopes, the defeat, and th terrible disorder of the postwar years.

"I am lazy," he proclaimed. "Mastroianni è pigro," they all say around him to explain many of his oddities. This laziness of his is now a legend. "I am lazy for many reasons—not to get involved in anything that I might regret later, not to make mistakes, not to be done in by smart people, not to rush into things I will regret." His vaunted lack of interest in women (and many women's lack of interest in him, when they finally meet him at close quarters) is incidentally due in part to his particular kind of laziness. "I like the movies," he confessed, "because I am lazy. They shelter you from everything. You go to the studio, stay there twelve hours a day, follow instructions, and worry about nothing." There are hundreds of stories illustrating this aspect of his character, some of them surely exaggerated, many circulated by him. Everybody who has worked with him has his favourite one. This is Fellini's: "Marcello comes on the set at eight but does not really wake up until ten. He sleeps when they make him up and does not know what

happens to him. Once he was rubbing his forehead and I told him: 'Look out, you are spoiling that beautiful bullet wound.' He had a round red bullet hole for one of the tentative ends of 8½ I was shooting. 'A bullet hole?' he asked incredulously, 'Where?'"

His apparent uncertainty, his pathetic and transparent loneliness in a complex world, his laziness are among the qualities which have made some of his impersonations memorable; they certainly contributed to his success, but not in the simple way critics believe. He does not memorize his part, for example, "because," he says, "I am lazy." It is true: he reads the script only once, just before shooting, or even before that, when he has to make up his mind about whether to play the part or not. He never looks at the script again. This is not really because he is lazy, as he pretends, or not entirely because he is lazy. What interests him is not the detail but the general design, the meaning of the character he is to portray in that particular kind of story. When his turn comes, he asks the script girl or the director: "What am I supposed to say here?" They tell him and he recites the longest lines with the necessary expression. He seldom repeats the exact words. "Movie dialogue is not important," he explains. "It's not literature." He improvises words of the kind the character would say in that particular situation. He invents his own expressions, uses exclamations and phrases which would come naturally to the man he is supposed to be. "I do what actors have always done in Italy," he explains. He also does what the heroic, old, stock company actors did, who always used to repeat what the prompter told them in whispers.

All this, the dozing between takes, the relaxed attitude, the joking in Roman dialect with the carpenters and the electricians, is really his method. When he acts on the spur of the moment, so to speak, keeping the character well in mind, everything takes on a fresh, improvised, spontaneous quality, which it would not have if he had repeated the words to himself a thousand times and rehearsed the gestures until numb. Monicelli says of him: "There is an 'Italian quality' about his acting which I can not define. He is not the caricature of an Italian as foreigners see him. He is measured and economical. He does not grimace and gesture. And yet, he portrays the Italian way of living, seeing things, doing things as nobody else can, in a way which is universally understood."

He is, of course, all the things journalists have said: a good actor, a Latin Lover of sorts, the symbol of lost humanity in the industrialized jungle, frightened and bored, a relaxed and lazy man. But his great quality is yet another. He says he must feel comfortable in the skin of the character he is to interpret. "Perhaps I, too, impersonate only myself," he explained, "time and again, but there are many more Mastroiannis than meet the eye." To do this he must choose the story very carefully. Some he keeps in mind for years and trusts to a favourite writer to hatch. A few are offered to him ready-made. He sometimes follows a favourite idea from embryo to finished script until he is absolutely certain of every detail. He endlessly and acutely debates scenes and fine psychological points with writers and directors. He wants to be convinced. For a lazy man, he admits he works very hard when choosing and preparing a script. "I read many stories; I see directors and producers for long conferences; I talk with the business people, I discuss everything with my wife and my friends," he recalled. And that is his real work. Without it he wouldn't be as famous. In the end there is only the acting to do, which he considers the easiest part. "Movies," he said, "are fun until you start shooting. After that everything is dull routine."

How does he choose the next story? "You have to be alive, live with people, listen to what is being said around you, sense what is in the air," he said. "If I lived away from Rome, the smell, the noise, the faces, the gossip, the air, the stones of Rome, the little *trattorie*, I would really become impotent. Movies are not made by one man alone, or by few men, but by everybody around you. They tell me I must go to America, they offer me fabulous contracts. I like America, for a visit, a holiday. I have been there five times in three years. I like Americans. They are friendly and without envy. I remember one day, in the lobby of a New York hotel, an elderly man stopped by me. He was well dressed and imposing. He said: 'Mastroianni? The Organizer? I admire you. I too was a socialist once.' And shook my hand. I could make one movie in America, as an adventure, as one goes on a safari or reaches the North Pole. But I

could not go to Hollywood for keeps, start all over again, as if I were twenty once more. I could not do it and survive as an actor."

And this, of course, is the clue. When you chat with him, *à bâtons rompus*, between takes in the cavernous darkness of a studio, at a small café at night, or walking with dogs in the Tuscan countryside, you discover a certain number of curious things. He uses an incredible wealth of apt and well chosen words (on the set, he improvises better lines than most of his writers can or dare to write); he uses by preference the informal jargon of Roman intellectuals among themselves, when they do not try to impress anybody; he defines things (emotions, persons, situations, colours, scenes) with uncanny precision. You have the sensation of facing a writer and not an actor.

In reality he is a weird modern variety of the writer, the man who does all the things a good novelist does except put pen on paper. Mastroianni is all this, a perceptive, inventive, and articulate artist, but also an intelligent human being. He is intelligent and aware that it is the kind of man he is (shaped by blood, Italy, experience, wife, family, love, and fear of life) who has somehow become a symbol of sorts. This man is made transparently accessible to the film-going public by his talent and his technique. But it is the man and not the talent and technique that the multitudes want to admire.

He is not the dominator, seducer, and winner of past decades. And yet he is not the perplexed, lost, frightened man some critics describe. He is a brave and lonely man, refusing to be taken in and enslaved by the idols of modern life: wealth, fame, the impeccably beautiful women, the many duties necessary to survive in the Organization. He could not care less. In life and in his pictures (those pictures he selects to fit him exactly) he does all the things a cautious man should not do if he wants to avoid defeat —and yet Mastroianni survives; does not get hurt too much, and sometimes even wins. That his success is due to this, the human stuff he is made of, he probably knows. Once he said to me: "When I choose a story, I contribute ideas to a script, I act, I must at all cost forget one thing. It is not easy. I must forget I am an actor. The moment I think of myself as an actor, I am finished. I must remember only that I am a man." Man is a big word.

Nabokov

A witty and profound study of Vladimir Nabokov, author of, among others, Lolita and Speak, Memory

BY PENELOPE GILLIATT

PHOTOGRAPHS BY PENN

"Is the Queen pregnant?" said Vladimir Nabokov.

"I don't believe so," I said.

"When I saw her on television at the World Cup watching football she kept making this gesture." He did a mime of smoothing a dress.

"She always does that."

"Oh, I see. A queenly movement. Permanently with child. With heir." He chuckled and looked interested.

We met in a distant part of Switzerland. I had said to him on the hotel telephone, sounding to myself ludicrously like a character in *Sherlock Holmes* but assuming that he wouldn't know it, that he could identify me downstairs in the lobby because I had red hair.

"I shall be carrying a copy of *Speak, Memory*," he had said back. (*Speak, Memory* is his autobiography.)

His ear for the idiom was instant and exact. It turned out later that his father had known Sherlock Holmes's creator, Sir Arthur Conan Doyle. ("Though Conan Doyle was much more proud of his intolerably boring books on South Africa.") Nabokov has a writer's passion for the physical details and likes Holmes's habit of passing half-a-crown through a chink in the cab to the cabdriver. He also has an intentness on the nuances of speech—Holmes's, mine, anyone's who uses English—that is made much more urgent by his exile from his own language.

Twenty nine years ago he abandoned his "untrammelled, rich, and infinitely docile Russian tongue," which he had already used to write novels unpublishable in the Soviet Union and so not published at all, for an English that he learned first from governesses. Perhaps his command of it now is partly due to the obstacle, as a man will often think more swiftly who speaks with an impediment. Nabokov now writes a dulcet and rash English that has found more of the secret springs of our language than most writers born to it can ever get under their fingers. For instance, he knows precisely the mechanism of an Anglo-Saxon use of bathos and rudeness, which will plant an anti-climactic word or a vernacular insult in a suave context where it goes off with a peculiar mixture of self-mockery and shabby bombast. For all that, his distress about losing Russian is obviously gnawing and will never be appeased. In the preface to *Lolita* he writes briefly about it as if he were an illusionist robbed of his luggage, performing on a stage where his plundered trickery has to be practised without any of the apparatus of association.

It occurs to me that perhaps this is exactly what makes him write better about love than any other novelist in modern English. The afflictions of exile carry a taste of theft that is the pang of intimacy itself. The tricked focus in the experience of loving, the one that hideously connects rapture with mortality and causes lovers to hoard the present as though it were already gone, bestows a psychic foretaste of loss that is close to the one that gave the privileged Russian children of Nabokov's age a genius for recollection. They lived their Russian youth with the intensity of the grown-up in love, mysteriously already knowing too much about losing it. The ache that clings to good fortune or great accord is one of time's ugly gags, like the grasping housewife already secreted in the rapturous frame of little Lolita.

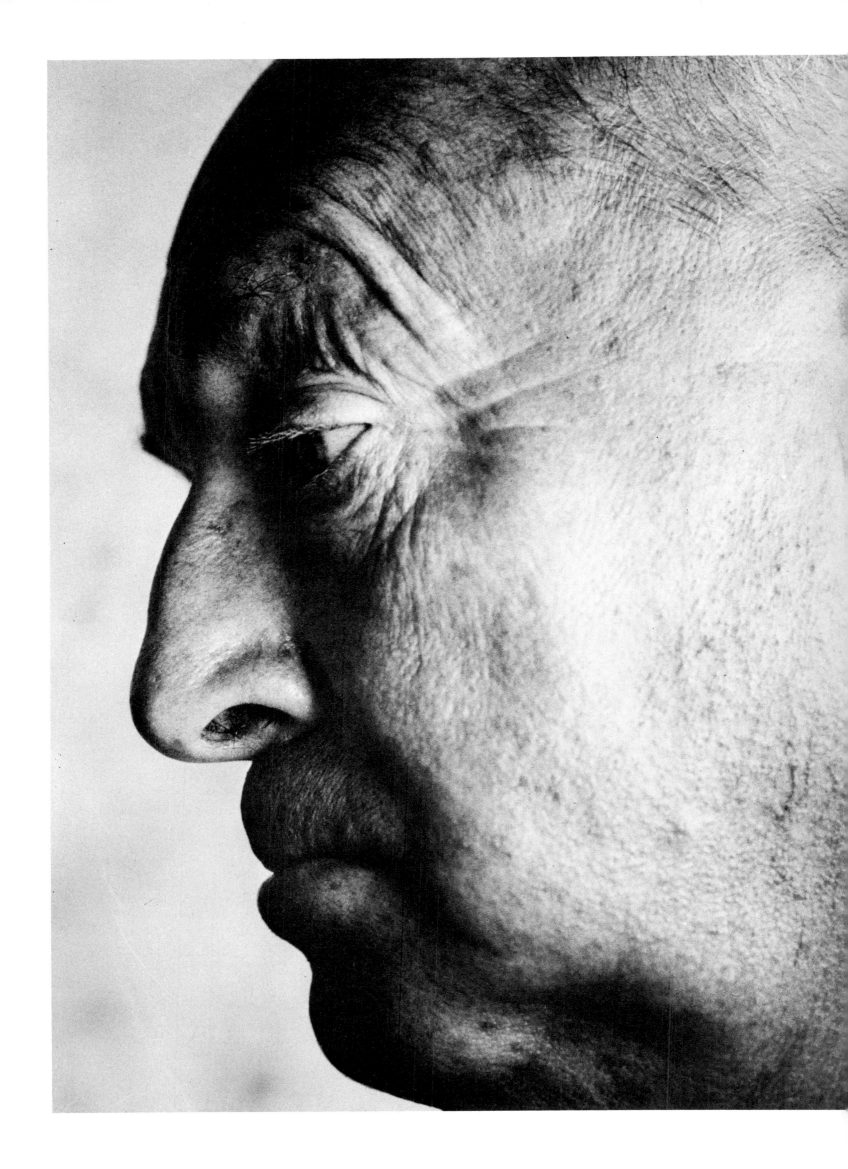

Humbert Humbert is in love with a booby trap. His whole situation hoaxes him. *Lolita* is an account of the passionate involvement of a man constantly ambushed by *dépaysement* and consigned to the plastic exile of motels. *Dépaysé:* de-countried: We need a word for it now in English far more than we need "deflowered." It isn't at all fully expressed by "alienation," or "rootlessness," for like the comic agony of love in *Lolita*, it is concept of loss that includes the knowledge of what it can be to possess. Before I met Nabokov I had wondered sometimes how it was possible for a writer to live permanently in hotels, as he has done since 1960, mostly in Switzerland; but it was a stupid speculation about a great novelist of *dépaysement* who carries his country in his skull. His landscape isn't Russia, but Russian literature.

His permanent address now is a hotel in Montreux that he described as "a lovely Edwardian heap." We met in the Engadine, where he and his wife had come for the butterflies, in another Edwardian heap with spa baths in the basement. He is a tall, loping man whose gait and way of peering reminded me faintly of Jacques Tati's.

"I am six foot," he said. "I have very thin bones. The rest is flesh." He picked at his arm as if it were a jacket.

In his autobiography he describes himself as having the Korff nose, passed on from his paternal grandmother's side: "A handsome Germanic organ with a boldly boned bridge and a slightly tilted, distinctly grooved, fleshy end." He wears spectacles, but switches to pince-nez after six to alter the ache in his nose. His accent is neither Russian nor American: I think it originates in the upper-class English undergraduate speech of immediately after the First World War, when he went to Cambridge. ("Cambridge, Cambridge, not Cambridge, Mass.," he said.) His French is delicate and pure. He hears it as dated: "The slang goes back to Maupassant." His Russian is the authentic sound of pre-Revolutionary St. Petersburg. He did a mischievously expressive example of the boneless accent of standard Pravda speech now. I don't suppose that either he or his wife can detect that their birth in itself is a distinct and commanding fact about them both; but then the

A passionate hunter of butterflies, Nabokov finds many of his specimens in the Swiss and Italian Alps.

IRVING PENN

upper-class people of Europe never do. It is only the rest who can see the difference, and the well-born truly believe themselves to be indistinguishable.

The Nabokovs think of going back to America to live, perhaps in California. They are looking for—what? A climate; and far more than that, a language. "We were in Italy, but we don't want to live there. I don't speak Italian. And the *scioperi* (strikes). . . . Véra found a château in France, but it would have cost a lot of money to convert it. It had drawbridges. It had its drawbridges and drawbacks." He has a habit of going back over what he has said and correcting it that is rather like the way he immediately uses an eraser on his notes. "I don't much care for De Gaulle. I fear things will happen there when he dies. I would go to Spain but I hate bullfights. Switzerland: lakes, charming people, stability. All my publishers pass through from one festival to another."

He had been up since six, as usual, and had a bath in the curative basement. "I discovered the secret of levitation," he said. "One puts the feet flat braced against the end of the bath and rises covered with bubbles like a fur. I felt like a bear. A memory of a former state."

We had a drink rather early in the morning. The whiskies looked small and he asked for soda. "Make the glass grow," he said, and then muttered: "The grass glow."

His books are written on card-index cards so that it is possible to start in the middle and insert scenes as he wants. He writes in 3B pencils that he says he sharpens compulsively. They have India rubbers on the ends which he uses to exorcise mistakes instead of simply crossing them out. My own error in writing with a pen struck him as technically cardinal. His pocket notebooks are made of paper squared like an arithmetic book. The formal pattern that might distract most people obviously stimulates him. I could understand this: It must be a little like seeing figments in the black and white tiles in public lavatories.

"Some of my best poems and chess problems have been composed in bathrooms looking at the floor," he said.

At some stage we started to play anagrams. I gave him "cart horse" (the solution is "orchestra"). He took the problem away on what

was meant to be a nap, and came bounding into the bar two hours later with an expression that was a very Russian mixture of buoyancy and sheepishness. The tartanned paper of his little note pad was covered with methodically wrong steps. "Her actors," he said, in try-on triumph, eyeing me, and knowing perfectly well that the answer had to be one word. Then he started to laugh at his picture of the creature whose property the actors would be. Bossy women strike him as irresistibly comic: They trudge through his books, absurd, cruel, creatures of inane placidity who see everything in the world as a mirror of their womanliness and who will speak sharply about something like Bolshevism as though it were an obvious minor nuisance, like mosquitoes, or the common cold. I believe his woman producer also amused him because he finds the theatre inherently funny when it is earnest: something to do with its thickness, I think, compared with the fine mesh of the novels he likes.

When he taught in America he lectured on *Anna Karenina*, Tolstoy's *The Death of Ivan Ilyitch*, *Ulysses*, Kafka's "The Metamorphosis," and Jane Austen's *Mansfield Park*, which was suggested by Edmund Wilson. The precise butterfly-pinner discovered that Tolstoy made the two families in *Anna Karenina* age on a different time scale, so that more years have passed for one than for the other. He also says that Joyce left out any reference to Bloom's coming back from the cemetery.

"I know Dublin exactly. I could draw a map of it. I know the Liffey like the Moskva. I have never been to Dublin but I know it as well as Moscow. Also I have never been to Moscow."

He and his wife both lived in St. Petersburg, but they met first in Berlin in exile. They could have met many times when they were children; at dancing class, perhaps; it bothers them and they go over it.

"Véra's coming down in a moment," he said. "She's lost something. A jacket, I think. When she loses things, it is always something very big." He started to shake again. His sense of humour is very Russian, and the sight of its taking him over is hugely pleasurable. There is a lot of the buffoon in it. He is one of the few people I have seen who literally does sometimes nearly fall off his chair with laughing.

"Véra has been doing 'cart horse' as well," he said. "Eventually she suggested 'horse-cart.' She hadn't much hope."

In the lounge there was an Edwardian mural of naked lovers, except that they were not naked and seemed to have nothing much to do with loving. The woman was vulgarly draped and the man wore, as well as a tulle scarf across his groin, a vapourish example of early Maidenform around his chest. After days of looking at the picture Nabokov still found it mildly interesting. It happened to be a rather obvious demonstration of the intimacy in art between silliness and prudery. The high-flying Philistinism of protected art tastes strikes him often as richly foolish. Long ago the Empress of Russia gave him pleasure by being an eager admirer of Ella Wheeler Wilcox. *Invitation to a Beheading*, one of his early Russian-language novels, has a sulphurous passage about an imaginary book considered to be "the acme of modern thought" in which world history is seen from the point of view of an elderly and apparently sagacious oak tree. Nabokov detests literature that has sweeping social pretensions. He also loathes prurience. The bad art of the past that has lost its power to bamboozle will often reveal that a large share of its badness consists in failing to go too far, which is the only course that is ever far enough in aesthetics. The streak of blue nerve in Nabokov's work is part of its quality. It has an effect that is close to the exhilaration of flair and courage in real conduct.

In the actual world, the vice for which Nabokov seems to have most loathing is brutality. He finds it in tank-shaped political bullies, "swine-toned radio music," the enjoyment of trained animals, the truisms of Freudianism, the abhorrence of Germany between the wars. (There is a German in one of his books who believes that "electrocution" is the root of "cute.") In the world of art his equivalent loathing is for mediocrity, which is perhaps only the aesthetic form of the same brutality. There are celebrated writers in whom he detects a naïveté that he obviously finds almost thuggish. He detests Zola, Stendhal, Balzac, Thomas Mann.

Nabokov spoke eagerly about the descriptions of the fish in Hemingway's *The Old Man and the Sea* and about the jungle passages and close physical descriptions in Graham Greene's *A Burnt-Out Case*. "The avant-garde French novels that I've read don't stir my artistic appetite. Only here and there. Even Shaw can do that." I asked him about Genet: "An interesting fairyland with good measurements." Ostrovsky, the Russian playwright, he described as having "a streak of poetry that he unfortunately put down because he was so intent on writing about the merchant class." Tin-eared translators torment him. *"Vive le pédant,"* he writes defiantly in one of his prefaces, "and down with the simpletons who think that all is well if the spirit is rendered (while the words go away by themselves on a naïve and vulgar spree—in the suburbs of Moscow for instance —and Shakespeare is again reduced to play the king's ghost)."

The English translations of his Russian novels have been done by Nabokov himself, generally with his son, Dmitri, who is a racing driver and a singer. Nabokov has just finished doing a Russian translation of *Lolita*, typeset in New York. "To be smuggled in, dropped by parachute, floating down on the blurb." His attachment to words is urgent and moving. A copy of the unabridged Webster's dictionary is carried about in the back of Nabokov's Lancia; in his hotel room on holiday it was open among the M's, halfway through, which is the way he leaves it so as to save the spine. In his autobiography he speaks of turning even now to the last page of any new grammar to find "that promised land where, at last, words are meant to mean what they mean."

"In Massachusetts once I was ill with food poisoning," he said. "I was being wheeled along a corridor. They left the trolley by a bookcase and I drew out a big medical dictionary and in the ward I drew the curtains around myself and read. It wasn't allowed because it looked as if I were dying. They took the book away. In hospitals there is still something of the eighteenth-century madhouse."

"Pasternak?" I asked. At once he talked very fast. "*Doctor Zhivago* is false, melodramatic, badly written. It is false to history and false to art. The people are dummies. That awful girl is absurd. It reminds me very much of novels written by Russians of, I am ashamed to say, the gentler sex. Pasternak is not a bad poet.

But in *Zhivago* he is vulgar. Simple. If you take his beautiful metaphors there is nothing behind them. Even in his poems: what is that line, Véra? 'To be a woman is a big step.' It is ridiculous." He laughed and looked stricken.

"This kind of thing recurs. Very typical of poems written in the Soviet era. A person of Zhivago's class and his set, he wouldn't stand in the snow and read about the Bolshevist régime and feel a tremendous glow. There was the *liberal* revolution at that time. Kerensky. If Kerensky had had more luck—but he was a liberal, you see, and he couldn't just clap the Bolsheviks into jail. It was not done. He was a very average man, I should say. The kind of person you might find in the Cabinet of any democratic country. He spoke very well, with his hand in his bosom like Napoleon because it had almost been broken by handshakes.

"Yet people like Edmund Wilson and Isaiah Berlin, they have to love *Zhivago* to prove that good writing can come out of Soviet Russia. They ignore that it is really a *bad book*. There are some absolutely ridiculous scenes. Scenes of eavesdropping, for instance. You know about eavesdropping. If it is not brought in as parody it is almost Philistine. It is the mark of the amateur in literature. And that marvellous scene where he had to get rid of the little girl to let the characters make love, and he sends her out skating. In *Siberia*. To keep warm they give her her mother's *scarf*. And then she sleeps deeply in a hut while there is all this going on. Obviously Pasternak just didn't know what to do with her. He's like Galsworthy. Galsworthy in one of his novels gave a character a cane and a dog and simply didn't know how to get rid of them.

"And the metaphors. Unattached comparisons. Suppose I were to say 'as passionately adored and insulted as a barometer in a mountain hotel," he said, looking out at the rain. "It would be a beautiful metaphor. But who is it about? The image is top-heavy. There is nothing to attach it to. And there is a pseudo-religious strain in the book which almost shocks me. *Zhivago* is so feminine that I sometimes wonder if it might have been partly written by Pasternak's mistress.

"As a translator of Shakespeare he is very poor. He is considered great only by people who don't know Russian. An example." His wife helped him to remember a line of a Pasternak translation. "What he has turned it into in Russian is this: 'all covered with grease and keeps wiping the pig-iron.' You see. It is ridiculous. What would be the original?"

"Greasy Joan doth keel the pot?"

"Yes. 'Keeps wiping the pig-iron!'" He expostulated and looked genuinely angry. "Pasternak himself has been very much *helped* by translation. Sometimes when you translate a cliché—you know, a cloud has a silver lining—it can sound like Milton because it is in another language."

"Isn't that what happened to Pushkin?" said Véra.

"He had translated the French writers of his day. The small coin of drawing-room poets and the slightly larger coin of Racine. In Russian it became breathtaking." I remarked that someone had once said to me that the first man who compared a woman to a flower was a genius and the second, a fool. "And the third, a knave," said Nabokov.

We went for a drive in the new Lancia through the mountains. Mrs. Nabokov drove, rather fast, mostly in third gear on a tricky road, in the face of jibes from her husband about the sheer drops that she had chosen on other days as suitable places to turn.

"Sometimes my son wishes I wouldn't joke so much," he said with melancholy.

I sat on the back seat, which was still insulated in cellophane, and took off my shoes to keep the cover intact. A hat for butterfly-hunting and walks was on the back shelf.

"You could cover your toes with my hat," said Mr. Nabokov.

He looked for good meadows for butterfly-hunting and memorized promising paths off the road. His feeling about nature is communicable even to people who don't share it. He is the only man I have ever heard who responds to mention of Los Angeles not with abuse of the city but with glory in the vegetation. He wrote once that when he hunted butterflies it was his highest experience of timelessness, a way "to picket nature" and "to rebel against the void fore and aft." I think it is also an expression of the great writer's passion to define.

We had lemon tea and cream cakes in another hotel looking out across the mountains. He was

The sensitive and strong hand of Nabokov, holding an Orion blue butterfly.

charming to a waitress who had seemed not to have heard the order and said peacefully after a long wait: "I can tell by the nape of her neck that the cakes are coming." He has a comic affection for girls' bodies that is rather like his tenderness for gaffes, as though the naked toes or napes of girls absorbed by other things fall unknowingly into a category of farcical and touching blunders.

I asked him whether Lolita would have turned into a boy if his own real child had been a girl.

"Oh, yes," he said at once. "If I had had a daughter Humbert Humbert would have been a pederast."

I thought perhaps that he might cherish a little hatred for *Lolita* now, as writers often do for books that have had more attention than anything else they have written, but his feelings seem not to have swerved. The book remains his favourite, though he says that *Pale Fire* was more difficult to write.

"I had written a short story with the same idea as *Lolita*. The man's name there is Arthur. They travel through France. I never published

it. The little girl wasn't alive. She hardly spoke. Little by little I managed to give her some semblance of reality. I was on my way to the incinerator one day with half the manuscript to burn it, and Véra said wait a minute. And I came back meekly."

"I don't remember that. Did I?" said Mrs. Nabokov.

"What was most difficult was putting myself . . . I am a normal man, you see. I travelled in school buses to listen to the talk of schoolgirls. I went to school on the pretext of placing our daughter. We have no daughter. For Lolita, I took one arm of a little girl who used to come to see Dmitri, one kneecap of another."

He says in the preface that the book originated in a story in *Paris-Soir* of an ape that had been taught to draw: Its first drawing was of the bars of its cage. The brawl around *Lolita* and the fierce humour that stylizes all of his work often seems to obscure the extreme tenderness that impels it. His sensitivity to suffering and the exploited makes the attention paid to the plot facts of *Lolita* seem even more brutishly literal-minded than usual. When he was

IRVING PENN

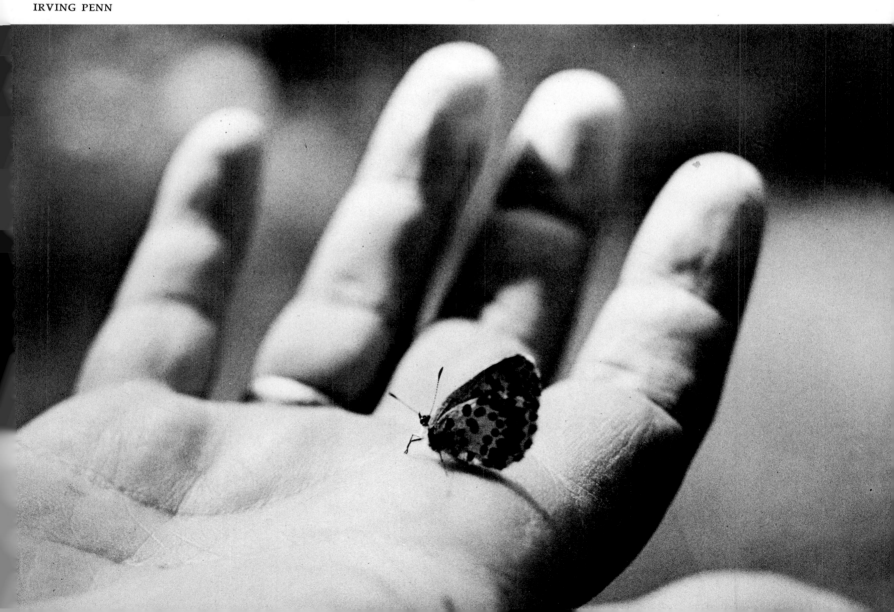

in Hollywood to do the script, the producers asked him to make Lolita and Humbert Humbert get married: Apparently this would have pulled some knot of embarrassment for them. The idea of the book being classified as obscene —as it still is in Burma, for instance—is much more gross than anything in most pornography, for it is a book that extends exceptional gentleness to the yearning and the out of step. Elsewhere, in his *Laughter in the Dark*, a murderer thinks "impossible to kill while she was taking off her shoe"; it is a modern equivalent of the moment in *Hamlet* when a man can not be murdered at prayer. In Nabokov's work sexuality stands for tenderness, and tenderness in the remaining sanctity.

In the car again I asked him about something he had once written about the author of *Alice in Wonderland.*

"I always call him Lewis Carroll Carroll," he said, "because he was the first Humbert Humbert. Have you seen those photographs of him with little girls? He would make arrangements with aunts and mothers to take the children out. He was never caught, except by one girl who wrote about him when she was much older."

He started to answer something I was saying, and turned it into an imitation of Edmund Wilson saying, "Yes, yes." Nabokov and Edmund Wilson are old friends, but they have recently conducted a waspish public fight about Mr. Wilson's knowledge of Russian, involving claims that seem fairly foolish in the face of a Russian-speaker. Nabokov's private feelings seem affectionately caustic. The imitated "Yes" involved a head-movement like a man trying to get down a pill when he is gagging on it." "Apparently consent with him is so difficult he must make a convulsive effort," said Nabokov warmly enough, and came back to *Lolita.*

"It was a great pleasure to write, but it was also very painful. I had to read so many case histories. Most of it was written in a car to have complete quiet." He says in *Speak, Memory* that "in first-rate work of fiction the real clash is not between the characters but between the author and the world." This is the force of *Lolita.* The most unsparing love-novel of our literature of glib and easy sex is about an obsession that is locally criminal, written by an alien attacking the numbness of a culture from the inside of the machine that best represents its numbness.

In Dreams: Does Seven Mean Conception?

BY FRANK O'CONNOR

EDITOR'S NOTE: *This article on dreams was among the last by Frank O'Connor, the great Irish storyteller who died March 10, 1966. Famous for his short stories, for his autobiography,* An Only Child, *O'Connor was an authoritative conversationalist with expertise as an Irish feudist, concentrated mostly on Dublin literary men. Putnam's published after his death his fascinating book* A Short History of Irish Literature.

Years ago, my wife overheard my small boy (as he then was) say sadly to another small boy, "Daddy isn't just interested in dreams. They're a disease with him." He is not the only one who has thought that, for a famous novelist once reproved me for what he thought was an aberration and said, "It doesn't go with your sort of work." Which, of course, is true. Neither he nor I would be happy writing novels in the manner of Kafka; we are both old-fashioned realists who believe that the close observation of character produces the closest approximation to truth of which literature is capable, or—as a brilliant professor of psychology once put it to me—"My students will learn more about the workings of the human mind from Tolstoy or Turgenev than from Freud or Jung."

All the same, I still continue to think that a function which takes up so much of our time can not be lightly dismissed. The trouble with it is that existing methods for studying it do not take the reader very far, and the reason is that they all have a purpose other than the study of dreams in themselves. In early times dreams were considered important because they were supposed to be prophetic; now they are considered important because they are believed to throw light on nervous ailments. If dreams *are* a form of language, if they really do communicate something to us, we should begin with the elements of the language and leave until later the question of their usefulness in anticipating a Derby winner, an air crash, or a nervous breakdown.

grew interested in the subject was, "Is there objective proof that dreams do, in fact, communicate something?" The test I set myself was a fascinating book by William Archer, a dramatic critic. Archer did not believe that dreams communicated anything; and, in reply to the psychoanalysts, he published a collection of his own dreams, selected from his records over a number of years and defied anyone to make sense of them. It seemed to me a fair test. I knew nothing of Archer beyond the fact that he was a dramatic critic and a friend of Shaw's, so I read his dreams many times and then wrote down my general conclusions. These were roughly that (1) for years before his death Archer suffered from an intestinal obstruction which he believed would be fatal; (2) that he had an only son whom he idolized and with whom he had had some disagreement; (3) that the son was killed in World War I, and (4) that the shock of the boy's death at a time when he believed himself to be dying put Archer off balance and turned his mind from rationalism to fantasy.

Most of this I was able to prove later. The only detail I had failed to notice was that, in his attempt at getting into communication with his dead son, the stout Scottish rationalist had taken up spiritualism. And yet, when I learned it, I saw that it was also recorded in the dreams. I had merely failed to notice it.

The moving little story that I traced through William Archer's dreams convinced me of one thing at least. Dreams *are* a language, and do communicate something factual and specific even if it is nothing so spectacular as a Derby winner. This is not necessarily something of which the dreamer is unaware. Very often, as with Archer, it is something of which he is already painfully aware. Nor does it necessarily mean something that he has repressed from his conscious mind or deal with subjects forbidden by that mythical character, the Censor.

Sometimes the subjects that dreams deal with are trite indeed, being no more than the expression of ideas or opinions that the dreamer holds. Here, for instance, is a dream of my own that I noted on waking. "I saw D. A. Binchy dressed like a sailor but only half his natural height." The meaning of this was clear to me even as I wrote it down, because it was merely a translation of a phrase I had used to a newspaper man who had interviewed me on the previous evening. I had talked of the loneliness of Irish writers and said that the only people they met who were their intellectual equals were the Celtic scholars, who had had training of a German type and consequently developed an international approach to scholarship, but even these were limited by the very narrowness of their subject.

D. A. Binchy is the great Celtic scholar, the dream shows him as the sailor, the international figure; but it shows him also as only half his height. The remark about the narrowness of the subject was actually Binchy's own. Anyhow, there is nothing here for the Censor to get his claws in. It is merely an idea like any other idea. The real importance of the dream is the way it shows us how an idea is expressed in dream language.

It is not often one can trace the origin of an idea dream as I was able to do with this one. The best dreams for study are functional dreams, dreams that occur when one has a toothache, palpitations, or bronchial difficulties because these allow no scope for subjective "interpretation." When one wakes up with one's nose stuffed, having dreamed that one had sent for the chimney sweep because the chimney was blocked, one realizes that "chimney" is a dream word for "nose."

In a similar way, dreams that occur during a gastric attack frequently make use of images that involve traffic congestion. In the William Archer dreams, the streets are frequently clogged with traffic, busses or horse-drawn; and, after the first hot dog I ever ate, I dreamed that "the Russians had taken over the railway lines." "Traffic" accordingly is a dream word for digestion. The most valuable type of functional dream is that which occurs in women during their periods, because, apart from its richly metaphorical character, it has a perfectly recognizable psychological content. It represents an ebbing vitality, a retreat to the womb, and—with different dream words—occurs in men as well as in women. In women it usually introduces the dreamer's mother or aunt; the womb is sometimes described as "a small back room"; it is sometimes set on a strand, and I have even noted punning allusions to the strand like "Land's End" and "Finisterre."

But the best way of proceeding objectively from the incontrovertible evidence of functional dreams into the unknown territory of dreams based on thoughts and feelings is by way of one's own family—parents, wife, husband, children. They can cause us just as much discomfort as any physical organ, so that one can often pin the dream down to the particular member of the family who is at the root of the trouble. Indeed, members of the family are often described in physical terms, and a woman will dream of an unsatisfactory husband as an aching tooth and imagine herself going to the dentist to have it extracted.

But between dreams of one's parents and dreams of other members of the family there is one enormous difference. We dream of our parents oftener than of anyone else, and we dream of them under a far greater number of disguises. It is true, as the dream books say, that the father appears in dreams as king, chairman, teacher, Pope, God, engineer, and policeman; but I have noticed that he is represented in different ways in different countries—in England, for instance, by any "author," or anyone called "Arthur" or "Pater." In Ireland he is "St. Patrick" and in America I have heard of dreams in which he is "George" or "Washington, D. C." He is also any "patron" or "pattern" or anyone who talks "patter" or behaves "patronizingly." The mother, on the other hand—usually queen, nurse, servant, housekeeper, the earth, a city, or an island—turns up in dreams I have seen as a hotel, a restaurant, a lounge bar, Eden, Edinburgh, anyone called "Edith," and any possible or impossible play on the word *mater*, like "matron," "matrix," "material," or even "mattress."

Here, semantics can probably teach us more than psychoanalysis. I have read a book by an eminent pupil of Jung's in which he proudly describes how he made a reluctant patient, a girl, associate the name "Edith" from one of her dreams with a juvenile delinquent she barely knew. If that unfortunate girl did not end up in a mental hospital, it was no fault of the analyst. "Edith" means "mother."

The reason for this confusion is that the father and mother of our dreams are only occasionally the real father and mother. The dream father is a pigeonhole, a category, a principle of authority who must at the same time represent God, the government, the dreamer's human father, the dreamer as father, and the dreamer—man or woman—as conscience or judgment. He usually appears on the dreamer's right-hand side as the mother appears on the left. To put your father on the left-hand side may mean, as in one or two dreams I have read, that you are trying to use instinct as a substitute for conscience—in other words that you are one of these people who, whenever

they do anything wrong, are inclined to say, "Well, you will admit it was natural." He seems to be the "public" as opposed to the "private" figure, the "front" as opposed to the "back." He is the real source and origin of life, protector of the moral law, civilization, and adaptation as opposed to the enduring, unchanging material embodied in the female principle.

Which aspect of the category the dreamer is discussing is usually neatly suggested by allusions. The person who accompanies us in a dream, or who accompanies the person we are dreaming of, is nearly always an allusion to some particular aspect of the dream. Thus when I dreamed that I was with C. P. Snow, it meant that I was discussing my problems as a writer, not my problems as husband, son, or father. In the same way, when the dreamer means "my human father," he usually says, "I was walking with my father and my uncle." When he means both his human father and himself as father—that is, when he is contrasting his behaviour to his father with his son's behaviour to him—he will dream something like "I was walking with *either* my brother or my son."

Here is a dream of mine which the reader should now be able to translate. "I am drugged and tortured. When I wake I am tied to a post. My left arm has been stabbed in a great many places and has withered. Mussolini stands before me with a penknife in his hand. Franco is standing some distance away with his back to me. Mussolini says compassionately, 'Franco did that. These Spaniards are so cruel.'"

And, just to show how dreams repeat themselves until we become aware of them, here is the same subject repeated a short time later.

This time it came in an extraordinary form, as a complete short story, so vivid and exciting that I at once began to write it. If I had finished writing it, I feel quite sure I should have had no difficulty in publishing it, and it would now be haunting me from the pages of some anthology, but fortunately I realized before I was done that what I was writing was really another version of the age-old theme of Dr. Jekyll and Mr. Hyde and that it criticized nothing except my own ugly character.

The period of the dream was 1798 when the Irish country people were being cruelly oppressed by English masters. The local land-owner had had estates in the West Indies from which he had brought back a young Negro coachman. After the landowner's death his son, the young master, had gathered about him a gang of ruffians who hunted the countryside at night, burning, torturing, and hanging. One night he set out with a coachload of these ruffians but, after searching cabin after cabin, found no victims because the country people had fled before them. Deprived of their sport, the gang decided to hang the Negro coachman instead. They hung him from a tree, and as the dawn broke, saw that the dead boy's face was identical with that of the young lord. They had hanged his brother.

I still think it is a striking subject, but if you examine the earlier dream you will see that the subject is the same; that the Negro coachman who is hanged is identical with the person in the first dream who has been tortured by Mussolini, and that in both dreams I am accusing my own judgment of crucifying my instincts. These are two dreams I felt I had to take seriously. Not that I should advise anyone else to take dreams as seriously as all that. So far as I understand their purpose, dreams are really a sort of built-in stabilizer that tries to reconcile the two sides of one's character, the masculine and feminine, the intellectual and intuitive. Each quality is necessary and important, but too much of either may be bad and lead to disastrous results.

If one thinks of paternal dreams as progressive and maternal dreams as regressive, but recognizes at the same time that progress and regress are necessary like flood and ebb, one can come to a reasonable understanding of what they mean. That is the principal interest of the women's dreams that I mentioned earlier—they are *all* regressive; they all represent a return to the womb, and in periods of low vitality men have them as much as women.

In men these dreams can usually be identified by the fact that the dreamer has rid himself of his clothes—at least, of all but his night clothes—and is searching for some place he has lost. Frequently the place he is searching for is painted green or has green upholstery—perhaps some vague prenatal memory of the amniotic fluid. But these dreams always end with a series of progressive dreams that represent a return to the father, represented very often by a bridge. Sometimes one can actually detect the end of the regressive phase by what I call a birth dream—one in which the dreamer seems to be falling down an elevator or a chute and wakes up with a gasp. For me, this always indicates a revulsion against the withdrawal from life. Birth really represents rebirth.

Death dreams are among the commonest of all dreams, and they have a language of their own. Archer, for instance, waiting for news of his son's death at the Front during World War I, describes how "a messenger boy from Wellington House with great difficulty forced himself into my room, carrying a locked case within which was a book. This was some book supposed to be contraband, and the glass case was the method adopted by the censorship to deliver it—and yet prevent it from doing any harm." If the reader is interested in dream language, he will now close this magazine and think carefully what "a book in a glass case" represents. The experience will teach him more about dream language than he will ever learn from psychoanalytic textbooks. He will find the answer in a note at the end of this article.

Sometimes, one sees the person whose death one dreads along with a dead person; sometimes in the company of a man with red hair. Here is another dream of Archer's where the two are linked. "I am looking at a bookstall in Charing Cross Road, and see a young actor whom I know (I forget who) go by in company with a man with a short red beard, in whom I recognize W. H. Vernon—an actor who died at least twenty years ago." For some reason which I do not understand, the redhead and the number four are the commonest of all images of death; they are also among the oldest. In a seventh-century Irish saga one of the tabus laid on a king is "never to go with three reds to the house of a red."

As I seem to be laying claim to more knowledge than anyone should possess, let me add that there are certain things about dreams that I don't understand at all. One is the significance of numbers. "Four," for instance, which is pretty generally recognized as having to do with death, has been rationalized as a reference to the number of men who carry a corpse. That looks highly improbable to me. What I *have* noticed is that odd numbers seem to be associated with the paternal side of the character, even numbers with the maternal.

"One" seems to mean the father, "two" the mother, "three" the individual (perhaps because he represents the sum of father and mother); "four" is certainly death; "five" may mean betrothal, "six" sexual divagation of one sort or another; "seven" conception, "eight" contraception or any other withdrawal from the responsibility of parenthood, "nine" almost certainly means children. To my mind, it looks remarkably like a general description of man's journey through life, but then I am only guessing at the meaning of certain dream words, and as for the various combinations of numerals that occur in everybody's dreams, like "six-eight time," "two and a half dollars," and "twenty past seven" I can not even begin to guess.

Colours are another part of the vocabulary that I find very difficult. "Green," as I have said, seems to be associated with birth; and again and again, for no reason that I can discover, I have found "blue" representing mourn-ing; but the other colours are beyond me. I have listed scores of examples of "brown" but I am still no nearer learning what it means.

The study of dream language has been bedevilled by people who look in dreams for specialized information; and, as always when one tackles a subject for the wrong reasons, real discovery has stopped dead. If you are one of those people—and there must be millions of us—who go round all day worrying about the meaning of a dream, treat it respectfully and don't expect it to tell you how to pick a winner or improve your character. Improve your vocabulary instead; and, when you have done that, consider, as I have tried to do, what the grammar of dreams is like. Perhaps it will show you how to make friends and influence people; but, even if it doesn't, you will at least have done something of value for the human race.

Note: "The book in a glass case" is a Roll of Honour.

Eighty-one-year-old Kahnweiler. A great adventurer in the arts, still "spry, beaky, amused, undeceived," at his directoire house, which he never allowed to be photographed until he gave permission to Lord Snowdon. The large Picasso painting here is "Spring," 1956.

The Man Who Invented Modern Art Dealing

DANIEL-HENRY KAHNWEILER, STILL PICASSO'S PREMIER DEALER

BY JOHN RUSSELL

PHOTOGRAPHS BY SNOWDON

People still think of art dealing predominantly as a matter of bluff and counter-bluff, midway between gangsterdom and the artificial comedy of Sheridan and Goldoni. The great art dealer, in this context, is a flamboyant and imperious figure: a man who hires someone like Bernard Berenson as an outraged husband hires Louis Nizer, goes through the great country houses as Nebuchadnezzar went through Jerusalem, lives better than many a Head of State, and ends up with a seat in the British House of Lords.

At the bottom of all this is S. N. Behrman's dazzling *Duveen*. Duveen was a great dealer—no doubt about that—and *Duveen* is as pretty a book as has been put together since the war. But there are other ways of being a great dealer, just as there are paintings other than the Titians and Gainsboroughs in which Duveen dealt, and clients other than Andrew Mellon and Henry Clay Frick.

Were this not so, Daniel-Henry Kahnweiler would soon have run through the small capital sum with which his family provided him in 1907; and no one would have come, in any

SNOWDON

140

case, to the tiny shop in Paris near the Madeleine which he had taken over from a derelict Polish tailor.

Kahnweiler's methods were, after all, the opposite of Duveen's. He dealt only in artists of his own age whom nobody else was after. (Already in 1907, for instance, Matisse seemed to him too old and too grand to bother with.) He bought cheap, and he sold cheap. He never advertised, never did anything to get his gallery talked about, and he never went out of his way to court a rich client. Duveen dealt in reassurance, as much as in works of art: buying a Bellini was the next best thing to buying a presentable ancestry. But there was nothing to be reassured about in the purchase of paintings by an unknown artist from a dealer born in Mannheim, Germany, apprenticed to the stock market in London, nicknamed "the little Japanese" by his acquaintances in Paris, and just twenty-three years old.

Had the unknown painters not been Picasso, Braque, Gris, Léger, Derain, and Vlaminck the venture would, in fact, have been a desperate one for all concerned. Kahnweiler knew nothing about the art trade. When he bought his first Fauve paintings by Derain and Vlaminck at the Salon des Indépendants in 1907, he paid the full asking price, not realizing that, in the first place, everyone bargained, and that as a dealer he was entitled to a further reduction. He knew no other dealers, no collectors, and no critics. He didn't even know any artists, although he soon made it his business to call on the ones he liked. "People told me," he said recently, "that I ought to learn 'the tricks of the trade.' Well, I still don't know what they are. No one ever told me. I just had five or six clients, after a while, who came in from time to time. I showed them what was on the wall, and either they bought, or they didn't. That was all there was to it."

From this it will be clear that if ever a deutero-Behrman tries to make a deutero-Duveen out of Kahnweiler he will have a hard job of it. Kahnweiler in conversation is one of the great uncomplicators. Never will he admit to the inner conflicts, the ups and downs of fortune, the moments of irresolution, and the brusque changes of intention which afflict the rest of us.

"I've always known what I wanted to do," is the message that comes across quietly and lucidly in French, German, and English, "and I've always managed to do it." Even the tribulations which came to him as a result of World Wars I and II are passed off with a practised and an unrancorous irony.

What Kahnweiler invented in 1907, and what has been practised ever since by the dealers who count for something in the history of living art, was a new kind of art dealing. In the nineteenth century the dealer employed a liveried doorman to keep the artists at bay; potted plants and a Moorish fountain reminded the client that this was a palace of art, not a common shop; formal dress and the dropping of august names reminded him, also, that his host was not so much a trader as a senior human being of style and substance. Behind and beneath all this, acknowledged by all though never stated openly, was the fact that in the last resort the dealer was there to satisfy an established need and for no other reason.

Kahnweiler substituted for this an informal, unpretentious relationship in which a profound emotional commitment was the thing that mattered most. Where the old-style dealer did his artists a favour by inviting them to luncheon, Kahnweiler lived with Picasso, Braque, Gris, Derain, and Vlaminck on a day-to-day, hour-to-hour basis.

The important thing was not so much that they should sell as that they should be free to get on with their work; and Kahnweiler, by making this possible, helped to bring into being what now seems to us the last great flowering of French art. Once again, his account of all this is a masterpiece of uncomplication. "My painters just wanted to get on with their work," he said not long ago in a radio interview. "They weren't like the Futurists, who were always getting into fights. They didn't even want to draw attention to themselves by holding exhibitions.

"I remember telling Picasso that one of our most faithful clients didn't like his new work. 'So much the better!' said Picasso. 'So he doesn't like it. Let's go on till *nobody* likes it.' My painters were quite certain that what they were doing would triumph in the end, and all they wanted to do was to live quietly and get on with it.

Fourteen-foot Picasso sculpture "Woman," 1962.

"It's a curious thing, but today, when I have a large staff in my gallery. I never have a moment to myself. Before 1914 I had nobody, and yet I had all the time in the world. I could play chess in the afternoon with Derain and Vlaminck, and at five o'clock Braque and Picasso would walk down from Montmartre, and we'd have dinner and go to the circus, or to the 'Lapin à Gill,' and on Sundays I'd go out on the Seine in one of the boats I shared with Vlaminck. . . ."

Picasso said once that neither he nor Braque could have done singlehanded what they did between 1907 and 1914: "It took teamwork." That Kahnweiler got the team together was a triumph of intuition and fine judgment. That he kept it together was also a triumph, and one owed as much to a sense of human quality as to an inherited sense for business.

The "five or six clients" of whom he speaks so casually included Hermann Rupf, thanks to whom Berne is taking its place among the world's foremost modern museum cities, and Roger Dutilleul, one of the last of the great French collectors, and Serge Schukin who built up, almost on his own, the twentieth-century French collections which make such an effect at the Pushkin Museum in Moscow and the Hermitage in Leningrad.

Up until the outbreak of war in 1914, these people were as much a part of "the team" as were the painters themselves; and it was thanks to Kahnweiler's dedicated management that the painters were able to live a little better, year by year.

"Not that they cared about luxury," Kahnweiler said. "Picasso got it exactly right when he said to me 'What I want is to be able to live like a poor man with plenty of money.' " Kahnweiler first came to know Picasso at the lowest moment in his fortunes, when "Les demoiselles d'Avignon" hung, derided, on the easel and the studio in the rue Ravignan was in an indescribable state of dilapidation, chaos, and decay.

"And the curious thing is that Picasso has always remained homesick for that studio. No matter how many houses he buys, he's always delighted when a bit of the ceiling falls down and he can say 'Just like the rue Ravignan.' "

Kahnweiler's position is based today, as it was in 1907, on the fact that he has first call on Picasso's production. For one reason and another the other painters in the team dropped away after 1918 (with the exception of Gris, who died in 1927); but from the heroic epoch there remains not merely some of the most beautiful canvases painted in the twentieth century but an enormous fund of reminiscence.

Kahnweiler at eighty-one is interested in everything, as he always was, and if he has charge of the conversation, it is as likely to turn on Italian opera, or on anthropology, as on his own career. But from time to time he gives a measured and unsentimental account of life when the "team" was in full activity.

In writing about the period, he has so far been more interested in evolving for himself a neo-Kantian aesthetic than in *la petite histoire*. Listeners to the French radio heard, however, how Vlaminck once made himself a wooden necktie, how Derain was dressed "American-style," in checked tweeds, derby hat, and bright-coloured tie, and how Braque's elegance was so discreet that only the connoisseur could take note of it.

"Braque wore very simple blue suits, cut in a way I have never seen before or since, black square-toed shoes that came, so he told me, from Abbeville, and a black string tie. Picasso was the only one who wore the classic artist's corduroys and velveteens."

Such concessions apart, Kahnweiler is more interested in characteristics that throw light on the inner life of the team. Picasso, for instance, is rarely seen with a book in his hand, and yet he turns out, on examination, to have read everything with the most perceptive attention. "Even in the early days, when he hardly knew French," Kahnweiler said, "he had an unfailing ear for French poetry."

And Kahnweiler, in this context, knows what he is talking about, for he has had an auxiliary career, and an immensely distinguished one, as a publisher. Once again his activity does not follow any accepted pattern, in that none of his books was published in editions of more than a hundred copies, but it should be remembered that he was the first person, anywhere, to publish Apollinaire, the first Frenchman to publish Gertrude Stein, the first publisher of André Malraux, and the initiator of books which count for a good deal in the careers of Picasso, Braque,

Gris, Léger, Derain, Marie Laurencin, André Masson, Raymond Radiguet, and Antonin Artaud.

Kahnweiler the musician (as a boy he dreamed of becoming a conductor) published Erik Satie's one-act operetta *Le Piège de Méduse* with coloured wood engravings by Braque; Kahnweiler the inspired traveller published André Masson's *Voyage à Venise;* and Kahnweiler the lifelong reader published in 1957 Picasso's eight lithographed portraits of Balzac with a text by Michel Leiris.

These books were not commercial enterprises, although many of them are now very valuable: they were ventures put together in moments of high enthusiasm. (Kahnweiler as a young man knew much of Apollinaire by heart.) The French cult of the *beau livre* applies as a rule to reprinted classics for which illustrations have been commissioned: Kahnweiler had to do only with texts never before published, and, often enough, with authors now famous who had never before been published at all.

The tradition was kept up even during the German occupation of 1940-44; for it was in Kahnweiler's Paris apartment, while he himself was in hiding near Limoges, that Picasso's play *Desire Caught by the Tail* was given its first reading, with Albert Camus as producer.

There is, in fact, no escaping Picasso where Kahnweiler is in question, even if it would be an illiteracy to speak of him primarily as "Picasso's dealer." At the entrance to his country house near Étampes a fourteen-foot-high sculpture by Picasso greets the visitor.

In the gallery in Paris which since the Occupation has borne the name of his sister-in-law Louise Leiris, the great event of each season is, beyond a doubt, the arrival of the new Picassos: sometimes a complete series, such as the variations on "Las Meninas," on "Les femmes d'Alger" of Delacroix, or on the "Rape of the Sabines," sometimes a miscellaneous group, sometimes an isolated sculpture to remind the visitor of Picasso's fantastic inventiveness in that domain.

Kahnweiler in old age has become, in self-protection and in spite of himself, someone who can be seen only by appointment; and the volume of business transacted by his gallery can hardly be less than that of the stockbrokers and the private banks with which he had to do in the days of his apprenticeship.

The forms of that business are, however, simplified as far as is possible: "If someone likes a picture, I look up the price, and he either pays it or he doesn't. No one bargains here, and I never make anyone a reduction."

You don't get where he is, and stay there, without a certain relish for the trade. One eminent colleague of Kahnweiler's once said to me: "I always know when he's really interested —his ears go just a little more pink." He is still tremendously active when the occasion warrants it. Towards most other dealers his mind was made up once and for all, I think, when his entire stock (it would now be worth around a hundred million dollars) was sold at auction by the French Government after 1918.

As a German national, he had had his gallery and its contents confiscated during the war. "One or two painters helped me," he once said, "and one or two collectors did their best. But my colleagues in the trade manifested an absolute hostility."

But if there have been dark moments in Kahnweiler's career, there is nothing forced or affected about the equanimity with which he regards past, present, and future. I know of few properties in France more uniformly agreeable than the one which he found a few years ago.

White doves tumble in the air above the long white Directoire house, the huge Picasso sculpture stands against the ruins of a thirteenth-century abbey, there is a touch almost of pedantry about the perfectly kept kitchen-garden, the gravel in the courtyard could not be more elegantly raked if it were a Japanese sand garden, and in the centre of it all is the master of the house: spry, beaky, amused, and undeceived.

His uncles were baffled when, in 1907, he passed up the chance of concerning himself with the gold and diamond mines which one of them had pioneered in South Africa. But somewhere behind that equanimity is the knowledge that, mine for mine, Daniel-Henry Kahnweiler's discoveries can compare with anyone's.

O'Keeffe

"Her extraordinary contribution to twentieth-century art . . . obscured by her fame."

BY E. C. GOOSSEN

Georgia O'Keeffe's name is engraved on the cornerstone of modern American art. It was placed there just a half century ago when the artist was thirty years old. As time goes on that name looms larger and larger.

O'Keeffe's painting is crucial to any competent understanding of the origins of recent styles, from the Abstract Expressionism of the late 1940's to the Hard Edge, Pop, Op, and "minimal" art of the 'fifties and 'sixties, Georgia O'Keeffe is a thoroughly representative American artist of the first rank with a vision that helps to define just where our art has been and where it might be going.

O'Keeffe herself is a phenomenon, not only because she is an extraordinary artist but also because she has survived the prejudice against her sex in art. This prejudice has been used on past occasions to diminish her contributions and her rôle in the art history of this century, and though this is no longer true, because of the changing manners and mores of the country, it has been effective enough to require an extensive re-evaluation of her work. Sometimes she was killed by kindness, by gentlemanly politeness; other times, the excessive praise of her "feminine" qualities as a painter, combined with a misreading of her subject matter, buried the truth that she stood head and shoulders above virtually all of her colleagues, male though they might be.

Alfred Stieglitz, art-world titan, pioneer photographer, and gallery owner, said upon first seeing her watercolours and drawings: "At last a woman on paper!" He is to be excused, for in 1916 the male world was still more surprised than threatened by the capacities of women. What he actually saw in these drawings was evidence of an exceptional personality and a truly adventurous spirit. O'Keeffe's response was delayed a few years, until her aims and strength became clearer. About 1924, the year she married Stieglitz, she "decided to *show* the boys."

The real O'Keeffe . . . O'Keeffe the artist . . . has been hidden behind a series of popular images. In the early days she was better known as Stieglitz's wife and model. His composite portrait of her, some five hundred candid shots, strongly influenced the art of photography. Then Freudian-minded journalists with little knowledge of art made her known as the woman who painted sexy pictures of flowers. In the 'thirties she moved to New Mexico, and since that time her pictures of deserts and bones have been coupled in the public mind with legends of her ability to kill rattlesnakes.

O'Keeffe can kill a rattlesnake, even in her eightieth year, with a hoe or whatever is handy. Just to survive seventy miles west of Santa Fe such deeds are frequently called for. But she rides from the new house in Abiquiu to her first Western home, the Ghost Ranch, in an air-conditioned automobile like any sensible Westerner. She rises early, eats lightly, has a figure any woman more than half her age would envy, dresses classically, simply, and appropriately for the climate and the out-of-doors. She wore trousers before Marlene Dietrich. No provincial in any sense, but thoroughly sophisticated, she has always been more modern than her contemporaries.

Her houses and studios are like everything else about her, kept immaculately, and designed by herself for modern comfort, efficiency, and austere grace. She is almost totally unsentimental and barely tolerates sentimentality in others. Her much-touted rock collection is really only a collection of hard forms which satisfy the eye and the hand. The only pictures she hangs in her ultramodern interiors are her own, for testing . . . and an occasional Arthur Dove, perhaps the only painter of her own generation and after whom she sincerely admires.

Of course, O'Keeffe has helped to create her public images. She displays the stamina and country qualities associated with those born in the nineteenth-century Midwest. For her huge fiftieth-year retrospective exhibition at the

CECIL BEATON

An O'Keeffe 1917 watercolour, "Light Coming on the Plains, No. 2," owned by the Amon Carter Museum, Fort Worth, Texas.

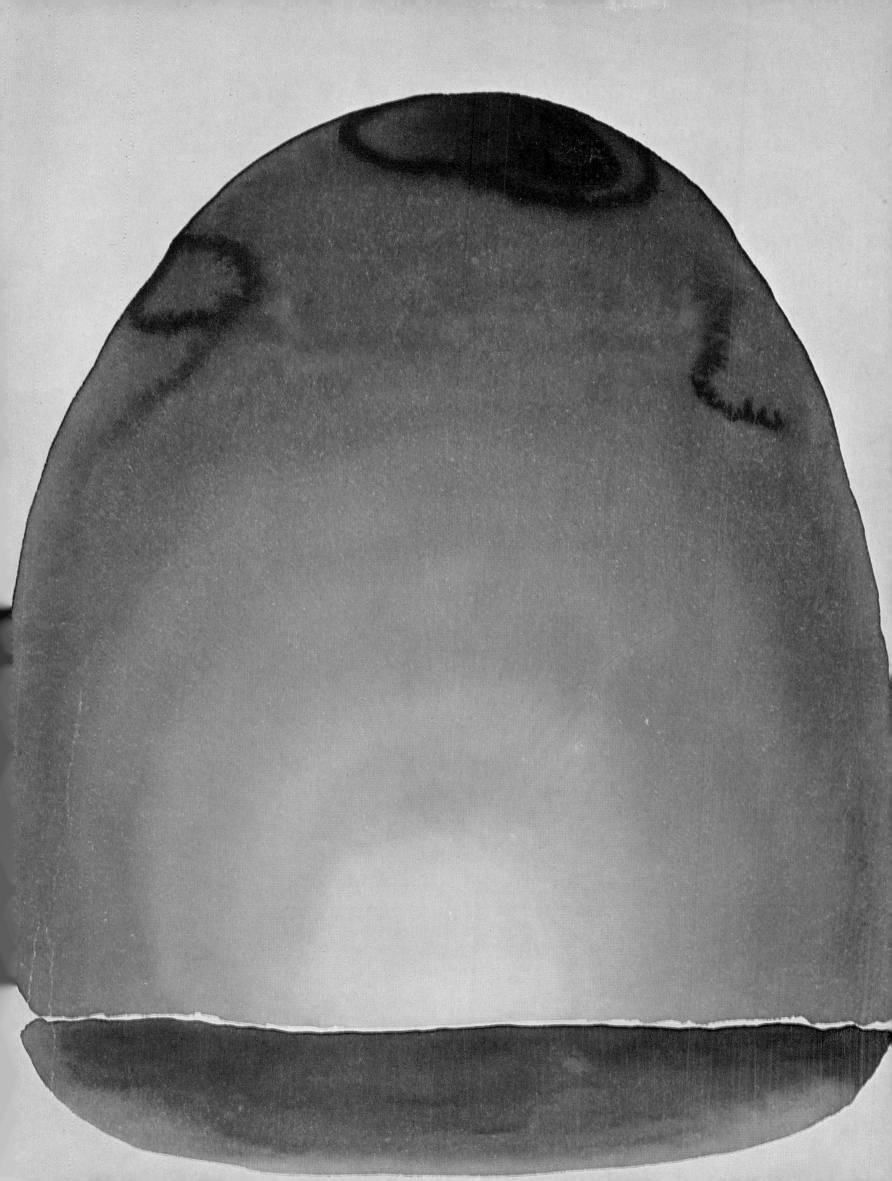

Amon Carter Museum in Forth Worth and, later, in Houston last spring, she painted the largest picture of her career, possibly larger than any produced in New York that year . . . a massive canvas twenty-four feet long and eight feet high. With one inexperienced helper she stretched this canvas herself. Any but the youngest and poorest New York artist would have turned the job over to the pros.

Despite the fact that all these characteristic images of O'Keeffe are true to a degree, they only adumbrate, but do not really illuminate her painting.

In the Metropolitan Museum there is a watercolour titled "Blue Lines, No. 10," painted in 1916 by a young schoolteacher. This picture contains simply two thin, freely painted blue lines drawn vertically down the middle to a flat blue bar across the bottom. It represents over a hundred related paintings and drawings which are perhaps the boldest and brashest avant-garde art done by an American in this century. "Blue Lines" was reproduced in 1946 as the frontispiece to one of the most well-read books of the postwar period, F. S. C. Northrop's *The Meeting of East and West*. For thirty years these pictures had remained prophetic. They were shown first in 1917 at the Alfred Stieglitz "291" gallery, a few again in 1934 and 1935, and then several were included in retrospectives of the artist's work at The Art Institute of Chicago in 1943 and The Museum of Modern Art in New York in 1946. Not until 1948, with the advent of the now historic Abstract Expressionist period, did contemporary art begin to catch up with them.

In 1912, after a half-dozen years of study in order to become an artist in her own right, Georgia O'Keeffe turned to art education as her vocation. She had satisfied all the requirements at The Art Institute of Chicago and the Art Students League in New York, but she remained discontented with her work because it seemed an empty echo of what had already been done. Her training had been academic. She had had relatively little contact with "modern" art as such.

However, she had come into contact, through Alon Bement at the University of Virginia, with certain theories put forth by the leading art educator of the first two decades of this century, Arthur Dow. In order to derive rational principles for the teaching of art to children and young students, Dow had analyzed both the Western and Oriental arts of design, painting, and architecture. From the 1890's on, he had shown that, if one understood the abstract character of the basic elements of art: line, colour, shape, rhythm, space relations, et cetera, not only did all world art open up to appreciation, quite apart from its place, time, and iconography, but that a new art could issue directly from these elements themselves. Dow's position placed him well ahead of the Cubists and the Futurists, and even the Russian, Malevitch. The implications of his theories were ripe for application and extension by the time O'Keeffe came under his influence.

Unlike Max Weber who had been an early and enthusiastic student of Dow's theories, O'Keeffe was lucky enough to get entirely away from the confusion of the New York art scene with its crosscurrents of imported Cubism and chauvinistic academicism. Without being aware of it, she had dropped into an atmosphere which would force her to invent a new kind of painting. West Texas . . . the Panhandle . . . is nothing but a rolling sage-covered openness where you can see the weather coming for a week. There was nothing for either her or her students to paint. She taught them to address an envelope, to find and draw a door, to make abstract designs, to draw from their imaginations. She threw out the textbooks which suggested exotic and useless subject matter and unfamiliar space situations. She herself began to draw and paint abstractions based upon her feeling for the experience of the openness, the verticality of the sky and the flatness of the land . . . with, in other words, the same elements around her which equalled Dow's elements of art . . . space, colour, line, and shape.

Though not all of the work of her years in West Texas is equally abstract, most of it, without the identifying titles, would appear so today. The watercolours are extraordinarily simple and direct. They are limited, as recent painting has been, to one, two, or three colours. The nightscapes are rich and dark in blues, greens, and reddish purples with a sense of inner light, yet the depth of each is so handled that it may be read as a stain of colour on a flat surface. She avoided deep space effects also by floating the whole image well inside the rectangle so that, even when it is composed only of colour and light, it still has the properties of shape. In all of them she moved easily from symmetrical arrangements to an asymmetrical system of balances weighted by appropriate shifts of colour intensities. In this grand simplicity there is a continuous display of knowledge and purpose. Nothing is left to chance. There are no gestural passages or exhibitionist techniques, yet the pictures are more emotion-laden than the wildest of the "expressionistic" paintings of this century.

O'Keeffe pinned down her vision by doing everything in series. Besides the dozen or so vertical blue lines which the philosopher-historian Northrop sees as a bridge between two aesthetic worlds, Eastern and Western, there are series of broad rectangular areas of soaked colour, of sweeping spirals, of opened grid patterns, of symmetrical ovoids. It is clear from this repetition of a theme and its format that she was no more interested in the phenomenon which provoked it than in the reduction of it to the most minimal and yet telling means she could discover.

Without perhaps being aware of it at the time, O'Keeffe was constructing for herself a group of what nowadays would be called "primes" and "form-classes," a morphology with which she would be preoccupied for the next fifty years. The vast amount of nonsense which has been written about her less abstract paintings of the 1920's and 1930's, associating her flower centres with sexual symbolism, her animal skulls with death, et cetera, begs questions of interpretation rather than answers questions of intent and visible results. Evidence has been growing every day that the evolutionary process of the twentieth century has been in the direction of a distillation of all forms of form and all forms of thought. Abstraction is the way art re-creates itself and strives to get down to simple universals from which new total styles can develop.

O'Keeffe's own procedure was to derive directly from nature basic shapes and structures consistent with the elements of pictorial design. From this vantage point she could reproduce nature or not, at will, without changing either her style or her forms. The fact that she has moved rather rhythmically back and forth between realism and abstraction has confused even her admirers. But she has always been a realist in the most American and pragmatic sense of the word. The strength of the American Realist tradition, characterizing our best art from the seventeenth-century Freake-type painters, through Copley, the Hudson River School, Harnett, and Eakins, lies in the fact that it was never interested in illusionism as such nor in the subjective aspects of subject matter, but rather in the honest presentation of form.

The impact of the huge, amorphous Armory Show of 1913 was perhaps one of the most unfortunate incidents in the history of modern art. It confused the issue just at the moment when American art was beginning to find its way out of the prewar chaos of styles. Moreover, the latest European art had already been shown in New York since 1908 by Alfred Stieglitz and others. Stieglitz, with the help of Edward Steichen, had exhibited work more advanced than that featured at the Armory . . . Matisse, Brancusi, Picabia, and the analytical Cubism of Picasso had all been shown before 1913. These reports on Europe, more particularly Paris, came in discreet quantities, enough to nudge and needle without overwhelming. (Who knows, for example, what damage has been done to budding movements in Argentina, Israel, and Japan by the onslaught of American Abstract Expressionism.) Seen in the right doses, the abstractionism developing abroad, though headed for its own disaster, was supportive of the deeper reorganization of the arts of design, painting, sculpture, and architecture going on here, stemming mainly from theories like those of Arthur Dow and Frank Lloyd Wright. The latter had sought a basis in "the nature of True form" for creating a new, indigenous, and wholly modern architecture. The difference between Wright's architecture and that of the later Bauhaus was precisely that the latter came out of Cubism and its system of geometric planes leading to interminable rearrangements of the rectangle. Wright, however, had studied Oriental, pre-Columbian, and other non-Western modes of design as well as the structures of nature, and was able to leap out of the purely Western tradition.

After the Armory Show attention was once again focused on Europe as the mystical source of creative power. The accumulated theoretical energy in America, virtually on the edge of large expression, was now penned up until the end of World War II. Expatriotism in the 1920's climbed like the stock market. The frenetic, reactionary arts of Dadaism and Surrealism captured the imagination of a public unable to distinguish the truly new from the nostalgic, unwilling to separate literature from art. Only O'Keeffe and Wright, and, to a degree, the painter Arthur Dove, were prepared for the trip through the long desert awaiting American art between the wars.

O'Keeffe's strong personality matched that of Wright, who was born, by the way, in 1869 in Wisconsin just sixty miles from Sun Prairie where she was born in 1887. Though she says today that her paintings are not the result of any theory, she agrees that Dow gave her the equipment to find a creative and yet orderly approach to the basic problems in art. She speaks of the extreme simplicity of his ideas and how they can be applied to any aspect of life where an aesthetic decision is required, "like selecting a tie, for example." This approach, once mastered and entered upon, made her impervious to fashion and gave her the assurance to withstand the criticism and misunderstanding that was to come. It probably also accounts for her habit of showing all the paintings done in any one year, often amounting to forty or more.

O'Keeffe had already established her basic approach to painting before she entered the Stieglitz circle which was comprised of such memorable figures of the time as Marin, Hartley, Paul Strand, Paul Rosenfeld, Charles Demuth, Dove, Hart Crane, and Sherwood Anderson. Rosenfeld and Hartley, who was a poet-painter, wrote essays on her work. But it was Dove who played the rôle of friend and fellow artist. With Stieglitz there seems to have been a constant and critical interchange of ideas. In their first years together, much time was spent at Lake George, the Stieglitz family summer home. The best pictures from this period are of fallen leaves, enlarged and painted as flat as they are in life. (In the 1960's Jasper Johns would paint a flat U.S. flag on a flat surface.) It was toward the end of the Lake George years (1927) that she painted a simple, flat portrait of the window in their house which now hangs in The Museum of Modern Art. Stieglitz made several fine photographs of parts of this house in the 'thirties, one including "her" window and another of a door she might have painted. But Stieglitz, as a photographer, was interested in pushing his camera work toward form in terms of contrasts of light and dark. O'Keeffe was looking for form in terms of line, edge, colour and design.

No one has yet given an adequate explanation for the explosion of American Abstract Expressionism on the world scene following World War II. Since the European-engendered styles, synthetic Cubism and Surrealism, and the dominant personalities of Picasso and Matisse had filled the interbellum period, and since several of the men who were to become known as the Abstract Expressionist painters had been pseudo-Surrealists or Picasso followers, the new American painting is usually traced, with guile and circumspection, to any variety of causes and sources. One thesis would give the credit to Adolph Hitler and Peggy Guggenheim because the latter assisted a large number of artist refugees to escape from the former. The appearance of these men on New York streets created, it seems, a little Paris, stimulating our provincial artists to new and great things. Another thesis credits Jackson Pollock's athleticism and psychic megalomania. More plausible is the one which credits the influence of Hans Hofmann and the rediscovery of the great chaotic Kandinskys in the old Guggenheim Museum. Least plausible are the explanations which find their sources in the mysteries of Surrealism.

Surrealism by definition is loaded with referential content. It was born in reaction to the increasing "contentlessness" of Cubism. As Clement Greenberg has remarked, "Picasso and Braque . . . in their collages of 1912 and 1913 . . . drew back from the utter abstractness for which analytical Cubism seemed headed."

That "utter abstractness" was the result of the Cubist attempt to reduce all form to a system of geometric planes *alien* to every form *except* geometric planes. Thus it found itself faced with a future dedicated to an infinite series of merely pleasing arrangements, of "good" designs. Most of what we think of as Bauhaus art and the International Style in architecture went along this road. Picasso, and later the Surrealists, unable to turn to a more viable system of design, and faced with "the death image of Egyptian geometry," as Barnett Newman has called it, stuffed "content" back into painting and went off on a thirty-year digression from the heights gained in the nineteenth century by European Impressionism and American Realism, styles of painting which had paved the way for abstract art by developing a cool attitude toward the subject.

The Surrealist imagination was certainly fertile and helped, in its way, to uproot the traditional notion of what a picture might be. It also helped to disassociate, *psychologically*, form from nature in the public mind. But its emphasis on "content" was the antithesis of that evolutionary process attempting to arrive at a basic, formal style. And simply as a mode it could never suit such a straightforward painter as O'Keeffe nor the literal rendering of the object which led Americans to Pop Art.

Had the analytical Cubists been able to top the roots of Dow's pragmatic and open-ended theories, they might have been able to come up with a systematic approach to the problem. Or had they been able to jettison their underlying sentimentality toward the objects they were flaying with their *"petits cubes,"* they might have found the way out. What saved, and saves, O'Keeffe, is that in the American Realist tradition, she has absolutely no sentiment whatsoever for the objects when she paints objects. She treats them as coldly as she does her abstracted shapes. She is an existentialist and so are her objects. Her paintings have no "content" in the European sense of the word. The occasional meaningful title has been someone else's idea.

The truly original Abstract Expressionist painting had nothing to do with Surrealism. It was the very act of abandonment by the artists of their Surrealist positions which made them into Abstract Expressionists. By dropping all content other than colour, line, shape, and space relationships, Pollock, Newman, Still, and Rothko, et al., by their attitude toward the canvas, rejoined the American Realist tradition and the issue where it had been left in 1917. The excitement and the sudden sense of freedom the leading painters of the late 1940's have recorded sounds very much like O'Keeffe's description of how she felt when she just decided to paint as she wanted to and made "Blue Lines" and "Light Coming on the Plains," and the others.

A great many of O'Keeffe's paintings from the 1915-18 years, if blown up to the heroic size of the Abstract Expressionists, could pass easily for slightly nature-oriented examples of this later period. In the broad colour pictures the hues go down smoothly, anonymously, soaking the surface; the colours are rich and deep like the Rothkos of the early 'fifties; others are stained in a brilliance and manner reminiscent of Morris Louis. The frontality, the openness, the symmetrical simplicity all belong as much to the later period as to her own.

Several of the artists in the newest wave of American painting have admitted a strong interest in O'Keeffe's work, among them the late Paul Feeley and Kenneth Noland. Feeley apparently picked up from O'Keeffe a technique he used for many years in his watercolours and later in his paintings of late 1959 and the 'sixties, namely the separation of each colour area from the next by a thin margin of unpainted surface . . . a method which prevents the actual and optical mixture of colours where they meet. Feeley also admired her coolness and control and imitated it in his last few years. Noland, whose original swirls of ragged colour evolved into clean-cut concentric circles in 1959-61, seems to have taken a definite interest in her centrifugally designed flower pictures. There is also an O'Keeffe of 1929, "At the Rodeo," an enlargement of a Mexican Indian ornament, wherein the centre recalls this whole Noland series.

One could go on . . . finding a number of Ellsworth Kelly's shapes of several years ago in the ovoidal openings O'Keeffe abstracted from pelvises; young Larry Poons's rhythmical grid patterns in her "Starlight Night" of 1917; and even younger Patricia Johanson's thin coloured line in the first 1916 series. But this would be stretching the point in terms of actual acquaintanceship on the part of these artists with all of her work. Suffice it to say that once a painter has had his effect, the reverberations continue from sheer logical development.

Possibly the real importance of O'Keeffe in American art history lies in her faithfulness to her first intuition that she had in her possession the key to a new and yet traditionally valid art. The winds of fashion must have been very strong over the years, but like Matisse and Mondrian she has remained herself. Moreover, from the evidence above, it appears she was right.

Lust for Tulips

BY ANTHONY WEST

The tulipomania is something that I have never had any difficulty in understanding, indeed, I suffer from periodical attacks of it myself. The necessary preconditions are a long, hard winter and the growth of that form of depression, or discontent, that comes of being starved of the particular forms of beauty that are nourished by the combination of heat and sunshine. This means that the madness often strikes in March, that terrible month in which spring delays and procrastinates until those, like myself, who are heat lovers often begin to wonder if a new ice age in which there will be no more summers can really have begun.

And then, suddenly, the tulips are there, and I know that, after all, everything is going to be all right; the world will soon be filled with sunburned women and children, and peaches, and nectarines, and ripe melons, and there will be shade under grape arbours, the birds will come back, and the sand will be hot under one's feet as one walks up the beach after swimming in the salt, green sea. To fully enjoy the foretaste of all these pleasures I have the tulips, not just a dozen or a couple of dozen, but armfuls, so that I can have them about the house in great bunches and watch them perform their peculiar miracle. They come from the florist in the strange, unflowerlike aspect that makes many people dislike them, looking as if they were goblets of wax placed on the ends of ramrods; and if they have been bought in a timid or niggardly fashion, they will look as leggy as spiders and about as attractive, until they wither meanly and call to be thrown out. But put them in large bowls, three or four dozen together, and they will cast aside the prudish,

puritan discipline that the growers have forced upon them by growing them in rows, each like her neighbours, and in a collective passion transform themselves into a bonfire of light and colour that will blaze joyfully on for days, to end gloriously in a shower of fallen petals. In a crowd they will reveal their secret. They are not really Nordics, and their Quakerish primness is an act. They are exotic Orientals from Persia and from northwestern India, and they worship the sun by storing its heat and transforming it into colour.

The legend of tulipomania ignores all this. The madness is said to have been a piece of Dutch folly, a mania for speculation in bulbs that swept Holland for three years—between 1634 and 1637—and led thousands of merchants and artisans to ruin themselves by throwing their money away on flowers. The English, in particular, are very fond of this picture of tulipomania and love to talk about the foolishness that was involved in such deals as the famous exchange in which, as Wilfrid Blunt records, a tulipomaniac gave two loads of wheat, four loads of rye, four fat oxen, eight fat pigs, twelve fat sheep, two hogsheads of wine, four barrels of beer, two barrels of butter, a thousand pounds of cheese, a bed, with mattress, pillows, and hangings, a suit of clothes, and a silver jug, all for one bulb of a variety of tulip named "Viceroy."

This is, no doubt, an extravagance. But a thousand pounds of cheese is just so much cheese, and for a man who has more than enough of that sort of thing, as this tulipomaniac clearly had, the exchange of quantities of the humdrum for something very special and

154

"In a collective passion tulips transform themselves into a bonfire of light and color." Here and on the following pages are tulips, rare and reliable, photographed by Irving Penn at their full blaze.

very beautiful could have been well worthwhile. The English, however, prefer laughing at the Dutch to considering this side of the question. When they have done laughing, they will pause to congratulate themselves on having escaped the tulipomania altogether, apparently they were intelligent enough to laugh themselves out of it. As Blunt says in his Penguin Book, "timely banter saved the day." But it is worth pointing out that, while the Dutch were giving themselves up to tulipomania, the English were busily getting themselves into the complicated mess that led them into their Civil War, brought Charles the First's neck under the headsman's axe, and gave them Cromwell as their military dictator. Given the choice between being mad for tulips and being mad for trouble, there is little doubt which a civilized man would prefer.

But the question remains, even if the tulipomania was not as foolish a thing as the English are fond of saying, what was the excitement about, and why did it happen just then, and not either sooner or later?

In spite of my own strong feelings of love and affection for tulips, I didn't fully understand the answer to the first part of this question until I happened to see the portrait of Rembrandt as a young man which is in the Museum of the History of Art in Vienna. This work, which shows the painter smiling shyly and, to tell the truth, a little oafishly from beneath a large floppy beret, is the product of a collaboration between Jan van den Hoecke, a flower painter, and a portraitist, Jan Lievens. It was painted when the tulipomania was at its height, and in what was also the heyday of the books of symbolic emblems, of rebuses, and riddling images, in the pleasant convention of the time by which a bust or half-length portrait was ornamented with a garland of flowers, giving it a frame within a frame.

While I was looking at this picture, I noticed that the garland which Van den Hoecke had placed round Lievens's head-and-shoulder portrait included more tulips than any other flower, and that these were all of the varieties that the Dutch called *bybloemen*. These have two colours on their petals, which are fantastically streaked in two ways, causing some *bybloemen* to be classified as flamed and others as feathered. It crossed my mind that this could have been a mere accident, and that Van den Hoecke

had perhaps put these flowers into his garland simply because they were the fashion of that moment. But as soon as I had formulated this notion, I could see that it must be wrong. The tulips are curiously emphatic in the garland, and they are obviously there to convey some message, to make some suggestion, or to serve, in keeping with the spirit of the times, as something in the nature of a crossword puzzle clue.

I bought a photograph of the picture, and when I returned to my home, I thought that a suitable place to keep it would be between the pages of Sir A. Daniel Hall's *Book of the Tulip*, and as I put it there I realized what Van den Hoecke's garland was saying.

Tulips can be reproduced in two ways: asexually, by taking offsets from their bulbs, or sexually, by taking seeds from pollinated flowers. The new bulbs obtained by the first method are, biologically speaking, parts of the parent identity, and, as might be expected, produce flowers almost exactly like those of the original bulb from which they came for as long as they can be persuaded to go on flowering.

When a tulip is grown from a seed, the result is a new identity. What sort of flower it will have will be a matter of speculation for seven years, when the plant will mature and bloom for the first time. What will then appear will be a self-coloured flower, as it might be, plain yellow, plain orange, plain rose-pink, plain lilac, or maroon. It will go on producing similar blooms for an indefinite period, but at last, sooner or later, it will "break," as no other flower does, and its plain flower will be replaced by a variegated one with the characteristic flamed or feathered petals that are found in *bybloemen* and parrot tulips. The garland round the Rembrandt portrait pays him, in fact, a fairly flowery compliment. It says in the language of visual metaphor: "Here is the young painter whose genius 'broke' and made him a nonpareil among Flemish painters, just as these tulips 'broke' from their original simplicity and plainness and became wonders of beauty. He has enlarged the world of pleasure for us just as have these marvellous and surprising new flowers."

The clue to the garland is also an important clue to the real meaning of the tulipomania of the sixteen thirties. The brief storm of speculation was much less of a gamble in bulbs than a display of excitement at the discovery of new pleasures and new beauties. It is one chapter, and only one, of many in the story of the development of Europe's secular culture, a fragment of that section of it that deals with the entry of the newly prosperous mercantile and artisan classes into the domains of leisure and luxury from which they had, until the later Middle Ages, been excluded.

In the fourteen hundreds their narrow and laborious lives were enriched by their discovery of the joy in flowers, and in flower gardening. This led, on the one hand, into the escape of a detail in religious painting—the crystal vase holding the Virgin's lilies—onto a canvas of its own as a flower painting, a secular subject painted for its own sake, and to the appearance of such specialist flower painters as Jan Bruegel van Velours, Daniel Seghers, Roelant Jocobsz Savery, Van den Hoecke, and so many others. On the other, it led to a search for new flowers that became world-wide as the age of exploration gave way to the age of international trade.

The tulip was one of the first great finds of that search, and the tulipomania was the product of the shock of recognition of a new source of delight. The flower was first brought into Europe from Turkey in 1554, when it reached Vienna. In 1561 it was being grown as an exotic rarity in the gardens of the Fuggers, the first of Europe's international bankers, at Augsburg.

A year later tulips came into the Netherlands. The phenomenon known as "breaking" was soon discovered, and not long after that European growers learned how to "fix" the new varieties so produced by taking offsets.

There is nothing quite like the satisfaction that a plant breeder feels when he can offer the world a new variety of flower that he has brought into being in his own garden and given a name. Nor is there anything quite like the keen amateur's appetite for a good new variety of a fine flower. Anyone who laughs at tulipomania really laughs at a holy passion, and a reasonable one: the desire to add to the world's sources of pleasure and delight.

The story of tulip growing, and of tulip gardening, so far as it is known, begins at Herat, in what is now Persia. There, sometime in the late fifteenth century, a certain Abu'l Ghazi Husayn Bayqara added the Bagh-i-Jahn-Ara—the Garden of the World Adorned—to the already numerous parks and gardens surrounding the town. It was unlike other Persian gardens in that it gave up a part of its hundred-acre extent to a display of massed red tulips.

This planting left its mark on the imagination of a restless and ambitious young man named Babur (1482-1530). He was touring Persia looking at gardens while he wondered what to do with his life. By the time he was twenty he had decided that he would emulate his ancestor Timur, the Tamburlaine of Christopher Marlowe's play, who had made a famous raid into India.

When Babur was twenty-one, he seized Kabul and the Punjab, and later he went on to seize the kingdom of Delhi, and to make himself the first Mogul Emperor. In Europe Timur is remembered as a great destroyer of civilizations, and in the East he is remembered as a creative spirit. Everywhere his armies went, his gardeners went also, and when he died in 1530 he had made Samarkand, Cairo, Damascus, Baghdad, Sultaniya, and Shiraz the most beautiful cities then in existence by ringing them with parks and gardens. He had invented that half-indoor, half-outdoor world of gorgeous carpets spread on flowery turf by scented fountains, of which the enchanting vision is preserved in Persian and Mogul miniatures.

His gardening efforts outside his first capital, Kabul, were initially unsuccessful. Under the much harsher Indian conditions all the familiar plants that he brought across the mountains from Persia sickened and died, even at Kabul, where water was plentiful. In his disappointment he turned to the local flowers, and since the Hindus had no flower gardening tradition to speak of, this meant botanizing and hunting for wild flowers suitable for garden use.

To Babur's delight he struck gold, horticulturally speaking, almost at once in the hills northwest of Kabul, where he found more than thirty different kinds of the flower that he had seen growing in the Garden of the World Adorned at Herat; among them, a rose-scented tulip. Inspired by this discovery and by others, Babur concentrated his efforts on a new form, the Gulistan, the garden for the concentrated display of particular flowers in their seasons.

Babur's new flowers, the Indian tulip varieties, and his new kind of garden became the fashion wherever his name was known. By the 1530's and 1540's the wild mountain flowers of northwestern India were the established garden favourites of the Ottoman Turks of Aleppo and

PHOTOGRAPHS ON THE FOLLOWING PAGES BY IRVING PENN

Constantinople and the scene was set for their conquest of Europe.

A steadily increasing number of secret, semi-secret, and overt emissaries from the Gothic north began to find their way to Constantinople from the 1530's onwards, and the barriers which had, for all practical purposes, excluded Christian traders and travellers from the Middle East since the days of the Crusades began to break down.

The early travellers from the North were shaken by their first experiences of Moslem culture. They had heard of little but the savage cruelty of the traditional enemies of Christendom, and they were surprised to find how much that was graceful, pleasant, and agreeable formed part of this alien way of life.

They were more impressed by the beauty of the formal gardens, the elegance of the garden pavilions, the pools, and the fountains, the wealth of flowers, the tree-lined walks, and the delight that both Turks and Persians took in using their gardens than by any other aspect of Moslem culture. They were fascinated, above all, by the seraglio of the Grand Turk, Sultan Mehmet III, the garden palace beside the Bosporus.

Thomas Dallam, a master craftsman from England, who had been sent to Constantinople to show the Turks how to operate an extremely elaborate clock-cum-mechanical organ that Queen Elizabeth had presented to the Sultan, was one of the first northerners to enter the inner courts which formed the Sultan's private quarters. Dallam learned that the Bustanji Bashi, the chief gardener, had a thousand men working for him and he was soon persuaded that there could be no better kept gardens in the world.

Dallam's clock, which featured a chime of sixteen bells, two trumpeters who played a tantarra on silver trumpets, a planetary display, an organ which played a selection of airs mechanically but which could also be played normally, and a bush full of mechanical birds which sang and flapped their wings, was a great success, and Dallam was rewarded for setting it up by being taken on a three-day tour of the secret splendours that no Free Christian had ever been allowed to see before. Towards the end of the last day his guide led him into a small court paved with marble and told him

that, if he wished, he might walk over to look through the iron grating set in the thick stone wall on its further side.

Dallam stepped forward and "saw a sighte that did please me wondrous well." Thirty young women were playing at ball in a garden beyond the wall. Their hair hung from beneath their caps of cloth of gold in long braids into which strands of seed pearls had been entwined, they were wearing jewelled earrings, and larger pearls in ropes round their necks.

Their slender bodies were concealed by high-waisted, richly embroidered sleeveless jackets beneath which they wore shortsleeved tunics, and loose knee-length shorts both of extremely fine white cloth through which Dallam could see the colour of their flesh. Some, who were bare-legged, wore heavy golden anklets, others wore long boots of Spanish leather.

These thirty girls, thus seen at play, were only a few of the twelve to fifteen hundred women who were kept in the seraglio for the Grand Turk's pleasure. His favourites among them had private apartments of their own but most of them, those who had not been fortunate enough to attract his attention or to bear him sons, lived and slept in great gallery dormitories which they shared with a hundred others. The patterns of living in this harem were exceedingly strange, but nothing about it was quite so curious as the form that was assumed by the tulipomania within its confines.

Once a year one of the courtyards of the seraglio was made the scene of an elaborate display of tulips and the women of the harem. The tulips were arranged in crystal vases on wooden stands round three sides of the court, and a sort of grandstand occupied the fourth side. When the Grand Turk and his attendants had taken their seats there, the women were turned into the courtyard to mime their delight and excitement at the beauty of the flowers. The woman whose appreciative gestures, movements, and cries, seemed to the Sultan to be most truly indicative of a passionate and responsive nature was taken off to his private apartments.

Because it was in this annual dance before the tulips that the average occupant of the harem had her sole opportunity of taking a sexual initiative that would bring her to the Sultan's notice and give her a chance of escaping from the crowded dormitories to enjoy the privileges of a favourite, the caresses, the endearments, the simulated frenzies lavished upon the flowers were often extravagant and bizarre in the extreme, and the renown of the seraglio's tulip show as an erotic spectacle spread through Europe.

It is difficult to imagine the impact of the discovery of a world of overt sensuality in which such a festival could be a normal part of court life on northerners who had never known the naked, sun-soaked gods of Greece and Rome. They had come from the world of Dürer, of the Holbeins, and they found themselves in that of the Persian and Mogul miniaturists and their earthly paradises. The tulips were a part of that vision and one that was especially easy to take home.

And that, esentially, was what the tulipomania was about. A frame of reference was broken. The northerners stepped out of the invisible prison of their still Gothic culture and discovered the world beyond Christendom. In the Moslem lands they discovered the secret that had died with paganism: That all life need not be darkened by thoughts of guilt and sin, that there are innocent pleasures . . . perhaps this is a highfalutin way of putting it, perhaps it would be better to say that in the seventeenth century the Dutch were happy because they were winning their fight to win their freedom from Spanish oppression, and that in their happiness they made the discovery that joy, beauty, pleasures are just as much necessities of life as cheese, and even freedom—that they are, in fact, the things that give freedom its meaning.

Janis Joplin, New Shout

Her nerves on the outside, nothing hidden, she is the young heroine of rock blues

Janis Joplin, the lead singer of the Big Brother and the Holding Company group, makes bunk of the history of singing the minute she opens her mouth and begins to scream, punish, and shake out her songs. Then, singing needs a new shocked definition, one that excludes precision, melody, and mellowness; her voice makes them obsolete. She adds turbulent wrath and rawness, produces a raucous rocking hysterical inspired sound that beats across the ears. The taste for her sound is an acquired one, making other voices sound insipid; her fans, spread across the nation, are fanatical, maniacal about her, claw and bite to get tickets for her concerts. She staggers audiences as well as staggering herself and at the end of a concert is always, in her own word, "spaced"—so high with excitement, noise, and response that she's delirious. "She's like plugged-in sandpaper," said Richard Avedon, photographing her in a peacock-coloured, jewelled troubadour cloak, a treasure that an anonymous fan, overcome with love, once draped over her shoulders.

Miss Joplin's lumpen extraordinary face has no makeup, her long brown hair doesn't shine, she screws her eyes up over constant cigarettes, and her lubrication and sustenance seem to be sickly Southern Comfort. Yet when she gets out there and starts to sing, she is a magnetic moving fireball lighting up the whole auditorium. Her appearance on stage is the total antithesis of the star entrance: She picks her way on in the dark with the four male members of the group; and when the lights go up, they are generally in a state of unperturbed confusion. Her clothes, which seem to have grown on her like strange fruit, are mostly made "by an important girl, who turns them out slowly and turns them out well, and turns them out only for those she likes." They are usually intricately embroidered, bejewelled, with lots of velvet and gold. Janis Joplin wears beads and bracelets and rings, arms and legs festooned with them. "They are important to me," she said, without guile. She is amazed, pleased, and unconcerned by her success. "If it's real, then it has little real effect on my mind; if it is real, then it is less and less like I thought it would be. It started, if it started, at the Monterey Festival last year, and so it's still a gas and I can't believe it; I've always been on the other side of society. . . ."

In fact, it all started in Port Arthur, Texas, where she was born twenty-five years ago. "But don't believe all that legendary stuff about my singing since I was a child. I started to sing when I was seventeen, with a bluegrass band in Austin, just for fun." After a visit to Los Angeles she returned to Austin where she studied at different colleges (she went to four in all) until Chet Helms, now the leader of the Family Dog rock group in San Francisco, stopped by. "He was a beatnik from Texas like me, and we headed for San Francisco. I stayed there for five years doing what young people do, finding out and changing and hanging out and bumming around, I guess you'd call it. Then I decided to go back home and straighten out, go back to college, even get married. But I didn't stay in Texas or get married; things change. But I can tell you this. I never wanted to be a big star singer." Now she is. "It means . . . I get an allowance now and I think that I got more when I was unemployed. It means . . . I have worries now but they are different worries. And I like working and rehearsing but don't know what to do when I'm not. Bob Dylan . . . he can do all by himself. But we are five people all pulling together, and pulling apart, and each doing each song differently. We have to work to get it all together. It's our weakness and it's our strength."

May 1968

RICHARD AVEDON

The Unique Ross

BY JANET FLANNER

EDITOR'S NOTE: Ross, The New Yorker and Me is an entertaining gossip of a book by Jane Grant, who was once married to Harold Ross and with him founded The New Yorker magazine which had its first issue on February 21, 1925. (Her book's introduction by Janet Flanner begins in the adjoining column; the book will be published this spring by Reynal & Company.) A small, fierce, brilliant, adroit woman who has been married to William B. Harris for the last twenty-eight years, and who is only known as Jane Grant at her stubborn insistence, she first met Harold Ross at a poker game when he was a private in the army, detached from the 18th Engineers, in Paris, where he was the managing editor of The Stars and Stripes near the end of World War I. Detached from The New York Times, she wore the uniform of the YMCA. Jane Grant started at the Times doing mop-up work in the society department for $10 a week, but when she moved into a reporter's job she had a raise.

Eventually the Times reporter and the newspaper man, who looked, said Alexander Woollcott, like a "dishonest Lincoln," married in 1920 and in time planned their greatest adventure, The New Yorker. The marriage and, later, the magazine were entirely surrounded by a buzz of wits, the most amusing people in New York, malicious, gentle, offside, and terrifying, with the buck-nose Woollcott the wolf of the pack, which at times contained Robert Benchley, Marc Connelly, George S. Kaufman, and other tooth sinkers. To start The New Yorker, Grant-Ross raised $25,000 on their own and persuaded Raoul H. Fleischmann to put up a gambling $25,000. From then on, nothing but trouble, threat of suspension, staff dismissals, until at last, through an additional $100,000 added by Fleischmann's mother and through the genius of Ross, The New Yorker ended its financial and staff crises and developed prosperous middle-aged spread. In her book Jane Grant's involvement with The New Yorker and her fun, love, despair, remarkable simplicity, and macédoine of anecdotes about Ross end with his death of an embolism in a Boston hospital on December 6, 1951.

The only directive Ross ever gave me for writing the Letter from Paris for his then new *New Yorker* magazine in the early summer of 1925 was succinct, characteristic, and perfect, and thus remained unchanged. "I don't want to know what *you* think about what goes on in Paris. I want to know what the French think," he instructed me. He was still trying to add the personal significance of his constructive, energetic mentality to his four-month-old frail, humorous periodical.

He was an eccentric, impressive man to look at or listen to, a big-boned Westerner from Colorado who talked in windy gusts which gave a sense of fresh weather to his conversation. His face was homely with a pendant lower lip, his teeth were far apart and when I first knew him after World War I, he wore his butternut-coloured thick hair in a high stiff pompadour like some wild gamecock's crest and he also wore anachronistic old-fashioned high-laced shoes because he thought Manhattan men dressed like what he called dudes. I had met him as I had met Jane Grant, who was later to marry him, through the artist Neysa McMein at her untidy hospitable studio in West Fifty-Seventh Street, frequented by the wits, poker and cribbage players, critics and writers who later became the famous Algonquin Round Table coterie of which certain members also became members of The New Yorker's staff.

In 1923, Neysa and Jane came for a summer visit to Paris, where I already lived by preference, because it was the capital of France, and Americans with little private incomes, like me, who wanted to write, could afford to live on their hopes and good bistro food on the Left Bank. When they returned to New York I occasionally wrote to Jane to tell her what was going on in the boulevard theatres and the Opéra to both of which she was addicted. In the summer of 1925, she wrote me saying, "You remember that magazine Ross always talked about starting? Well, he has it in print at last. Why don't you write a fortnightly Paris letter for us?" I wrote back asking what Ross's magazine was called and if it was any good, to which Jane replied it was called The New Yorker and was not any good as yet, but that Ross was labouring over it, on some days believed in it optimistically and particularly in some of his new ideas. I sent two sample Letters from Paris which were also not good, especially after Ross condensed them into one which, when I finally saw it, published early in September, somewhat surprised me by being signed "Genêt," apparently my nom de plume. Months later, out of curiosity, I wrote and asked him which of the three well-known rather objectionable Genêts he had had in mind in choosing it. Had he named me for Citizen Genêt, the first minister from the First French Republic sent to the United States after the French Revolution whose recall was demanded by President George Washington as a brash French diplomat historically noted for his tactless lack of democratic diplomacy?

Or had he named me for the yellow broom flower, that leguminous weed that overruns French heaths and is viewed by peasants as a pest? The third I cited was the feline genêt or civet, a small French relative of the polecat. Ross very sensibly ignored my letter. Office gossip in New York reported that it seemed unlikely he had ever heard of any of the three Genêts. He had apparently fallen on the name at random, and to his eyes and ears seemed like a Frenchification of Janet, so it was merely a pleasant compliment after all.

For the first two years practically all The New Yorker's few regular contributors wrote under pseudonyms because they had regular jobs as writers elsewhere, two of them on Frank Crowninshield's notably brilliant monthly Vanity Fair, where they signed their pieces with their own well-known names which had a value that magazine willingly paid for. What they wrote semi-anonymously for The New Yorker, which was practically unknown, was a sub rosa friendly favour to Ross and for pin money. Ross paid on the nail when he could—his financial backing dried up more than once before his magazine caught on—and when he could not even give the modest check he customarily offered, he paid in New Yorker stock, then of uncertain value but which today is gilt-edged and would make any surviving member of the old-guard original writers rather rich, had Ross only been out of funds even oftener. Robert Benchley of Vanity Fair wrote his witty nonsense under the signature of Searchlight and his colleague Dorothy Parker signed her brilliantly bilious New Yorker book reviews as Constant Reader. In her review of a new A. A. Milne book in which she found his whimsy especially nauseating, she reached the point at which she wrote "Tonstant Weader fwowed up," the most hypersensitive literary criticism the magazine ever published, and the best known.

Ross was a strange, fascinating character, sympathetic, lovable, often explosively funny, and a good talker who was the most blasphemous good talker on record. Once, on holiday from Paris, and at The New Yorker office, I heard him chatting in the corridor. I called out to him that his profanity was really excessive, to which he said in surprise, "Jesus Christ, I haven't said a God damn thing." His swearing was automatic, unconscious, always chaste, never coarse, and merely continuous. He had been a dropout in his mid-high-school years in the Far West to become a roving young provincial newspaper reporter, his aim being an eventual job in New York, which in his early period he never got any closer to than New Jersey. He matured as a habitual autodidact. In his twenty-six years as chief in his *New Yorker* office he was an unremitting reader of *Webster's New International Dictionary* (second edition), the magazine's official lexicon. He was in love with and fascinated by the English language. Dictionary reading had become an endless comfort to his restless mind. Endowed, as he was, with inquisitiveness and interest, mixed, the exactitudes of words and their definitions were his continuing passion and pleasure.

While on the hunt for an exactly right and suitable word for some writer's manuscript he was editing, Ross enjoyed having his assistant editor read *Roget's International Thesaurus* aloud to him, relishing its rich variations. He was an insatiable enquirer and, probably because of his incompleted education of which he remained self-conscious, was always unsure of himself and of his own answers, was both blessed and cursed by an endless uncertainty which drove him on constantly framing questions. His queries were proverbial around the office. Even if it were only a question of where to place a comma, to which he knew the answer better than anyone else being a punctuation fiend, he always wanted opinions. He was a vitally intelligent man composed of instantaneous mental reactions. The speed with which his brain functioned probably strengthened his habit of indulging in uncertainties as a delay in which to think things over a little. On the pages of his magazine he demanded impeccably correct grammar for which he had a fetish. He said that, when he was a boy, his mother had given him grammar lessons at home, teaching him to parse sentences in the old rigorous country schoolhouse style. When he discovered in *The New Yorker* that few of his writers with college educations were good grammarians, almost as a revenge, he took it on himself to edit and correct their copy. Fowler's *Modern English Usage* became the office book of law. In obedience to the famous Fowler guidance on when to use *that* or when to use *which* in relative clauses, the magazine faithfully pursued what

its copy readers today still call "the which hunt," a jollity Ross did not appreciate since he despised puns. To him, an error of fact, grammar, spelling, citation, or punctuation that found its way into print in his magazine, "makes me heartsick," he said, as if describing a painful physical symptom.

Ross was a perfectionist. His aim was literally the publication of a technically flawless copy of *The New Yorker* every week which, as time and experience accumulated, he and the experts he assembled around him usually achieved. The unassailable grammar and skillful editing that soon marked the maturing *New Yorker* created the solid skeleton he set in place, on which he and his writers framed its special prose style which ranks as a contemporary American classic. His own development duplicated that of *The New Yorker*, whose increasing culture rubbed off onto him; they matured together like dual identities, man and magazine.

Something visibly and communicatively new took place in the mid-twenties of postwar Manhattan which was summed up in the word *sophistication*. This was what Ross aimed for. He had paid little attention to art in any form till then, yet the most important drawings he chose to publish were practically avant garde. He was a magnet for intelligent people, and once in his orbit they remained fixtures. The drawings of the unknown Peter Arno became the magazine's first success in sophistication—eye-catching in their strong modernist draftsmanship and in a certain sensuality and sense of satire, with voluptuous-looking, handsome young women talking in bed to their effete, inert husbands, or the same Matisse-like curvaceous beauties depicted in nightclubs with rich, attentive, predatory satyrs in top hats, both the conjugal and the public scenes offering implications then new and piquant to Manhattan humour. Art, in *The New Yorker*, became a special department with its particular director.

The Tuesday art meeting to view and choose the new drawings was like a board of directors' meeting with Ross and the main editors in attendance held in the magazine's only spacious room which was reserved for this purpose, while the writers and under-editors remained crowded in the rabbit-warren cubbyholes that became legendary. (Much later, during World War II, Truman Capote, who had been determined to work on *The New Yorker* and had become the office boy in charge of presenting Tuesday's new art on an easel, would anxiously focus on Ross to see if he favoured any drawing that Truman himself specially liked, and if Ross snorted, "God damn awful" as he brandished the long knitting needle that he customarily used as a pointer, Truman was known to have shaken his blond head and clucked, "Tch, tch," the only office boy on that magazine who ever dared cluck at the editor-in-chief.)

In the special protection the magazine gave its artists, they developed their own idiom and at the same time the magazine's, which created for *The New Yorker* its particular influential graphic art. The first two magazines it influenced were its only competitors, the old so-called humorous weeklies, *Life* and *Judge*, with their antiquated He and She cartoons and vapid jokes, both of which soon folded up and went out of business.

Ross's brilliant invention was the Single Line joke, in which the commentary was furnished in the single line spoken by one individual in a duo or group who, on order from Ross, a realist, had to have his or her mouth ajar to indicate who was speaking. One drawing handed in showed two elephants conversing. "Fix pix," Ross ordered, his laconic office jargon, spoken or written, for "tell the artist to improve the picture." "I can't make out which elephant is talking," Ross complained.

The other popular Arno drawings were the Whoops Sisters, old-fashioned camp characters like *Punch*'s London charladies with their feathers in their bonnets and their plates of tripe. The Whoops Sisters, whom Ross ran three times a month for three years, sold the magazine on the newsstands. In its over-all makeup Ross had leaned considerably on parts of *Punch*'s format, borrowing its itemized London gossip which he transformed into Talk of the Town, its casual bits of fiction (still known in *The New Yorker* office as Casuals) and the occasional character studies which he developed into Profiles. During World War II the *Punch* editors came on a brief visit to New York and its magazine world, which received them with honour. The outstanding event for them and Ross was their stately call on *The New Yorker*, where he candidly declared to *Punch*'s editor, "We owe *Punch* a great deal," and *Punch*'s edi-

tor said, "And you have greatly influenced *Punch*," which Ross had noticed in its recent modernization where there were indeed certain reflections of his own magazine.

Ross made so many rules for running *The New Yorker* that he spent his time making exceptions to them so things could work. However, his complicated departmentalisms, the technical, social, regional, and linguistic expertisms did actually mesh and work admirably, all set up in his restless insistence on further perfectionism. Five of his carefully selected editors had special competences which served for background knowledge and reporting. One was an expert on New York clubs and real estate, another knew the Junior League crowd, sports, and the purlieus of the rich (in whom Ross was always interested); a third had been an Oxford University man, knew England and the old-fashioned New York upper class to which he belonged. The fourth knew Broadway and Greenwich Village, was a railroad buff and a master proofreader, and the fifth was from Philadelphia, knew its society, and also spoke French as his second language.

In the checking department, for verification of every fact or reference, were university men who also spoke French, Italian, or German. Ross established as archivist a woman who had the best memory he ever met, he said. His proofreaders were a female club of experts who had the value almost of ghost editors, making the magazine what they still say is "the most intensively edited magazine in the Western world." On top of this, as a journalist himself, he picked writers who were an élite crack crew of journalists and could produce anything needed that World War II later demanded. On the fall of France, which Ross heard of when he was under the weather at his country place near Stamford, he went in his pyjamas to the nearby printing plant and remade the opening pages of the magazine.

As the invasion by the American Army grew near, Ross was asked by an Army friend, who was a general, to help on the printed pocket guide to France, which our American soldiers were to carry with them, along with everything else, when they crossed the Normandy beachheads. Ross asked me to write this little brochure and asked Ludwig Bemelmans to draw the illustrations—a female writer and an artist of an Austrian enemy-alien family, both quietly working for the United States Army. My chapter on the dangers of social diseases was considered weak by the general, whom I later met at a party. When I asked him to let me see the finished booklet, he whispered, "Sh, its contents are top secret."

"But I know what's in it, General," I said, "I wrote it. Don't you remember?"

When the time came for me to try to go back to Paris after the Liberation, Ross talked about sending me back on a small boat carrying dynamite to Denmark, so I turned to Jane Grant who, though she and Ross were no longer married, was still devoted to the magazine that she had helped found, and who was then editing the "pony" or midget editions of *The New Yorker* for the Army Library Service. "Nonsense," she said, "He doesn't know the right generals. Do you fly?"

"I never have, but I will," I said.

"Get your uniforms ready. You will probably leave in three or four days in an Army plane. I will phone my generals in Washington to fix things up."

When I said goodbye to Ross in the office, he said, "Do you mind signing your Paris letter with your own name from now on? Maybe it's high time for you to be yourself." But on receipt of my next Paris letter he cabled, "Do you mind signing it Genêt as usual, it looks more natural." Which it did to me, too.

After the war, *The New Yorker* seemed like a senior citizen compared to the old days. It carried news from pretty well all over Europe, Africa, and the British dominions, and special articles from such an extension of American and English writers that it was no longer what Ross had developed as "a New York paper," which is what he always called it. It had become a famous, important, transatlantic reportorial weekly, a fact that afforded him his greatest satisfaction. Of all the non-New York material that it carried—lengthy, authoritative articles, and topics and ideas so special that they could have been printed in specializing magazines—one contribution was extraordinary in that it had nothing to do with any cities or countries or nations. This was Rachel Carson's *The Sea Around Us*, which dealt with the evolution of land rising from the waters—the essential primaeval news of a world.

Ross remained unchanged. He still prowled around the corridors in the late afternoon, looking things over and looking in on those who worked for him and about whom he was always paternally curious. He would drop in on them, chat and swear, and usually make them laugh. As an official chief, he was a humanly observing kind of man. He shared himself especially with the new young writers on his staff. He would bang on their doors, walk in, and say, "Ross" as his introduction. He also maintained his eccentricities. He never liked to be spoken to in the elevator, not even to have anybody say, "Good morning." He didn't like anybody to whistle in the corridors. He still remained available when he was in his office. We could walk in to talk. Often he sat there with his head resting on his hand, looking thoughtful, sitting quietly, as if he were prospecting in his thoughts. In his career he had never changed himself or his elements. In his developments he did not become a literary man or an intellectual. In his maturities he remained the journalist *par excellence*. Within his limited class he was a double paragon. He was born with a kind of genius for being the great editor-journalist as other men might be born lyric poets. Of the two, his endowment was rarer.

A Reference for
Lady Chatterley's Lover

BY ANTHONY POWELL

EDITOR'S NOTE: *What happened to Mellors, the gamekeeper, and to Lady Chatterley, after D. H. Lawrence dropped the story? Keeping to details from the novel as carefully as if they were clues in an archaeological dig, Anthony Powell came up with this startling twist, a 1966 domestic reference for Mellors given by Lady Chatterley. One of England's most distinguished writers, author of the imposing series of novels* A Dance to the Music of Time, *Mr. Powell recently finished the eighth in line:* The Soldier's Art, *to be published in a year or so by Little, Brown and Company. In his novels, as in this wryly presumed aftermath to one of the world's most famous love stories, Mr. Powell's comedy is an unsettling mix of the absurd and the all too humanly possible.*

A long, low house in brown stone. Wragby Hall looked much as one had been led to expect. It was set among trees from which the rain still dripped forlornly onto tangled undergrowth. The oaks stood silent and tired, like old, worn-out seekers after pleasure, unable to keep up in this grimy, mechanized world of ours. The weather was sultry, and from where Tevershall pit bank was burning, a scent of coal dust and sulphur charged the atmosphere, while lowering, mackintosh-coloured clouds gave warning that another heavy downpour might at any moment take place. Away beyond the park at the far end of the drive, a hooter gave three short blasts, and there came the noise of shunting trucks, the whistle of colliery locomotives, and the voices of men, bitter and discontented; loud, rasping voices raised in conflict. Ashes had been thrown down in front of the entrance to the house to fill the cavities of the gravel in which pools of brackish water had accumulated. He rang an iron bell and waited, trying to remove from one eye a small piece of grit, blown downwind from the furnaces. After some minutes the door was opened by a good-looking, middle-aged woman, dressed in black.

"Lady Chatterley?"

She smiled slowly, sphinx-like.

"Her Ladyship is expecting you."

She took the hat and overcoat.

"Her Ladyship is in her own sitting room. She said I was to show you straight up."

Some concealed implication of enquiry seemed to rest in those rather defiant grey eyes. No doubt it was a little uncommon for a guest to be given access to that intimate, inviolate apartment; or some hint such as this was at least conveyed by her look, a questioning of the favoured stranger's credentials it might be. Turning on her heel, she led the way up the main staircase, and along a passage hung with stark oil paintings and then up more stairs. On one of the landings, the door of a lumber room was ajar and behind a pile of hatboxes, suitcases, vestry chests, rosewood cradles, and engravings from Landseer's works, was the glimpse of a contraption which seemed at first sight an unusual form of mowing machine, but declared itself almost immediately as Sir Clifford Chatterley's wheelchair. It was rusty and covered with dust; and piled high with riding boots and old golf clubs. Clearly it had lain unused for years.

"Sir Clifford won't be back for some weeks?"

"He's in London, sir. He often has to go there now on business."

"He has become an important figure in coal."

"He has indeed, sir."

"I suppose he is—perfectly all right now."

"Oh yes, sir. Absolutely."

She laughed quietly to herself as if this were a rather foolish question to have asked, and she knew the answer all right. She was a thick-set, healthy-looking woman, speaking with a broad Derbyshire burr, with keen eyes and a strong, supple body, like a tigress moving through some dark, thick undergrowth.

"Oh yes. Sir Clifford is absolutely all right now."

She gave another of those secretive, excludatory laughs as she opened a door on the third floor and showed him into a small room decorated in pink and yellow distemper, upon the walls of which hung huge German reproductions of paintings by Renoir and Cézanne. He had the impression of entering a bright, up-to-date schoolroom where lessons are enjoyed.

Constance Chatterley was standing by the window, looking down onto the park. She turned slowly, and held out her hand with a movement that carried with it a challenge of hidden energies; fair, blue-eyed, with some occasional freckles. A faint fragrance of wood-violet perfume was wafted across the room.

"So you found your way here in spite of the rain."

The other woman paused at the door.

"Will you have tea here or in the drawing room, m'Lady?"

"In the drawing room, Mrs. Bolton."

"At five o'clock or earlier, m'Lady?"

"I will ring when we are ready for it."

"Very good, m'Lady."

Lingering, almost rebelling, Mrs. Bolton left the room hesitantly, as if unwilling to submit to this assertion of a subtler will than her own. Lady Chatterley was certainly handsome. Not in a too demure or dull way. On the contrary, she had put on plenty of lipstick, and her clothes looked almost over-smart for the country. At the same time she gave an impression of a person at ease with herself and her surroundings, a person not easily embarrassed. This was a relief because it might be necessary to make enquiries that would sound—in the ordinary way—inquisitive. She held out a box of gold-tipped cigarettes.

"Do sit down," she said. "You wanted to see me about a reference?"

Best to go straight to the point. There was nothing to be gained by beating about the bush; especially with someone so unaffected.

"A friend of mine is looking for a suitable man for a post in one of the national game preserves of the Dominions. He has had an applicant who seems to be the right type and who gave your name as a reference. Hearing that I was staying with neighbours of yours my friend suggested that you wouldn't mind if I came over, and had a talk about this man."

"But of course—"

"There were certain points my friend wanted to make sure about before he engages anyone. It is quite an important position, you know, and—coming under the Government—you will appreciate that one has to make the fullest enquiries. The man is a former employee of your husband's I understand. Mellors. I take it he gave your name as he knew Sir Clifford was away from home."

For a moment she frowned, as if at a loss.

"Mellors?"

"Mellors," he said. "Oliver Mellors. A gamekeeper."

"Mellors, it was Parkin. Wasn't it Parkin? Or was it Mellors? I dimly recall the name Parkin, and yet Mellors is familiar, too. Anyway, I remember the man you mean, I'm sure. I am so glad he is in the way of getting a good job. He never seemed somehow very happy here. But such a nice man."

"My friend says he appears to be an excellent type. I believe he had a commission in India during the war."

"Yes, a quartermaster, I think, or do they call it the Army Service Corps? Clifford told me, but I forget. Clifford says he always laughs when he thinks of Mellors handing out stores. You'd have had to have been a real old soldier to have got by Mellors, Clifford always says."

"That sounds promising. He will be able to deal with the clerical side."

"Oh yes, Mellors started in an office—but I think he liked to remember his army days. He always saluted if one came across him in the grounds."

"I suppose he has the usual formal requirements—honest, sober, hard-working, an early riser—I mean he won't be too much of an old soldier?"

"Honest to a fault. An absolutely reliable man. Sober, too—and didn't at all mind getting up early. I believe as a matter of fact he had rather a weak head."

She pouted archly.

"Was there some trouble? Tipsy at the tenants' dance or something of the sort."

"Really I have only the vaguest reason for saying he had a weak head. Perhaps I shouldn't have mentioned it. Only after he left us, my father happened to run into Mellors in the street in London. They had seen a good deal of each other because Papa has a passion for the rough shooting round here."

"Your father is Sir Malcolm Reid, R. A., of course."

"Like most artists he is a bit of an eccentric. He took Mellors to a sort of Bohemian club he belongs to in Soho and gave him lunch. Papa always likes to do himself well—and he said that by the end of the meal poor Mellors got rather red in the face and kept on telling the same story over and over again about how when he was in the army in India he would have been a captain if it hadn't been for the dark gods."

"I suppose the Indians had been getting on his nerves."

"Visits to temples or something, I expect. Perhaps he had seen queer Oriental carvings—I myself have been shown some that might easily upset a highly strung person. Anyway it was all rather a shame to my mind—but Papa is quite shameless where it's a question of having too many liqueurs after luncheon."

"This was obviously a most exceptional occasion. But he is a hard worker—Mellors?"

"As far as he goes, he is a very hard worker. Of course, you realize that he is not a strong man. I remember in the days when my husband used a wheelchair, the engine that drove the chair went wrong. Mellors tried to push it as if it were a bath chair, and really got quite breathless, poor fellow. That breathlessness was really why Clifford's father had arranged for him to have the job in the first place."

"So he dates back to your father-in-law's time?"

"Oh, he was quite an old retainer."

"And knew his job well?"

"There was not a great deal to do, you see, as we couldn't afford big parties—just an occasional old friend like Mr. Michaelis, the playwright, for a night or two. In fact Clifford always said it was a terrible piece of extravagance employing a gamekeeper at all in those days, but he went on because he thought it would give Mellors time to himself for reading and so on."

"Why reading?"

"Mellors was quite a highbrow in his way. He was a scholarship boy at Sheffield Grammar School and always had the air of having come down in the world a bit. We wanted to do anything we could for him."

"His father was a local blacksmith, wasn't he?"

"Oh, surely not! A schoolmaster, I think. On second thought, I believe he did shoe horses for a time—to demonstrate the dignity of manual labour. Mellors had a lot of those rather William Morris-y ideas too, you know."

"But I understand that he described himself as of 'mining stock'?"

"His grandfather—or possibly his great-grandfather—had something to do with the mine—surface work of some sort. It's quite true. Mellors was very proud of being 'mining stock'—all the more because he himself was a bit of a highbrow. In fact I believe he even had something published in *The New Statesman* once—a little piece of verse, or his impressions, or something of the sort."

"I had no idea. . . ."

"He had quite a small library of books in the cottage he lived in here—we might have gone to see it if it hadn't begun to rain so hard, it's rather snug. There were books about the causes of earthquakes, and electrons, and curious Indian customs—the 'dark gods,' perhaps—and Karl Marx, Freud, every sort of thing."

"He sounds an out-of-the-way fellow."

"Oh, Mellors was a real character. And then he loved dressing up. That was why he always wore a sort of green velveteen uniform and gaiters. Clifford made rather a fuss about the expense of getting it for him, but in the end he gave in, and Mellors got his way—as he usually did in things he had set his heart on."

"He must have looked quite picturesque."

"He did say to me once that he thought men ought to wear close red trousers and little short white jackets—but really we had to draw the line there. Unfortunately, the Chatterley livery is a rather sombre affair of black and drab so there was nothing much to be done for him in that direction. However, I think he was fairly happy with his green velveteens."

There was a pause. Lady Chatterley looked out again towards the park, as if trying to re-call more information about Mellors that might be of assistance to his new employers. Now the rain was coming down in sheets, thudding like artillery against the windowpanes.

"There was another—rather delicate question."

"Yes?"

"A considerable female staff is employed on certain clerical and other duties connected with the scientific observation of the habits of the animals within the preserve in question. Mellors, I am sure, could be trusted not . . . not to make a fool of himself. . . . Only there was a rumour about some sort of a scandal in connection with his wife—that is only why I ask. No doubt gossip and much exaggerated."

"I am sure it was. That was certainly our impression here. I should say he was entirely trustworthy—unless some quite unusual circumstances were to arise."

"Excellent."

"In fact your question would make our housekeeper, Mrs. Bolton—who let you in—laugh a great deal."

"She had a poor opinion of Mellors?"

"I'm afraid she used to laugh about him sometimes."

"Then we need to go no further into the matter of his wife?"

"I don't think the trouble about Mrs. Mellors was to be taken too seriously—although, of course, there was a certain amount of talk in the village at the time. The Mellorses had all sorts of what were then thought to be rather 'ad-

vanced' ideas. For example, he always used to refer to her by her maiden name as 'Bertha Coutts.' "

"No relation to the banking family?"

"If so, very distant. There were endless—and I believe rather unnecessarily public—discussions as to whether or not, for example, it was better for husband and wife to have separate rooms; whether companionate marriage was a prudent preliminary; how large families should be, and if it was desirable for a married couple to spend a certain time apart from one another in the course of the year."

"She was rather a highbrow too?"

"She had lived in Birmingham. I think she moved in circles on the outskirts of the Repertory Theatre."

"One can understand that all this was not wholly appreciated in the neighbourhood."

"It was during one of Mellor's temporary separations from his wife that he returned to his situation with us."

"You say 'temporary'—did he go back to his wife then?"

"In the end they decided in favour of a divorce—but without any hard feelings on either side."

"Were there any children?"

"A little girl. Mrs. Mellors held rather decided views as to how her daughter should be brought up, and was very anxious that no early harm should be done by frustration. I understand there were signs of—well—a bit of a father fixation. Besides Mrs. Mellors was conscientiously opposed to blood sports, which created difficulties vis-à-vis her husband's profession."

"There would be no question of Mrs. Mellors wanting to accompany him if he took up this post?"

"On the contrary. During their periods apart Mrs. Mellors found herself increasingly influenced by the personality of one of the colliers at Stacks Gate—a prominent figure in local Chapel circles. They used to discuss social and economic questions with others in the village interested in such matters. In the end they married."

"So Mellors is entirely without encumbrances."

"It is a long time since I have seen him—but this talk of ours has made me remember a lot of things about him. When he finally parted company with his wife there was some vague question of his getting married again—to someone younger than himself and in rather a different walk of life."

"Indeed."

"It would not, I think, have been particularly suitable!"

"A local girl?"

"I believe. . . . It was after he left us. They used to meet in London."

"Did anything come of it?"

"Very sensibly, the understanding was broken off by mutual consent."

"No doubt all for the best."

"After that, Mellors let it be known that he very definitely intended to remain single. He was quite happy, he used to say, with his wild flowers and his animals—and the wonderful imitations he used to give—when he had an audience—of the local dialect, in the origins of which he was keenly interested."

"Why did he actually leave your service, finally?"

Lady Chatterley considered for a moment.

"Temperament," she said at last. "It was a question of temperament. And, after all, most of us want a change at times. I suppose Mellors was like the rest of the world and enjoyed a little variety at intervals. He used to say, there are black days coming for all of us and for everybody. In some ways he was a very moody man. An unusually moody man."

There was another pause.

"I am really most grateful to you. I think you have told me quite enough to assure me that he would fill the vacancy admirably—that is, if his health holds up."

"That is the question," she said, very quietly, "if his health holds up."

She swung her feet onto the sofa, and lay back, stretching towards an ashtray to extinguish the stub of her cigarette. One of her suède slippers fell to the ground. She did not bother to recapture it. Outside the rain had ceased and a dull sun showed through the heavy cloudbanks. Below the window the hazel brake was misted with green, and under it the dark counterpane of dog's mercury edged the velvet of the sward. Still the breeze bore on its wings the scent of tar, and all the time came the thud, thud, thud of industrial afternoon in the Midlands; while the gentle perfume of wood violet was more than ever apparent above the insistent incense of the undying furnaces.

Notes on Leningrad

The Irrational Voyage

BY PAULINE DE ROTHSCHILD

We arrived in Leningrad late at night. The airport was soundless, covered in snow, white, except for low blue lights flickering near the ground. A tall blond young man took us through customs. The customs men looked at nothing, appeared uninterested. I had been told that it would seem unflattering to bring no jewellery, or only imitation, but to take merely what one could wear or carry in one bag and, above all, to declare it.

"I have some jewellery," I said, and pulled out a pair of diamond earrings shaped like ribbon bows and a flower made of diamonds and sapphires. When they were stretched out on the palm of his hand the tall young man glanced at them. "Small diamonds," he said, and handed them back to me, smiling.

We were off, in an old-fashioned limousine with hardly any luggage space, so we sat bolt upright, in a sort of grotto of suitcases. The streets were still brightly lit. People were walking about, rather slowly, talking and posturing in the bitter cold. Shopping. The big stores stay open until ten, the food shops, always very full, until eleven. "Otherwise," asked our driver, "when would you do your marketing?" When, indeed.

Off to our first winter in Russia. Like children arriving at a new school, we knew nothing, who or what of the faces we would meet in the next two months. And like children in some old-fashioned world, we were immediately put in the hands of our nannies.

The nannies are the Intourist people. They nest downstairs in every large hotel. From afar, when you are asked precisely, oh, so precisely, when and where and what you wish to see, you wonder if this particular Travel Bureau is not a little over-interested in travel, your travel. In reality, the Intourists are a group of excellent governesses. "Full-breasted, agreeable ladies," said Philippe. Not very different from agreeable, full-breasted ladies anywhere, except for their higher heels and their soft caressing Russian voices. Low, almost grave, these voices have the beat of poems in them, and in the men's an almost feminine tenderness. They are as susceptible to their own voices as we are. Standing on street corners, they talk to each other as if the one wished to enchant the other.

The nannies try to make everything easy for you, treating you as attractive children who must be protected. From the cold, from lack of knowledge, from a ballet that is not quite perfect. Like all good nannies, they are firm about time, good manners, and the dates of your comings and goings. They hesitate a little before telling you a thing is possible, which reminds you still further of your childhood. It is only when you wish to change your dates that they develop neurasthenia. Because over one hundred million Russians travel, at all times, filling all planes and most trains, in a country of a baffling size. One central office in Moscow, floating somewhere high above the local offices, takes care of all this. It works, but it is delicate. Changes are discouraged.

We listened. Your guide is your interpreter. You have a car and an interpreter three hours a day. After that, you may keep the interpreter, but to keep the car you will have to pay extra. There are tickets for your meals; almost all restaurants accept them. When you have no more tickets, you have to pay. (Almost impossible, even with lengthy meals and many guests, to get through the tickets.) Why did you choose to come in the winter? But we love the cold! And where can Philippe get that sort of fur hat? A *shapka?* (Fur hat with earmuffs.) Two or three lovely smiles. We are almost Russians.

Not very attractive, the rooms of that first night. Small, with stencilled walls imitating a brocade, a fashion of the turn of the century, not very good to start with. Narrow beds, possessed of the dreariest of printed blankets. The lamps were consoling: tall, winged, Napoleonic gilded ladies, carrying lampshades. They must, at one time, have been candelabra in a great house.

The following day, after remarking to the Intourist ladies that we were too large for our rooms, did they not think so, too, we were moved to an apartment, small but superb. Its dark-blue and bright-red drawing room housed, for the purpose of contemplation, twenty-one bronzed bears. On dressing tables in big hotels, a luxury unknown to ours: handsome silver boxes, small silver trays, occasional silver-backed brushes. They are the flotsam and jetsam of pre-1917 travelling cases, the redistributed bureau sets. Each object in the room bears a small metal inventory number, a kind of dog tag, one item of the immense Inventory of the State.

Before we went to sleep, we observed with interest the first sign of the great Russian cold. Double windows, of course. What was interesting was a strip of paper two inches wide, glued all along the cracks and hinges on the inside of the outer window. A man comes and puts these strips on about October fifteenth.

The windows remain sealed till spring. All windows. As you walk along the streets, you see that a few adventurous souls have an occasional small pane that can be opened. But it is usually sufficient, to cool or air a room, to open the inner window.

It is 9:15 in the morning. The day is the colour of soft brown fur, under a gentle, widely spaced snow. The night-lights are still on; they illuminate the broad five-sided square bordered by flesh-coloured houses with their flat white pilasters. A snowplow goes by. The ground becomes immediately white again. Light never seems to strike a surface but appears to come through walls as something latent and luminous. Not unlike Glenway Wescott's description of a woman's beauty; "A skin you can read by," said Glenway. A spotlight hits, high and solitary over a roof, a small square of red cloth of the brightest and lightest red, taut in the wind, beating.

Downstairs, our interpreter waited. A strong young woman who enjoyed her good looks, she wore a stiff fur hat straight across her brow. She liked this hat very much and never took it off. We would take our car to the Neva. In the car, there was no question of opening the windows, completely frosted over. This did not disturb our interpreter, who would point out the buildings, St. Isaac's, the Admiralty, the Winter Palace, as we passed, blind and bowing, behind our ice-bound windows.

That day at lunch, for the first time, we heard of the Scapegoat.

Everything in our interpreter's face was round. A round nose, a round mouth, round pink cheeks, and wide-apart brown eyes. She complained a little of her lipstick. Like all Soviet cosmetics, it blurred, and did not last. She and her young husband were buying an apartment. In a stone house, which was more expensive and for which one had to wait longer, but which was nicer. Philippe asked her what they were paying for it. It came to somewhere around three thousand dollars. This seemed a great deal for a young couple.

"My mother-in-law is helping us," she said. "She inherited some money when my father-in-law died."

"Inherited?"

"Yes. He was a good engineer and they were very well off. It was only for a while that she was very poor. When he was in a concentration camp. Yes, he was in a concentration camp, and yet he was a militant Communist."

"What happened, then?"

"A denunciation. A denunciation was sufficient in those days. We never knew from whom."

"It was never questioned?"

"Oh no. But that was in Stalin's day. . . ."

"Ah, but since Stalin that has changed. We are no longer. . . ." We were to hear this time and time again. When Khrushchev laid bare the bones of his predecessor, he raised a Culprit for all to see. Stalin could be blamed for everything that had gone wrong with the régime and, since the régime runs your daily life, for what had gone wrong with your life. All that had been borne in silence, the costs that had been too high to pay but had been paid. They would always be thankful to the garrulous old man for letting so much air into the country. It is healthy, they now said, to recognize what is wrong. The old Fox had died and become the Scapegoat. No amount of rehabilitating will take the spots out of those hands.

The voluptuousness of having one's eyelashes lengthen with frost and one's furs crinkling a little when one breathes. We walked, first one way, then back, then back again, the better to see, to see.

There is a curious quality about the past in Russia, not the presence but the immediacy. Peter the Great is here, and Catherine, and Lenin. The War and the Revolution. These people are image-makers at work. They have the conjurer's gift. The Revolution is here, the War is there. Elsa Triolet, the Russian-born French writer, said that they go from the daily to the legendary faster than most.

This is an immaterial city. Suspended, light, and quivering over the marshes it has replaced. One forgets that in winter all its canals, all its rivers are white, long white veins, and along this white, the riverbanks are softened out so that there is no difference between earth and water. Along them the broad flanks of its houses: moss green, buff, and the colour, cream-with-coffee-in-it, that Théophile Gautier called

ventre-de-biche. Then more furry greens, one apricot, then the rectangular walls of four houses and a low palace, red.

But this is nothing. This is only what the eye breaks against on the ground. There is another city above this one, weightless, spired and domed, divided from the other by mists. Across the river, over the fortress of Peter and Paul, a long golden needle, slim and still, floats alone, disembodied.

When Peter the Great wished his new city to grow, he passed a law: No one in all the Russias could build a stone house, except in St. Petersburg. Because of fires a second law imposed wide spaces between the houses. So that you get along the river an alternate pattern of wall and air, a checkerboard of colour and snow.

Philippe said to our interpreter: "Peter the Great imagined this city, created it, pulled it out of the marshes. He called it St. Petersburg. He had earned this. Why did you change its name to Leningrad?"

"When Lenin died, we wanted to give him the very best we had. So we gave him this city."

Advantages and disadvantages of the sheltered life. No foreign newspapers, except two Communist dailies, one in English, resembling the *Daily Worker,* and the other, the French *L' Humanité.* No foreign-language weeklies, except one. This is prepared in Moscow for some preconditioned foreigners and is of an unbelievably low intellectual standard, written in *Prince Igor* English.

No telephone books. There were none printed.

There was no way of ringing anyone up if you hadn't the number.

Letters reached us in about three weeks. For customary visitors to Russia, letters take about eight days. These delays are slightly illogical, since there seems to be no censorship on cables, and you can telephone anywhere in the world —within a quarter of an hour, if you are in Moscow; if you are away from Moscow, within the hour—for as long as you wish the conversation to last.

At the Hermitage Museum, we presented our credentials to Madame Edovina. A sort of bridge of tact and warmth between the invisible directors of the museum and the outside world.

Her office had enormously high windows giving on the Neva, and the usual Russian desks, most comforting as they seem big enough to lie down on. We would meet there twice a day, and she would plan our day for us. We would have conversations, very worldly in the sense of light and teasing questions and answers that did not take you very far afield. She said that she would have liked to invite us for lunch on New Year's Day, but that couldn't be, and she offered us some delicious chocolates disguised as large gold coins. There began a series of relationships, more bewitching even than the works of art.

There was, for instance, the Meteor. She was the head of the Byzantine department, a world-renowned scholar, and we had been most anxious to see her. No appointments had been feasible. She came upon us one day in a long gallery. "I am a meteor," she said, and vanished. Eventually she gave us a long afternoon's care, way past closing time, and, as a proper meteor, she would turn to light up dark rooms and dim cases. We told her that we knew less than nothing about Byzantine art, and instead of boring her this seemed to refresh her spirits. After this, when we were with other curators, she would suddenly appear for a few seconds' conversation. There was something long and English about the shape of her face, and she combined languor with speed as the English so often do.

Then, there was the passing glimpse of the Rich People. Madame I.'s gay voice and witty looks had brought her three husbands. The last one, a brilliantly intelligent Armenian, had been the director of the Hermitage. "Very intelligent, but what a temper! Impossible in the house, that temper," she said. She then touched the grey lamb of her small fur cuffs and collar and swung faster the pleats of her grey tweed skirt. Perhaps one should love some husbands for show, others for use. We passed a Bonnard. "This landscape was given to us by a collector," she said, "two years ago."

"People here still have collections?" asked Philippe.

"Why not? Of course," sounded the happy voice. "We have everything here, even Rich People."

"And they have collections?"

"Of course." With an undertone, rather offended, of: Do-you-think-capitalists-the-only-ones-to-have-collections?

The inn at Tsarskoye Selo, (the Czar's Hamlet, now called Pushkin) is a simple, square, three-storeyed wooden building, painted white, rather like the Massachusetts houses of the early nineteenth century. The room in which we sat for lunch was light, high, rather like a schoolroom. Through its long windows and the interlacing of the furry white branches of the frozen trees, the domes of Catherine's chapel could be counted. Freshly gilded in the sun against a Mary-Mother-of-God blue sky. Five, seven onion domes, sometimes nine, never anywhere an even number.

Madame N., a great beauty, had large grey-green eyes, straight black lashes, dark hair brought back into a knot, pearl earrings through her pierced ears. She wore a soft cardigan of the type we all own buttoned up to the neck. When she walked or stood she kept her arms close to her ribs, which increased her length and narrowness. A tweed skirt. A small jewel. Nothing, yet *le comble de l'élégance* as the French say. Which is wrongly translated, I think, as the "height of elegance." It is more: "elegance fulfilled."

All Russians have patriotic principles. Madame N.'s came out rather unexpectedly. A Frenchwoman, across the table, spoke of the past of Catherine the Great somewhat wistfully. How well the Empress had organized herself, reigning, collecting, taking her pick of any men at court, *se tapant* (the equivalent of helping yourself a little too quickly and recklessly but with thorough enjoyment), "se tapant les ambassadeurs."

"No, I've never heard that about Catherine the Great," came the prompt reply, "she never slept with foreigners."

One is struck by the number of green-coloured houses. Everything Rastrelli, Catherine's architect, built, is blue-green or green, so of course the Winter Palace returned to its original green after 1917. The inventor of Boeuf Stroganov lived in a charming green eighteenth-century palace on a wide canal. The café called the Frogs, where one goes to eat ices, is green. On the other hand the nineteenth century is mostly yellow and white, like the Youssoupoff

IN LENINGRAD: THE KIROV BALLET

The adored, superbly trained corps de ballet
at the Maryinski Theatre—here in "Swan Lake," danced
exactly as it was at the première on this stage in 1895.

BRUCE DAVIDSON

house from which Rasputin was dragged, a very large man to die in so small a river.

At Tsarskoye Selo, Catherine's head gardener lived next to the palace in a large house of the most exquisite proportions, the colour of a heart of artichoke, and corresponded there with Thomas Jefferson. Just to look at this house is a form of happiness.

"On the 24th of October, 1917," reads the sign, "this palace was open to the people."

It is curious how the Soviets manage to convince the crowds that all that they see belongs to them; I have never felt this to be true elsewhere in any other national collections. Perhaps if the Metropolitan Museum of Art in New York put up a small sign saying, "In 1870 this museum was open to the people," it would have an agreeable effect.

At times, curators of other departments would join us at Tsarskoye Selo and, as they were all friends, would make comments. This was a sort of refresher course for them and would make of our visit a trip through strangeness, with people getting on and off the bus. There was the morning when the Head of the Decorative Arts was to shepherd us. The decorative arts were to include silver, porcelain, glass, such apartments as the Czarina's, and furniture, too, perhaps, though I was never to find out. This very tall and imposing gentleman showed us the Sévres a certain Czar ordered, the silver tureens Count Orlov, the most interesting of the lovers, had brought back from his visit to Paris. Philippe showed no signs of excitement.

Once or twice he would ask, "Isn't Madame N. joining us?"

We passed the great silver service made by Louis XV's silversmith, Germain. Philippe's indifference, I thought, was perhaps due to the silver's being black, as Russian museums never clean their silver.

Philippe turned to the serious and by then somewhat silent man. "I am not interested in Germain," said Philippe.

The serious man quickly stepped to a telephone and dialled a number. "M. de Rothschild only wants to look at Madame N.," he said. "So would you please ask her to come down."

The street is a street of bankers. The men are all in fur hats, handsome fur collars on their overcoats, the most modest driver or delivery man has the most perfect astrakhan. They wear their fur *shapkas* with the ear covers not tied down but standing out. This makes them look like dogs on their hind legs, their fine ears flapping. When the high dogs with the flapping ears go home, the streets seem still more brightly lit.

What makes one turn one's head is the courtesy of the Russians one to the other. Relationships are gentle. This is a holiday time, and people stop to congratulate each other. The men kiss the women's hands. I don't know if this is just the festive time, or customary.

Under their warmth, a sort of compassion.

The routine of the happy days began to take shape.

The Hermitage would close. Every evening there would be theatre, but first tea and my Russian lesson. We would walk home through the square under the trees, each branch two or three times its size with a shagginess of iced snow standing up on it, like hair on end.

Tea came with a sea of strawberry jam. There is a discussion, in Tolstoy, I think, on how to make jam. Liquid, hardly cooked in the Russian manner, or the German-Western-European way, more long lasting. In our jam the strawberries were left whole, as if you had just picked them and left them about for an hour. The hot toast would be brought. Crushed with their own weight, the berries had the sweet sleepy smell of the fields about them.

My teacher was a university professor, the mother of a small girl of six. She could easily have played Joan of Arc in Anouilh's *L'Alouette*, and she would give us brilliant foreshortened accounts of the play we would be seeing that night, whole sentences made recognizable at key points. She had a straightforward beauty and dignity. Philippe would watch her from under his eyelids, not knowing quite what to make of such good looks and such timidity, without any self-consciousness whatever. Yet with banners flying somewhere.

She would draw for me outlines in red ink of the throat and the palate, to get me to place sounds where no sounds had come from before. As a reward I would be allowed to translate, oh how badly, a Tolstoy fable for children. What I preferred was when she talked of her husband and child, suddenly, very quietly, as if these wonderful creatures were in the next room. When we left Leningrad she gave me one of my favourite presents: a recording of Chekhov spoken by his actress-wife.

The word Revolution is worn like a flower in the buttonhole. People speak of the Revolution the way mediaeval poets speak of the Spring. The Revolution is a sort of nationality, a country of the mind, their success and their strength.

In the back of our minds, however, remains the thought that there is something of Lucifer in the Revolution and that the Revolutionaries are the Fallen Angels. Something very faint, an astonishment once removed, comes over us when the Fallen Angels are sitting down at table, successful, happy, laughing.

The Fallen Angels, bright and cheerful at home, meet with strange reactions in other countries.

Two women curators of the Hermitage were in Paris. They found that if they said they were Russians, they would be taken for White Russians. This they did not want. "Of course we are *not*," they explained, "and when the nice man staying at the same hotel said to us in the elevator, 'What are you?' we answered, 'U.S.S.R. We are Soviet citizens.' The man leaned against the wall of the small elevator and loosened his tie."

We had brought our books, what we thought necessary for travelling. In truth a library. Herodotus—very useful, with his Scythian-Russians of the fifth century B.C.; Théophile Gautier's *Voyage en Russie*, in the winter of 1858; Maurice Baring up to 1912; some recent writers like Paustovsky and Chklovsky (his marvellous *Letters That Do Not Speak of Love*). No books on the revolution, no information on the present day. The surprise came late at night, reading on the spot, in the flesh so to speak, the great Russians. Aristocratic Tolstoy's novels *Anna Karenina* and *Resurrection* become social tracts; the cosmopolitan Turgenev writes with controlled despair; the revolution is present in each line of the self-taught Gorky, and Chekhov the doctor asks for a more hopeful tomorrow. Dissimilar talents, dissimilar stations of life, and everywhere the same roar and the same lament.

There seemed to be no way out of this sickness, this waste. Lenin's book: *What Is To Be Done?* Except for a handful too rich, or too powerful, or too stupid, every class wished for a change, could not get it, and knew the revolution to be inevitable. Now that the pain had gone it resembles a fresh beginning, a spring. Not a resurrection but a coming to life.

At a quarter to five in the morning Philippe came into my room. I had been having one of those delicious nights of insomnia, when, if you put out the light for a minute or two, you know that you will not sleep and can hardly wait to go on with your reading. Philippe stood in the doorway and said, "What are you doing? I have been in pain since two o'clock. I don't know what's the matter with me. I have never had this pain before." His face was grey and he moaned a little. He went back to his room. The hotel was half dark. The night watchman almost asleep. Anyway, whom would he call? Better to wait. Until nine o'clock when the Intourist desk would open.

I would walk from Philippe's room back to mine listening to the silence and then again the spasms of cries. During the intervals when he was not suffering Philippe would say, "I have come to Russia to die."

The doctor arrived at ten. I opened the door. Three people stood in front of me, all dressed in white operating gowns and caps. One woman, who was the doctor, and two huge young men who turned out to be interns. I said rather loudly, so Philippe would not be frightened, "Must you be so many? Could you not come in one at a time?" No. They seemed to have brought a great deal of material in tin suitcases. One of the interns had studied in Holland and was disappointed because I did not speak Dutch. In the meantime, two calls to Paris came in, one to Philippe's doctor, one to his surgeon (he had been operated on six months before). The three diagnoses coincided. The Russian doctor gave him an injection and then insisted he would be better taken care of in the hospital. Philippe acquiesced. Off we went. In the ambulance, sitting up, he felt the pain come on again, grabbed and held tightly to the hand of the dark young intern. The young man took his hand and patted it seriously and gently as he would his own child's. In the

IN LENINGRAD: THE BLAZE OF MATISSE

Among the glories of the Hermitage Museum are thirty paintings by Henri Matisse,
all done between 1897 and 1913. They fill two rooms, are the delight of Leningrad children
who cluster there, their hair in nylon bows. *Right,* Matisse's "Red Room" of 1908,
originally commissioned by a Moscow collector and brought to that city by Matisse himself.

hospital, there was no waiting and in no time Philippe was sitting up in bed surrounded by three women doctors, all very large and all stroking his bare stomach. He seemed enchanted. He soon went to sleep. One of the shots they had given him was to help dissolve the stone in the kidney, I believe they said, and he could go home in a few hours.

I stayed in the hospital watching the new arrivals.

A boy of about fifteen was brought in. He had been hit by a car, unwounded, but white, suffering from shock. He was given the same warm care, and tenderly covered. Philippe was not allowed to pay for his X rays or medicines. The boy's father before going away had left two packages of cigarettes and some matches.

The next day I returned to thank them and to bring some tokens of appreciation. (In this case small packages of pairs of silk stockings.) My women doctors were out. It was their day off. I was taken to see the chief nurse and two others, very large and kind, and we sat down with my interpreter for the usual exchange of small talk. I remarked that what impressed me the most during this whole affair was just that, the extraordinary kindness. The head nurse straightened herself behind her desk and said, "Everywhere in the U.S.S.R. you will meet with kindness." The conversation seemed to have taken on weight. Not dazzling, as Lady Murasaki would have said.

I bowed, hand on the heart, and left.

The heart is much to the fore. One constantly puts one's hand on one's heart, sometimes both hands, especially women. Lucid thought is not to be trusted as much as this heart's instinct, this quickness.

When you see a queue you may be quite sure that it is either in front of a tobacco shop or of a bookstore. The line-up in front of bookstores before the morning or afternoon opening is startling. Women with white blouses over their heavy winter clothes, enormous as balloons, stand at street corners behind hampers filled with the latest edition of a new book and sell these as they would oranges, and just as fast.

The longest queue in Leningrad is in front of a pastry shop in the Nevsky Prospekt with the best cakes in all Russia. If anyone is travel-ling home, or has a birthday, or a small feast, one brings a pastry from this famous shop.

People say, yes, but Rastrelli, an Italian, built the Winter Palace. Cameron, a Scotsman (and what a Scot, with a great classical education, and a taste for flowers in decoration made so fresh in their varieties that they would ravish a botanist), built Pavlosk. In short, foreign architects. But how long do they remain foreign. One should remember how one's eye changes in another country with a different weight of light and sky, and certainly a different weight of patron. With a different length of purse strings.

The city lights have three round frosted-glass globes, at a little over the height of a man. When they are lit, two are of a lilac pink, one of the palest green. They give off what Turgenev saw in the country and described as "a pale and floating lilac colour" or a little further down the page as a "lilac-coloured mist." The snow becomes more phosphorescent.

Here go the young, leaving the Hermitage at dusk, ten, twenty boys and girls in their grey flannel suits, with around their necks their bright-scarlet scarfs tied in Byronic knots, the ends flickering, as their eyes.

In this light, as they run one to the other the eyes are like streaks of grey. The faces have the look of young Russian skins in winter, a pale smoothness, which is the unexpected result of the cold together with hothouse temperatures. The women's hands, for instance, are never red.

By now the Matisse rooms in the Hermitage are so famous that one might keep quiet about them. If one could. The photograph Vogue published in 1964 of three Matisses with the young girls sitting in front of them, their coloured nylon bows on top of their heads—it is just like that. You go up quite a long way to the top floor, then two large grey rooms with low ceilings, and there they are, a wild number of Matisses. What are these colours, this incredible freshness? There is something of the early morning of creation still on them. You are given these colours so that you will be present at a feast. The picture was worked out and suddenly the feast was on. The feast of painting. You must see and you must take part. You begin to understand how God felt when He first saw a green field.

Then, there was the Skeptic. The Skeptic was also a Sage. He unwittingly gave us a view of ourselves which is universal in the U.S.S.R. This view disturbs them more than it does us.

The Skeptic was very short and round and strong, the shape of St. Thomas probably, the sort of bald man who seems to have refused hair at birth. He had firm, mocking views about everything. Except women. With them he was an instant success, probably because they could charm him almost at will. So he had snared with the greatest of ease three or perhaps four beautiful wives. His great love, like Berenson's, was Italian painting. He had travelled much and often to Italy, to conferences of art historians, and to many other countries where research was done, where ideas were being exchanged. This last to show you that he was not an insular, but a travelled man.

One evening, very much later, after our return from Moscow, I found myself, owing to the warmth, the general happiness, the green-yellow Georgian wine, saying to him, as an American: What a terrifying waste this is, our two countries still almost sealed off from one another, when no two people's qualities on this earth are more an extension of one another's. Why should we not know their use of the heart; their elegance of mind; the gentle, rapid sensitivity of their understanding; the vitality of their love of people, just people. They share with us an extraordinary sense of tomorrow. We are perhaps more generous than they, our machine is less cumbersome in letting talent and intelligence come to the surface; and, having had no spectacular prophets, we know more about what makes the modern world tick. Isn't there a formula of some sort, political or economic, that would make a bridge between their world and ours over which we could both safely pass?

"Oh," he answered, "no formula. Above all, no formula. Let us slip, when possible, between difficulties. But no formula. You see, my dear, if you were to say for instance that there is a great deal of liberty here, I would have to say, no, that is not so. On the other hand, if you were to say that you did not exploit the workers, I would have to say that that is not so, either."

A marvellous looking young woman, reddish hair, quite a bit of eye makeup and red lipstick, was holding at arm's length her strong baby. She and the priest were in the act of immersing him several times and the child howled accordingly. At the other end, coffins, opened at the place of the head, the profile of the dead raised against the light. "Philippe, you can not take part in the baptism rites and also join the mourners. Especially the mourners."

"Why not?" asked Philippe. "They don't mind."

They didn't.

During the World War II siege, the people who lived on the top floors died first. They no longer had the strength to go up and down. It was a very cold winter and the doctors counselled people to live all together in one room of the apartment if they wished to survive, each one giving out some heat to the other. At first, the dead were taken down into the courtyard to be fetched by the city trucks. Later people became too weak to carry the corpses down and they simply dragged them to some unused room at the end of a corridor and left them there. The window panes had been broken by the bombardments and the windows were boarded up.

Our friend was only sixteen or seventeen at the time of the siege. She and her mother survived because the mother stayed in bed near the small stove that had been rigged up for them by a man, in exchange for a gold watch and a ring. She would wait in line two to three days for a distribution of bread. People would replace each other in order to warm themselves and then return to the line. The friendships made waiting in those lines still last.

The women in the factories sometimes stayed at their benches, too tired and weak from underfeeding to go home at night, afraid they would not get back.

All over the world, alas, most saleswomen in big popular-price stores are disagreeable. In Russia, a sort of aloof grandeur is added to this. They are functionaries of their government, and what are you? It is a little like going to the Pentagon for one's hairpins. One would expect them to look surprised, but not pleased. So it is with the Soviet saleswoman, a sacred member of the State, keeper of the missing article.

Philippe, who is always dinning into me the abuses of religion (obscurantism, brakes on scientific discovery, furtherance of ignorance), was made into a believer by a visit to the Museum of Atheism.

I suppose that one of the secrets of a successful life is to be made to hear as a child much that you do not understand. In the winter mornings, at half past ten, one goes to the children's performances, not, as in my childhood, children's plays, but the great ballets and the great operas. In this manner we saw Tchaikovsky's *Eugene Onegin* and *Queen of Spades* in the Kirov, the huge pale-blue and silver theatre, packed with children. Leningrad, the most elegant of all cities, has two or three blue-and-gold or blue-and-silver theatres the colours of those of Versailles. There was a little girl with a thin face and a heavy plait wearing a winged apron which came beyond her ears. On her narrow chest was pinned a decoration. People fussed over her and she looked superior and rather disagreeable. Perhaps a hero of school studies.

The realism in the Russian theatre is so strong that it gives you a feeling of unreality.
The flat surfaces become three-dimentional, the lighting disquietingly exact, the actor himself ages under the old man's makeup. And where are you? Forty years back. No, perhaps one hundred.
The result is pleasant but old-fashioned. Though at times marvellously suggestive. In *The Barbarians* of Gorky, there is a dinner-party in a garden, a remarkable, to us nostalgic, scene of rich, aimless, and irretrievable country life.
The Russians are a complicated people, unafraid of complications. A welcome change after the French, who insist on clarity till the thought dries up, and after the Anglo-Saxon in fear of splitting hairs.

"They did not need brains, since they had felicity," once wrote Karen Blixen of the Danish aristocracy.

A country can perhaps best be judged by its children. Here they are, playing under the snow-iced trees, strong and fat cheeked, bundled in little fur coats of black seal, more likely rabbit, but so sharp against the snow, topped by the favoured green or some other colour wool scarf tied at the back. Their fathers pull them in small sleds along the street and they lie back, clear-skinned lords of all they survey. They are hoisted to the top of the toboggan slide, sled and all, and they flash down and spin again and again at the bottom without a trace of anxiety. Calm and collected, true kings.

The night before we left we gave a small dinner party in our apartment. The head waitress brought us some frail dark hyacinths, the very first. Just enough for a glass and a few on the tablecloth. Philippe and I will never forget those small fresh sprigs.
We loved that apartment. It was at the top of the Astoria, floating in sun. Philippe slept in the study off the sitting room, surrounded with leather upholstered birchwood seats. My room had been done vaguely in the modern manner and resembled a girl's room in a reformatory. In the centre a small, but splendid, drawing room. I wished we could take this apartment every winter of our lives.
We walked for the last time to the Neva, invisible and covered in mists, then back by a small cut through the children's park. Children were playing in the half-light under the iced trees. I thought of the passage in *The Tale of Genji*, the little girls sweeping the snow with the tips of their long black hair as they ran about.
Travellers bring home regret, a nostalgic desire, more or less effective, to return. With Russia it is total infidelity. You wish to go there, and never to come home. And you don't know quite why, which is the worst sort of infidelity, the kind that does not bear self-examination.

The Hidden Force of Black African Art

BY H. E. LÉOPOLD SÉDAR SENGHOR,
President of the Republic of Senegal, and
a famous poet

EDITOR'S NOTE: *An architect of African independence and Africa's greatest French-language poet, Léopold Sédar Senghor is in his second term as President of the Republic of Senegal. As a poet, his work has been translated into seven languages, including Russian and Chinese. Here, Atheneum published his book of brilliantly cadenced poetry,* Selected Poems; *Praeger, his book* On African Socialism. *This excerpt is from the chapter, "L'Esthétique Négro-Africaine," in President Senghor's latest book,* Liberté I, Négritude et Humanisme, *published by Éditions Du Seuil in France.*

Literature and art are not separated from man's basic activities and notably not from work techniques in which theirs is the most efficacious rôle. One need only remember, in Camera Laye's *The Dark Child*, Laye's father as he hammers out a gold ornament. The prayer, or rather the poem, that he recites, the hymn of praise that the *griot* [the balladeer] sings as the goldsmith works the gold, the dance of the smith when his task is completed: It is all these—poem, song, dance —that over and beyond the actions of the craftsman accomplish the work and make it a masterpiece.

From this same perspective, all the arts are seen to be interconnected. Sculpture fully achieves its purpose only with the aid of the dance and the poem that is sung. Or consider the man who, behind the mask of Bélier, incarnates Nyamié, the Spirit Sun of the Baoulé. He dances the deeds of Bélier to the rhythms of the orchestra, while the singers chant the poem of the deeds of the Spirit.

This is an example of what may be called functional art. The masked dancer must identify himself with the Spirit-Sun-Bélier and, like the sacrificing priest, cause his force to flow over the spectators who participate in the drama.

This brings us to another characteristic of the poem. There are professionals in literature and art, of course. In Sudanese countries, the *griots* are simultaneously historians, poets, and storytellers. In Guinea and the Congo, the sculptors who are employed in the princely courts wear the mallet on the shoulder as a mark of honour. In all areas, the smith, the polytechnician of magic and art, according to a *Dogon* myth, was the first artist to use the rhythm of the tamtam to cause rain to fall from the sky. Existing side by side with these professionals, however, are the people, the anonymous crowd, who sing, dance, sculpt, and paint.

In Black Africa, a man's school is his initiation; as he leaves childhood, he assimilates, together with the skills of the tribe, the techniques of literature and art. The two examples given above indicate, on the other hand, that every art manifestation is collective—made for all with the participation of all.

Because they are functional and collective, Black African literature and art are engagé. They commit the persona—not merely the individual—through and to the community in the sense that they are existentializing techniques. They engage man in a future that will be present to him henceforth as an integrating part of his self. This is why, contrary to what has often been said, the Black African work of art is not a copy of an endlessly repeated arche-type. Specific objects exist, of course, each

The Astonishing Thrones of Bamileke

Unique, sacred, and treasured, the *Kuo Koko*, or state thrones, were the sensation of a great exhibition of African art in Paris. To see them was to marvel. The heritage of the Bamileke Chieftains, the tribal kings of the hardy highland people of the Northern Cameroons, these beaded, superbly ornamented figures are life-size. For this secret art, each craftsman guards his patrimonial patterns, passed on from generation to generation. Unless there is a royal reason, these jewelled rarities are seldom seen They are kept locked away in the Chieftainship Treasury with other beaded artifacts and brought out to dazzle only at Bamileke ritual festivals. Right, bearded in diamanté bangles, a head of a *trône perlé*.

Mysterious and mystical, double images stand imperiously on this throne, with, at its base, the royal insignia: a leopard, bare-fanged, open-clawed, ready to pounce.

IRVING PENN

of which expresses a life force. But what strikes one is the variety of execution, determined by personal temperament and circumstance.

The artisan-poet is rooted, and his work engages not only himself but *his* ethnicity, *his* history, *his* geography. He utilizes the materials he has at hand and the events that make up the web of his daily existence, but he rejects what is simply anecdotal, because the anecdotal is devoid of feeling and does not commit him. Whether painter or sculptor, when the opportunity is offered, he will use tools and materials imported from Europe; he does not hesitate to represent that great pride of the West, the machine; he will go so far as to dress this or that ancestral spirit in European style.

In the new African society, the storyteller will give money its rightful, primary place as the incarnation of Evil. But because the Black African artisan-poet is committed, unlike the European he is not worried about producing for all eternity. A work of art is perishable. The moment an earlier work passes from fashion or is destroyed, it is promptly replaced, and although spirit and style are preserved, it is updated. This is one way of saying that in Black Africa "art for art's sake" does not exist. All art is social.

However, Black African art and literature are not merely utilitarian, and one would mistake their essence by supposing that the Black lacks a sense of beauty. Quite the contrary. The truth is, the Black African assimilates beauty with goodness and especially with efficacity. The Wolof of Senegal is a case in point. The words *târ* and *rafet*, "beauty" and "beautiful," are applied preferably to human beings. For art works, the Wolof will use epithets such as *dyêka, yèm, mat*, which I would translate as "that is suitable," "that is proportioned," "that is perfect."

The beautiful mask, the beautiful poem, is the mask or poem that produces the desired emotion in the public—sorrow, joy, hilarity, terror. Significant in this regard is the word *baxai* (pronounced baa-kaa-ee), or "goodness," by which young dandies designate a pretty girl. Which is to say that for them beauty is "the promise of happiness." On the other hand, a good deed is often termed "beautiful."

The poem produces the right effect when it finds an echo in the mind and sensibility of its listeners. This is why the Peuls define a poem as "words pleasing to the heart and ear." But if both the Black African and the European concur that "the great rule is to please," the two do not find pleasure in the same things. In Black Africa, art is explication and knowledge of the world; that is, sensitive participation in the reality that subtends the universe—participation in surreality or, more exactly, in the life forces that animate the universe.

The European takes pleasure in recognizing the world through reproduction of the object—which he refers to as the subject. The Black African takes pleasure in knowing the world through image and rhythm. With the European, the thread of the senses leads to the heart and head; with the Black African, it leads to the heart and guts, to the very root of life. Bélier's mask pleases Baoulé spectators because it incarnates the Spirit Sun in a plastic, rhythmic language.

Image and rhythm—these are the two fundamental characteristics of Black African art.

First, image. We must, however clarify the nature and function of language to grasp the import of the Black African image. For us, the Word is the chief instrument of thought, feeling, and action. Speaking of a painting of white and red geometric forms that represented a concert of birds sitting on a tree at sunrise, the artist explained, "They're some wings, some songs; they are birds."

The most notable characteristic of Black African languages is richness of vocabulary. There are ten, sometimes twenty, words to denote an action depending on whether it is single or multiple, weak or intense, beginning or ending. Words are always pregnant with images; behind the sign value, the sense value always shows through.

Accordingly, the Black African image is a surrealist image. The object does not mean what it represents but what it suggests, what it creates. The Elephant is Force; the Spider, Prudence; horns are the Moon, and the Moon is fertility. Not only is the image-figuration a symbol but so is the material—the stone, earth, copper, gold, fibre—and so, even more, are line and colour. All language that does not fabulize bores the Black African.

African surrealism differs from European surrealism. The latter is empirical, the former mystical, metaphysical. The Negro analogy presupposes and makes manifest the hierarchized universe of life forces.

Potency of the image; potency of the Word. For example, in Dahomey, the Kings of the Fon tribe at every cardinal event of their reign used to devise rhythmic maxims, the chief words of which served as their new names. "The Pineapple laughs at the drought." Whereupon the word and the Pineapple would be despotically inscribed in wood, clay, gold, bronze, ivory, on the throne, the headdresses, the royal sceptre, the palace walls—everywhere—and made into image.

Take music, which is a tissue of images: In Black Africa, the primary rôle of music is not to be a concert, an enchantment for the ears, but to accompany a poem, or that dynamic sculpture which is the dance. Or take narrative—myth, legend, tale, fable, and even the proverb and riddle. The Black African narrative assumes the forms of the parabola, of the image in motion through time and space. Animal is rarely a totem: He is such and such a person, whom everyone in the village knows well—the tyrannical and stupid, or the wise and good King; the Young Man, redresser of wrongs; Kumba-the-little-Orphan.

The facts are images and they have instructive value. Hence the pace of the story, its progression by leaps and bounds, its material improbabilities, and the absence of psychological explanations.

What is rhythm? Rhythm is the vibratory shock, the force that, through the senses, seizes us at the very root of being. It is expressed by the most material, the most sensual means—lines, surfaces, colours; volume in architecture, sculpture, and painting; stress in poetry and music; movement in the dance. But it directs all this concreteness toward the light of the Spirit. If the Black African becomes incarnate in sensuality, to the same degree rhythm illustrates the Spirit for him. In the African dance, bodily contact is repugnant. But watch the dancers. The lower body is agitated by the most sensual tremors, but the head shares in the serene beauty of masks, of the Dead.

This, then, is the Black African for whom the world *is* by virtue of reflexive action. He does not state that he thinks; he senses that he senses, he senses his existence, he senses himself. Because he senses himself, he senses the Other, and because he senses the Other, he moves in the rhythm of the Other, toward the Other, to be reborn in him and in the world. Thus, the act of rebirth is a harmonious accord with the world, a simultaneous awareness and creation of the world in its indivisible unity. This élan of life force is what the religious and social life of the Black African expresses, for which literature and art are the most efficacious instruments. And the poet cries: "Aheeah! perfect circle of the world and concord therein."

TRANSLATED BY ADRIENNE FOULKE

George Segal

a new realist, is an artist with an eccentric
method of sculpture and the internal power to
impose his compelling vision on museums, collectors, and galleries that range from Brazil
to Sweden. These days, that impassioned, satis-
fying but curious reality that is not real has
been seen in Paris. Düsseldorf, Stockholm, the
Museum of Modern Art in New York, the Sid-
ney Janis Gallery, where this photograph was
taken, and at the factory of the Schweber Elec-
tronics company. His black room, with the word
Cinema in red lights and the plaster figure back-
lighted, has just been bought by the Albright-
Knox Art Gallery in Buffalo. (Segal's head
shows here at the entrance.) In fact, this room
is the realization of Segal's simple, reasonable,
and logical intentions. "I put figures and objects into a space, and then invite you to walk
within that space and encounter these figures in
many different relationships. The air between
the objects, its density, is just as much a part
of the whole as the solid objects." What is odd
is Segal's method. For "Cinema" he wrapped
a friend of his—a machinist—in cheesecloth
squares dipped in plaster of Paris, let the cheesecloth set, then removed the whole thing to
reassemble the fragments into a figure about an
eighth-of-an-inch larger than the machinist.
After a long bout with abstraction, which had
led him to a painting impasse, he took up
chicken farming in New Jersey and later taught
high-school students English and mechanical
drawing. A man of unconscious attractiveness,
light humour, and easy laughter, Segal at thirty-
nine has found a route to doing what he wants
with, in Melville's phrase, "pasteboard reality."

IRVING PENN

Isaac Bashevis Singer

perhaps the greatest living Yiddish writer, has become in the last few years recognized as one of the great living American writers—almost always in translation, done by Singer and a collaborator. A tall, bald man with a healthy pink scalp and skin, Singer has a slow, temperate voice, his English knowing, and his opinions definite. It was only in the early fifties, however, that anyone outside of the readers of the newspaper *Jewish Daily Forward* really cared about his opinions. Now he lectures to college students, gives amusing talks around the country, and writes for a variety of magazines. But all that Singer wants to do is to entertain with his tales. He does not believe in writings that are only symbolism. He does believe in the actuality of the supernatural. That double Singer stance has given him special influence lately among younger American writers. He is a storyteller who in the process of entertaining is at sixty-one famous but not rich. Instead, in his mild and charming way he is happy since his works have been translated into English, French, Russian, Hebrew, Finnish, Dutch, Italian, and Norwegian. Back in 1935, he left Warsaw where he was born to settle in New York with his brother, I. J. Singer, the famous author of *The Brothers Ashkenazi* and *Yoshe Kalb*. Here he continued writing his short stories set in small Polish villages before World War I. He would begin a story thus: "In the town of Lashnik, not far from Lublin, there lived a man and his wife." From there the tale would continue about someone who had been talked to so much that he got "water on the ear," or Singer would explain that a woman looked "as though the mouth had aged all by itself." Singer's people lived in a world of matter-of-fact fantasy, with demons, Hidden Powers, dybbuks, magic. Everyone in the villages lived remarkably rich lives, each traced with the supernatural, including the Jews with their Chassidic, joyous, wonder-working rabbis. A non-Chassidic rabbi in fact was Singer's father, the central figure in the new Singer book, *In My Father's Court*, an autobiography full of extraordinary stories that Farrar, Straus & Giroux will publish in May. At one point Singer stopped writing for five years as he felt there was no one to write *for*. Since that hiatus he has kept writing in "a mad way." The net of all his writings is a shelf of books—eight translated into English—in his New York apartment with so many short stories that he can not remember them all.

IRVING PENN

Eunice Kennedy Shriver, the Spark

*She causes action, flashes with brilliance,
and, like all sparks, sometimes hurts.*

BY POLLY DEVLIN

Eunice Kennedy Shriver's personality is so strong that it greets you before she does. Not an ounce or ray of this strength is wasted; she channels it so that all the activities of her life are fuelled and flamed with maximum efficiency.

As Executive Vice-President of the Joseph P. Kennedy, Jr., Foundation, set up by Joseph P. Kennedy, Sr., in 1946 as a memorial to his eldest son killed in the Second World War, and devoted to aiding and preventing mental retardation in children, Mrs. Shriver has helped change the present, the future, and the whole national atmosphere for retarded children. "Make no mistake about her rôle," said a doctor who has specialized in work with mental defectives independently and with the Kennedy Foundation. "She *is* the Kennedy Foundation."

Part of Mrs. Shriver's secret is that she can inspire others with her inspiration, infuse others with her enthusiasm, convert others with her faith. Not many people, though, can keep pace with her speed, and it is fortunate that her husband's energies match her own. Robert Sargent Shriver, Jr., formerly Director of the Peace Corps, now is Director of the Office of Economic Opportunity and Executive Director of the Kennedy Foundation.

Although the Kennedy Foundation takes up a taxing part of Mrs. Shriver's time and energy, she still manages to make short work of other full-time jobs. These include travelling throughout the United States and abroad explaining how retarded children can be helped and enlisting constructive aid from organizations and teachers; helping to organize an international conference on abortion so that experts can try to resolve some of the staggering difficulties which surround this subject; and, especially, campaigning for more recognition of motherhood as a profession. This seems a slight paradox until one meets her five children, ranging from two to thirteen years old. Handsome, glowing with the strong personalities of their parents, they are splendidly self-confident, quite terrifyingly good examples of how children ought to be.

Mrs. Shriver has also worked as a member of the National Advisory Child Health and Human Development Council, as a consultant to the President's Panel on Retardation, as a member of the Board of Governors of the Menninger Foundation, and as a social worker in a Federal penitentiary for women. She has a B.S. in Sociology from Stanford University. Her honorary degrees include Doctor of Letters, Doctor of Humane Letters, and Doctor of Laws, the first from the University of Santa Clara, in California; the second from both Manhattanville College of the Sacred Heart, Purchase, New York, and D'Youville College, Buffalo, New York; the last from Regis College, Weston, Massachusetts.

In November, 1966, when Mrs. Shriver was presented with The Albert Lasker Public Service Award in Health, the citation emphasized that it was as the result of *her* urging and efforts that the Congress in 1963 enacted two monumental pieces of legislation aimed to correct decades of neglect of the retarded and to provide funds to help them in the future. The award was presented in recognition of Mrs. Shriver's "leadership in encouragement of national legislation against retardation and the

new hope she has brought to the blighted lives of millions."

A friend said of her: "I've never seen anyone like her for getting things done. She goes to the heart of the matter, cutting through obscure issues instantly. Whatever she does, she does wholeheartedly, bearing down on any particular goal with a keen curiosity and fearful energy. One can hear her dynamo humming. She doesn't keep energies in reserve, or switch from a private to a public life; she maintains the same energy and manner all the time. But when she relaxes, she *is* relaxed, without nerviness, without bother. She knows how to rest. Lord knows where the energy comes from—that Shriver house hums with it, perhaps because everyone there goes to bed so early. Certainly not many people have seen the Shrivers on foot after half past ten. If you go to a party in their house, you leave early, else they'll be halfway up the stairs."

Another friend said: "She has an infallible sense of knowing who will be *the* asset in getting some project done, who will need the coaxing, who the pushing. It doesn't *look* like manipulation the way she controls people—but that's what makes her such a good politician—which she is—shrewd, tough, ready, and committed."

This formidable feminine powerhouse, so daunting in description, turns out to be a marvellously boned, high-cheeked, slender woman with the appearance and movements of someone whose habitat is the open air, who looks too big in any room, for then her limbs look trammelled. She has a lean and free-moving body with the smoothness and unity usually seen only in professional athletes, and although she is forty-eight, one can see immediately why everyone in describing her always uses the word "girl." She is the third Kennedy "girl," and her whole look is so much an amalgamation of the famed physical characteristics of all the Kennedys that one's view of her vigour and determination, her springing hair and gleaming teeth, her hopeful voice concerts exactly with one's views and idea of the whole Kennedy clan.

Indeed, watching, Mrs. Shriver pace up and down in the middle of a large lawn, head down, talking quickly, emphatically, saying, "*Now, this is what I think important,*" and each time turning on the tenth pace as though confined by walls or a hearthrug, is like watching an actor overact a Kennedy. But although this energy radiates and pulsates around her, she comes across as a gentle woman.

What no actor could imitate is the famous, flashing, direct look; in her, this regard is rare, relentless, and startling, using the full power behind the eyes, a look both intimate and defensive. But it *is* rare and generally she simply glances, missing nothing.

Because Mrs. Shriver can be extremely abrupt, some people are wary of her, and there are many whom she has disconcerted once too often with her frankness. "Not only does she not suffer fools gladly," said an acquaintance ruefully, "she doesn't suffer one's odd foolish lapse either, perhaps because she lives up to her own high standards. She might be more sympathetic and more tolerable were she less of her own paragon and more tolerant."

She watches her children with an abstract attentiveness. For example, Anthony, who is two and blond, climbed onto the slippery rungs of the swimming-pool ladder—a pool full of dark six-foot depths and autumn leaves. He was warned of the hazards involved and then left to get on with it. Whether or not he came to minor grief was his choice; although she would be there to rescue him.

The Shriver house, large, congenial, comfortable, in Maryland, near Washington, overlooking rolling white-fenced country, has rooms full of noise and light and children; people come and go all the time; doors are always open. Mrs. Shriver deals with the major part of her work from her office here, usually in the afternoon when the younger children are asleep, and once a week goes into the Foundation's office in Washington where a staff of eight deals with the work. Her own secretary works in the Foundation office part of the time.

It is a magnificent measure of Mrs. Shriver's achievement and of the success of the Kennedy Foundation that in December, 1967, she went to the White House to witness the signing of the Mental Retardation Amendments. These amendments to Federal law appropriated a total of 243 million dollars over the next three years for projects that benefit the retarded, including the construction of professional training facilities at universities, the construction of schools and service facilities by communities, the training of teachers and the staffing of these facilities, with ten million dollars specifically earmarked for use in a physical fitness and recreation program. This last amendment was proposed by Senator Edward Kennedy and through his work was adopted by Congress.

A few years earlier, Mrs. Shriver, with the backing of the Foundation, encouraged President Kennedy and Congress to initiate the National Institute of Child Health and Human Development and to serve on its advisory council; and it was on her suggestion that President Kennedy appointed a panel on mental retardation to study the plight of the retarded and make a set of recommendations to help them live normal lives. (Senator Robert Kennedy once said that President Kennedy fought so hard for these bills in order to get his sister Eunice off his back; now the same might be said of Ted.)

The Kennedy family first got involved with the problems of mental retardation when, looking for an enlightened and congenial home for Rosemary Kennedy who is mentally retarded, they saw the appalling conditions in most state institutions. Save for a few dedicated doctors, some privately run institutions, and Connecticut's Southbury Training School (established in 1940, where patients live in cottages and carry on productive lives), little was being done to make the lives of the retarded even bearable, never mind happy.

Mrs. Shriver has described one of these mediavel prisons thus: "I remember mostly the smell—the overpowering smell of lye squirted from hoses to flush down the concrete floors. I remember the mentally retarded patients with nothing to do—standing, staring, grotesque . . . like misshapen statues." When Joseph Kennedy, Sr., established his Foundation, he could discover no private foundations devoting funds to research in this field and only a small amount of Federal money was allotted to aid the retarded; indeed mental retardation was not recognized as a national problem. In fact, there are over five million retarded Americans, and by 1970 the number is expected to reach six million.

For some time Joseph Kennedy, Sr., directed the Foundation from his office; but as the Foundation developed, as the proportions of the problem grew more apparent, the Foundation set up in its own offices and the Shrivers took over.

Mrs. Shriver said: "We worked right from the beginning in the belief that *care* was the essential thing. From the moment we started, we got hundreds of letters every week from mothers asking could we help them, could we take their children in. We were making only the smallest dent in the problem and we decided that we must help research prevent the problem."

Initially the Kennedy Foundation helped build and support homes and schools for retarded children, but after the building of the 125-bed Joseph P. Kennedy, Jr., Children's Memorial Hospital for pediatric rehabilitation in Massachusetts and under Mrs. Shriver's guidance, the Foundation moved into another phase, which culminated in its helping to establish the Kennedy Child Study Center in New York and the Kennedy Institute in Washington, D. C.

"One of the things nearest Mrs. Shriver's heart," said a colleague, "is physical training for the retarded. She really works hard at that."

"For years," said Mrs. Shriver, "mentally retarded children were left out of games all over the country. They were in very bad physical shape. It's understandable—games are so competitive and they aren't good enough at catching or they get muddled and then people become impatient and tell them to sit out and watch. But games are so good for them and are among the things that they can revel in, that they can find rewards in. So we launched this fitness campaign with medals and goals and projects and we aim to make champions of them."

Mrs. Shriver practises what she preaches. She wanted retarded children to enjoy the pleasure and activities of summer camp; there weren't any, so she opened up her own house; and now every year forty or more children come for three weeks to the Shriver summer day camp, supervised by twenty or thirty voluntary workers. Her own children join in, and it's all a great success. Last year the day-camp basketball team won nine out of ten games played against local teams.

"I think the most important thing that has happened," Mrs. Shriver said, "is that there is a whole new atmosphere of hope now; people are beginning to recognize that eighty-five per cent of retarded children can make a contribution to society. They don't have to be passive or helpless. They can be a productive part of any family. The next marvellous thing would be if retarded children could get as much and as many of life's essentials and attentions as normal children do. They certainly need them at least as much, crave them more. Who's to say that only normal children shall have these things and no one else."

Mrs. Shriver discards any suggestion that she should have a sense of achievement, shakes herself loose of praise as though she were being trapped into staying still.

"I don't think what I do is at all unusual," she said. "The time has gone for that. All the women I know in Washington, whose husbands are busy, work very hard—I think particularly of Mrs. Katzenbach and Mrs. McNamara. *Now* is the greatest time to be a woman, when we are doing more for others and doing it more effectively than ever before. And not just middleclass professional women—poor women, too, are finally having a say in their local community's affairs, are sitting on committees and saying: 'We'll tell you what we want and need.'

"But what does concern me terribly is the enormous responsibility women have towards children; in some states the monthly mainte-nance for a mother and child is fifty dollars. So she has to go out and earn enough money to support her child in a nursery while she works —situations like this are so crazy, so widespread, and so hard to change; and not just at Government level—at all levels.

"I've been trying for years to get schools to give credits in child development and care. They even give credits in driving—and think how infinitely more important and intellectually stimulating pediatrics and child care is; but schools simply will not do it.

"I think it's fine to build new buildings for research, but I would like to see existing environments improved and more practical knowledge applied. There are still so many things to be done; there is a huge neglect of pregnant mothers in cities. Some forty thousand women in one Eastern city had their babies last year without *any* pre- or post-natal care.

"There are passive mothers who will not take their children for the Salk vaccine nor to the hospital for jaundice. Measles can cause retardation in children if contracted at a certain age under certain conditions. We *must* prevent children's getting them. There are so many things to do and getting that 243 million dollars, far from meaning we can stop, means that only now can we really start rolling."

Arthur Schlesinger, Jr., said of Mrs. Shriver: "She is a wonderful girl. Whoever she was, she could never be satisfied simply being a wife and a mother. She quickens things, she galvanizes people. How could that energy be latent?"

David Smith:
A Major American Sculptor

BY ROBERT MOTHERWELL

"I hope you can interpret—try . . . you know me and how I speak—add it up and guess when in doubt." David Smith, the great contemporary American sculptor, wrote that to an English critic in a letter. Smith is referring to his handwriting, which, in fact, is clear enough. And so is his sculpture, based as it is on the Cubist collage, with welding replacing glue, with three dimensions functioning instead of two, with an aesthetic weight and largeness of scale that Parisian Cubists never dreamed of. That in turn makes Smith not only the sculptor most related to our native Abstract Expressionism, but a major American sculptor of international esteem and influence.

I have known him for many years, ever since that afternoon that we met by prearrangement (but unknown to each other) early in 1950. We instinctively tried to drink each other under the table on Irish whiskey and Guinness stout. We left each other late at night, wobbly but walking. In those days I was full of French Symbolist aesthetics, of Rimbaud and Mallarmé, and of André Breton, of the possibilities of representing reality indirectly but passionately in one's medium. I still can see David saying, with his characteristic bluntness and inalterable sense of his own identity, "I don't know about those guys, I don't read French, but I don't need them. I've read James Joyce!" He was

right, all of it *is* in *Ulysses*, and I looked at him with a sudden intellectual respect that has not diminished as my affection for him has continually grown.

When, as a young American sculptor in the 1930's, David added Picasso to Joyce for his points of reference, when he was possessed of a continual fascination with the ancient sculpture of the Near East, and, when from economic necessity, during the Depression, he learned the welding of iron in locomotive and automotive works, he had as economical, relevant, and adequate background for making an essential contribution to modern art—with its proper obsession with the nature of the medium—as could be imagined. That background has served him well. When you see his burly figure in workman's clothes, you sense a cultivated man who knows his ancient and modern art intimately, including all the most recent developments. When you see him in Irish tweeds and with Monte Cristo cigars these past years, you are aware still of a man who spends most of his days cutting and welding hunks of steel often far too heavy for a single man to lift, driving his professional helpers as hard as himself, knowing that the workings of the greatest national economy the world has ever known are inadequate, not only to absorb his prodigious amount of work, but even to exhibit much of it.

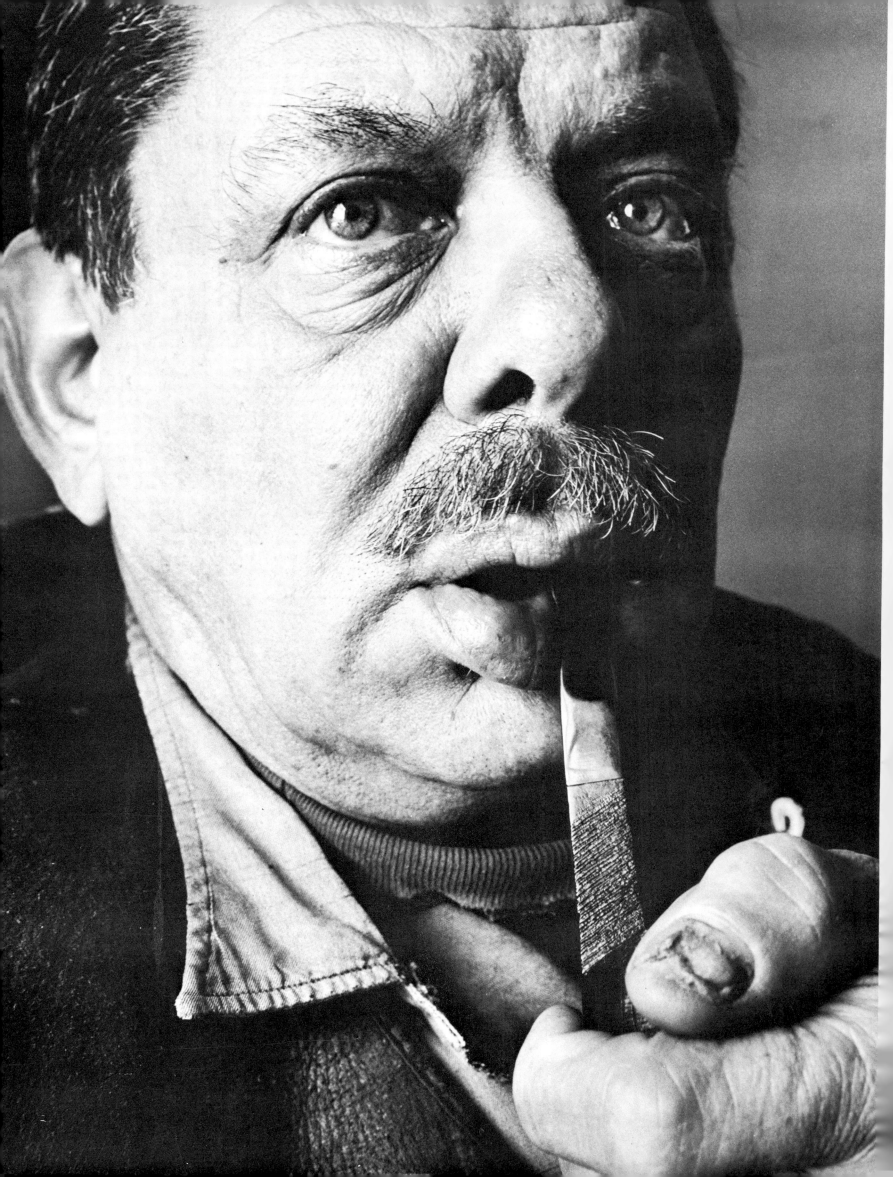

Some of his recent great iron "wagons" on wheels are too large and heavy even to be moved unless there were a fantastic private railroad spur to the Adirondack mountain place where he lives and works.

(He bought hundreds of acres in the mountains there for a few dollars during the Depression. He himself built the studio-house out of concrete blocks and iron, to which in recent years he has added further factory-like studios.)

It is not an especially comfortable place, especially for women, but on its grounds, like sentinels, stands the greatest permanent one-man show of heroic contemporary sculpture in the Americas. A folk song runs: "It takes a worried man to sing a worried song." Well, it takes an iron will to have made all those weighty iron sculptures strewn about his mountain landscape, each silhouetted against an enormous sky.

Typically, his bitterness about his years of struggle during the Depression and the 1940's is mainly about his inability to afford then to make as monumental sculpture as he can now.

Lately he has been buying up ancient tractors with gigantic steel wheels, and even an enormous old road grader. He wants to incorporate them into sculpture, sculpture so tremendous that this industrial machinery will have no larger rôle in the whole sculptures than the clockworks have in a grandfather clock, or the elevator in an elevator shaft.

He is originally a Hoosier from Indiana, and a streak of Paul Bunyan lives on. But this is only part of a more generalized American trait, that, given world enough and time, anything is possible. In his case, he has made a quantity of great sculpture of a size never realized by an individual before nor of such weight—immobilized by weight, even when mounted on bronze wheels.

Or, speaking of quantity, consider his involvement in the Spoleto Festival in Italy, organized by Gian Carlo Menotti.

In the spring of 1962, David Smith, along with such celebrated sculptors as Alexander Calder and Henry Moore, was invited to go to Italy. (No doubt to save transportation costs—it is cheaper to move a man than a monument.) The sculptors were to make a monumental steel sculpture or two to be shown at the Festival. "Having neither job nor love to hold me here—went to Genoa. . . . Given everything I asked for

—residence 'Colombia-Excelsior'—interpreter—chauffeur—six workmen—chose abandoned factories at Voltri to work," said Smith.

At first Smith was overcome by his reception. By enough help for the first time, by being allowed to use any of the vast numbers of steel parts left in the abandoned factories by "Italsider," the Italian National Steel Trust, which supplied his help.

He had the fire in the forge started. In four weeks he made twenty-six monumental sculptures from six to twenty feet high. Smith said later: "Worked twelve hours a day seven days a week—not knowing Italian, I had not known I had been asked to make one to two pieces—'Italsider' let me roam all the factories—pick out whatever I wanted—let me work without interruption—I still do not understand how this confidence and generosity generated. I was never bothered with officials, questions, teas, social affairs, or checkups—somehow word was extended that I had privileges—I have never made so much—so good, so easy, in such a condensed time as in my thirty-day Italian phase—that was damn near a piece a day."

Part of David Smith's productivity certainly had to do with his beautiful relationship with the workers who, as we all learn, are apt to treat abstract art with diffidence or ridicule. Every abstract painter knows, from the way they handle his work, that moving men are unconsciously art critics, and not very discerning ones.

David Smith has said: "I felt in full ease with the workmen despite different language—I learned some Italian (Berlitz)—they some English—I am as much factory as professor, having worked in auto and locomotive factories in U. S. for a living roughly equal to teaching time—I enjoyed the confidence of the workmen—they brought in the [food] specialities of Voltri and home cuisine for our 3:00 P.M. wine break—mussels, snails, birds, fungi—we ate together, exchanged confidences—differences. I think we were all a little sad that it ended."

The twenty-six sculptures were sent from Voltri to Spoleto by train. David had wanted to make one of the sculptures out of an abandoned flatcar, but it was too ancient to travel the tracks. Four sculptures were mounted in the town, the others in the old Roman amphitheatre. Smith who gave one to Spoleto on behalf of "Italsider," told me: "The mayor said he

IRVING PENN

David Smith, a noble and hard-working artist of tremendous appetites and stamina, in welding clothes. He produces much more sculpture than is physically and economically possible to exhibit: "because I have to."

Landscape with four raw iron sculptures by David Smith based on the theme of the circle. They rest on his grounds at Bolton Landing on Lake George, New York. These sculptures, done in 1962-3, are in a state of "preliminary painting" after months of contemplation and changes in their colour, done with auto paint. Smith hopes to arrive at exactitude of colour for each sculpture, perhaps by the summer of 1965, after several years of aesthetic "seasoning." Smith (far left) is shown sketching the circle pieces with an eye to colour changes.

liked it and all seemed acceptable when I left in late June—Professor Carandente installed it so well it looked as if it belonged."

In reflecting on his Italian experience, David said: "Perhaps it was the climate—locale—at least it seems to me that my Italian work took on a different feeling than my U.S.A. work ever had—yet it was natural and without intention. . . . Certain things are not possible here—there is no affinity of the government or industry for my work (other artists as well)."

From his mountain fastness at Bolton Landing, Smith makes periodic forays to New York City, often staying with my wife and me ("I miss a household"); often at the Plaza Hotel ("I like the comforts of the Plaza, I have none at home: often dinner burns while I read or work or drink or dream"). While here, he invariably spends at least one night at a jazz joint, The Five Spot, and visits the museums, bookshops, record shops, and Dunhill's for his cigars.

At other times, when loneliness gets him, he crosses the state line from Bolton Landing over to Vermont to visit the painter, Kenneth Noland, who lives near Bennington, where Smith has taught, and where Anthony Caro, a superb young English sculptor, now teaches. Smith and Noland drink whiskey and play chess.

On the way home, Smith stops at junkyards looking for old farm machinery or anything metal that will fit his "Agricola" concepts, a series of machine sculptures that began exactly twenty years ago.

For some years now during daylight hours, David Smith works on four separate streams of sculptural concepts simultaneously—painted pieces in which colour is of major importance, stainless steel structures, a series of iron "wagons" with bronze wheels, and heavy, welded structures of raw iron. At night, he continues an endless series of drawings ("the delicate pursuit of my life"). These are often nudes from life.

Oh David! You are as delicate as Vivaldi, and as strong as a Mack truck.

One of the few great meals I have had outside France was at David's last spring: fresh lettuce with red edges from his garden, a pink leg of lamb roasted in a marinade of ginger, soy sauce, and Madeira, fresh black bread, sweet butter, and bottles of 1953 Pommard. We mourn the passing of Henri Soulé's The Côte Basque in New York City, but David's real love is Boston's Locke-Ober.

The other day in my kitchen in New York we were talking. He became as eloquent as Homer: "I like to eat, I like to see people eat, I don't like the presence of women in restaurants, they pick, and where they are, the portions are smaller. . . . Of any place outside Italy, I like Locke-Ober's Men's Bar best. Hunger is a masculine experience. I have eaten during the Depression twenty-five-cent meat loaf with free salad and rolls, and with gin and a small beer chaser (ten cents). I've made my sculpture that way too, before love or food. Only my small daughters have priority over anything.

"Locke-Ober's! Lobster bisque, baked oysters. Broiled bay scallops with bacon—to hell with greens! You stick a quarter of lemon under the scallop serving pan to give out odour. Black bread with frosty edges. Sweet butter. Things I don't get in the mountains. Hot Indian Pudding with vanilla ice cream melting in the centre. And true chicken broth, great before fried soft-shell crabs, both preceded by icy dry Martinis. Better than France!"

Maybe. But what matter? A man expresses himself, his personal taste. His sculpture is universal.

Autumn 1964

Has Anyone
Found the Beast in Us?

BY JULES HENRY

EDITOR'S NOTE: *Professor of sociology and anthropology at Washington University in St. Louis, Missouri, Dr. Jules Henry is, he said, "a people-watcher." After receiving his Doctor of Philosophy degree at Columbia University, he went first, in 1933, to people-watch the Kaingáng Indians, living with them, learning their language, and writing about them the book* Jungle People. *Later he and his wife lived with the Pilagá Indians near the border of Argentina and Paraguay studying relations between parents and children. Children are often the people Dr. Henry watches. On a grant from the United States Office of Education he is studying "the natural history of the deprived Negro child. We want to find out, as exactly as we can, why some of these kids make it and some do not." His newest book,* Pathways to Madness, *to be published this autumn by Random House, is a study of families with psychotic children. Whomever he is watching, Dr. Henry works in "human ethology—though, of course, we do not deal with innate but rather with learned traits."*

Outside the big glass door of our kitchen-dining room, high on the side of a steep hill in Portola Valley, California, was the patio-dining room of the animals that came to eat what my wife and I put out there. As we ate breakfast or lunch, we watched the birds and squirrels. We saw that some birds would come only when the coast was clear; that some would take only tiny crumbs, while others would eat only big ones. We became angry with the squirrels, because they were so timid that the jays would take all the peanuts while the squirrels were getting up enough courage to come down off the trees. Even though

we were but a short time in California, we became like Californians in detesting jays, because the birds were so "aggressive" and "greedy."

One night, during a party, when the company was gay from pre-dinner Martinis and a *garrafa* of wonderful Spanish wine, a single raccoon appeared inexplicably out of the night and regarded us from within the circle of light that fell on her from the dining room-kitchen. Immediately we lost interest in one another and rushed about to feed "Racky." The handiest food was the Malayan chicken (chicken seared in olive oil, plus orange juice, ripe olives, water chestnuts, et cetera) my wife had prepared; and we gave that to "Racky" and, in silence, watched the animal eat it and come back for more. Ever after that, until we left, Racky returned to be fed every night between ten and eleven. It was so moving to see her appear quietly out of the darkness and approach us, in simple trust. It was moving to feed her (we think she was pregnant and *very* hungry) and have her come so close—almost into the house. We discovered that Racky would eat practically anything: mostaccioli, cottage cheese, supermarket rolls (ugh!)—anything. She drank milk and water, and when she finished she would vanish.

From such simple beginnings—man's primordial feeling of closeness to animals, his fascination with their habits and their mystery, and his inherent tendency to attribute his own emotions to them—has grown the branch of zoology called ethology. Ethologists are not men and women who watch occasionally from inside their breakfast rooms but are scientists who usually spend years studying the same animal (bird, fish, insect, mammal), first in the wild state and then often in the laboratory. Ethologists are primarily interested in discovering the innate—the inborn—social-behaviour patterns of animals: The more the behaviour of the animal seems determined by intelligence and experience rather than by what is inborn, the less attention ethologists have given the animal. Hence study of the gibbon, orangutan, gorilla, and chimpanzee—the animals closest to man in physique and intelligence—has been left largely to anthropologists and comparative psychologists.

Two of the most distinguished names in ethology are Niko Tinbergen and Konrad Lorenz. In "Der Kumpan in der Umwelt des Vogels" ("the companion in the birds' world"), published in 1935, Lorenz described "imprinting," a phenomenon it took the scientific world just about twenty-five years to examine and understand. Lorenz discovered that if one presents a bird with almost any moving object at all shortly after birth—before it has had contact with one of its own species, it will follow that object all its life. This discovery raised the important question of the "critical period" when any animal learns best and indelibly. Tinbergen has been less spectacular and is less known, but his work in ethology is fundamental and gripping. Here is something on courting among herring gulls from his *Social Behaviour in Animals:*

> In spring the flock visits the breeding grounds in the sand dunes together. When they settle, after having circled in the air above for some time, they segregate into pairs, which settle on territories within the colony's range. Not all birds are paired, however; many gather in so-called "clubs." Long and consistent study of marked individuals has proved that new pairs form in these clubs. The female takes the initiative in pair formation. An unmated female approaches a male in a peculiar attitude. She withdraws her neck, points her bill forward and slightly upward; and, adopting a horizontal attitude, she walks slowly round the male of her choice.

There is an equally meticulous description of what the male does and of the final mating.

Superficial similarities between animal and human behaviour have led many who should know better, including the great Lorenz himself, to draw parallels between animal and human behaviour. One of the numerous objections to drawing a parallel between herring-gull and human flirtation is that in the herring gull the behaviour pattern is largely innate, whereas in man it is culturally determined. One may see something like the herring-gull manoeuvre at a cocktail party in our culture but not in a Kaingáng Indian or Pilagá Indian village; one may see it in a middle- or upper-class living room but not in an igloo. Herring gulls have no choice; man has a million—and has made them all.

There is scarcely an issue of *Science*, organ of the American Association for the Advancement of Science, that does not contain at least one article on ethology. Consider just the following:

> "Defensive Use of a 'Fecal Shield' by a Beetle Larva:" by T. Eisner, E. van Tassell, J. E. Carrel. December 15, 1967. Abstract:

> "The larva of *Cassida rubiginosa* carries a tight packet of cast skins and feces on a fork held over its back. The packet is a manoeuvrable shield used by the larva to protect itself against attack. It is highly effective in blocking the bite of ants."

> "The Accessory Burrows of Digger Wasps:" by H. E. Evans. April 22, 1966. This major paper is "a condensation of material to be included in Dr. Evans's forthcoming book, *The Comparative Ethology and Evolution of the Sand Wasps.*" The first sentence of the article reads, "Students of solitary wasps have long been intrigued by the varied and elaborate behaviour patterns associated with nest closure and concealment."

In the same issue of *Science* there is an article about research on the speed of porpoises, financed by the Navy, and one on courtship among spiders, funded in part by the National Science Foundation.

Thus ethology is a major field of study in zoology, and even students of solitary wasps, it would appear, are not alone. It will be remembered that the late Alfred Kinsey was a student of wasps before he started to study human sexual behaviour.

With few exceptions, ethologists have been happy to concentrate on lower animals, fascinated by their mystery or concerned to fit animal behaviour into an evolutionary scheme. But

Konrad Lorenz has not been satisfied to love his greylag geese, his jackdaws, and his ducks: He wants ethology to mean something in human affairs; he is in agony over the condition of man, and he thinks—he hopes—that ethology has suggestions of what to do about man's "aggression" against man—about human killing and cruelty. To this subject he has devoted his book *On Aggression*. It was published in 1963, when, having lived through two world wars and seen his Germany first create a holocaust and then go down in rubble and flames, and when, in the shadow of the bomb and the impending tragedy in Viet Nam, he began to feel that perhaps there was no hope for survival at all. He looked to ethology for a solution. Lorenz is a suffering man who wants to save *mankind*.

Starting with a lovely word picture of the Florida keys, as he swims among the fishes and the flora in the warm water, Lorenz takes us through a stunning array of animal life, from fishes to mammals, showing us, above all, how intraspecies aggression is controlled just at the killing point in the animal world. That is the main thrust of this fascinating book. With species after species he shows that in lower animals aggression within the same species usually eventuates in bluff and no animal is hurt. A marvellous and intricate section on the greylag goose shows how what was originally a "triumph ceremony," in which a triumphant goose displayed its "pride" over a defeated rival, became transformed, in the course of evolution, into a "family ritual" so that each greylag goose family—father, mother, and children—now identifies its members by their own private family ritual. It is not territory that unites these wondrous birds, but a common sharing of the symbol.

Why can not man invent mere bluffs and rituals that will divert aggression and proclaim solidarity with his fellow men? Why is *Homo sapiens* the only species that pursues intraspecific aggression to the death? This is Lorenz's question; and he has no convincing answer. He urges that men should develop rituals that will sidetrack and sublimate killing. He thinks, for example, that sport is a good way of draining off aggression and, on an international scale, could be used as a substitute for killing.

A striking fact about Lorenz's proposals is that some are well-known at the tribal level.

For example, among my friends the Pilagá Indians of Argentina, with whom my wife and I lived for a year, hockey (a game invented by South American Indians) is played as mock warfare between antagonistic villages. The men dress up in war paint and panoplies, play for high stakes, and, in the course of the game, treat one another so savagely that the women and children act as medics, ministering to the kicked and the bashed. No one is ever seriously injured, however. In other tribes, ritual spear throwing is a way of working off tensions between members of different villages. Sometimes someone is wounded, but the ritual is to dodge the spears. On the other hand, however, serious inter- and even intratribal wars are common in some parts of the primitive world. Before the colonization of South America, a common, perhaps the most usual, warfare was between different segments of the same tribe. (See my *Jungle People*, Random House, 1965.) Hans Staden, a German seaman, captured by the Tupí Indians of Brazil in about 1552, wrote a rare book containing cannibal recipes. They are based on Tupí Indians' eating of other Tupís.

Human beings have tried Lorenz's formula from time to time; but in the contemporary world, with so much wealth and power at stake, ritualized aggression is a feather against the walls of Hell. Meanwhile, I respect Lorenz for his suffering and for the sincerity of his anguish.

Matters are different with Robert Ardrey, another person who has looked to ethology for answers to human problems. His book *The Territorial Imperative* is free-enterprise, private-property ideology "based on" the findings of ethology, though he is not an ethologist himself. He says he had some training as an anthropologist—though it surely was very long ago and it did not stick; and he has written plays and at least one other book. Ardrey believes that, as an absolute instinctual imperative, everybody has to have private property ("territory"); and he uses the findings of ethology to "prove" it.

In sociological thought, an ideology is a system of notions that grows up to bolster a predetermined position. If I am a communist, I will have an unshakeable system of ideas in which I believe heart and soul, no matter how many holes one can punch in it; if I am a free-enterpriser, I will have an opposite set of ideas, equally "impregnable," equally inaccessible to reason. Ardrey uses the biological fact that many species of animals appropriate, inhibit, and defend fixed territories to support his private-property ideology. He is thus a very different animal from Lorenz, and his goals are different. Lorenz weeps for all violent death. Ardrey says he is in favour of what the United States is doing in Viet Nam, but that we are bound to lose, because we are violating the primaeval biological reality of Viet Nam by invading Vietnamese territory. Soviet agriculture has been a "catastrophe," says Ardrey, because it is communized and the individual farm has been abolished. The Republic of South Africa is bound to grow more and more powerful as long as we keep insulting their right to lead their own lives in their own way, on their own territory. "The principal cause of modern warfare," he says, "arises from the failure of an intruding power correctly to estimate the defensive resources of a territorial defender."

Thus, arguing from the fact that numerous animals—deer, robins, many fish, monkeys, lemurs, et cetera—are innately territorial, Ardrey concludes that the ownership and defense of "property" is instinctive in all animals, humans included, and that we violate this instinct at our peril.

What does he do when he comes to the gorilla and the chimpanzee, the animals closest to us in physique and intelligence, and discovers that they have and defend no territory, *i.e.*, are not "territorial"? Why, he says, these animals, whom he absolutely detests, are "evolutionary failures" and are becoming extinct. The reason they may be on their way to extinction, however, I would point out, has nothing to do with their lack of innate "territoriality" but rather with their being hunted and trapped by men for food and for sale to zoos and to experimental laboratories, and with the encroachment of man on their feeding grounds.

Let me quote from an article by Raymond A. Dart, the great palaeoanthropologist in *Current Anthropology*, July, 1960, entitled "Can the Mountain Gorillas Be Saved?" Professor Dart is one of Ardrey's heroes. In the article Dart pleads for the gorilla and appends a letter from the Institut des Parcs Nationaux du Congo Belge to UNESCO and a report by Professor George B. Schaller of the University of Wiscon-

sin, a distinguished student of primate behaviour. I give some relevant passages from Professor Schaller:

> The gorilla sanctuary is situated partly in the Congo and partly in Ruanda-Urundi. Unfortunately, in Ruanda a cult of cattle is practised, introduced by the Watutsi. . . . The social importance of the proprietor [of the cattle] is dependent upon the number of heads of cattle he possesses; further, no beasts are sacrificed for . . . food. This fruitless pasturage has led to a total disappearance of wooded vegetation . . . [and] induced the herdsmen to thrust their herds into the forests of the Parc National Albert. . . . Today, after twenty-five years of protective efforts, the mountain gorillas in their sanctuary are threatened with irremediable destruction. . . .
>
> Habitat destruction is the greatest danger facing gorillas in the Virunga volcanoes.

A book Ardrey is fond of quoting is *Primate Behavior*, edited by Irven DeVore and published by Holt, Rinehart and Winston in 1965. Yet, Ardrey has overlooked passages in that book that would challenge his thesis that the gorilla is becoming extinct because it is not territorial. For example:

> p. 327: Populations of gorillas probably drift or are pushed about as local conditions change. The most important disturbance to the region during the past 200 or more years has been the repeated clearing of the forest for cultivation. . . .
> p. 334: Some Bantu tribes persistently snare, spear, shoot, or net gorillas for food and to protect their crops, making man the only major predator on the apes.
> p. 335: Gorilla groups varied in size from 2 to about 30 animals.
> C. Cordier, an animal dealer, has trapped or seen groups of 4, 13, 14, 15, 19, and 25 animals in the lowland rain forests near Utu.
> p. 336: It is possible that in the absence of predation by man such factors as availability and type of forage influence the size of groups.

Similar considerations apply to the chimpanzee.

But it is all so absurd . . . everyone knows that nearly *all* wild animals are becoming extinct in Africa and that the Negro may be on his way out, too: the breakdown of tribal culture, starvation, disease, intertribal warfare, exploitation by whites, including the massing of Negroes in immense concentration camps . . . all are hastening the disappearance of this great race. What we shall have left eventually in Africa is a race of steely-eyed whites, gripping their rifles and surrounded by a devastation they call "civilization" . . . supported, perhaps, by "foreign aid."

CONCLUSIONS AND REFLECTIONS

Since the Middle Ages and before, men have developed biologically based ideologies—blind prejudices—to "explain" and support things as they are. In the Middle Ages the preferred biological model was the human body—the king or the pope was the head; and the limbs, et cetera, were servants carrying out the wishes of the sovereign. Hence, like the body, the state of things on earth was necessarily well-ordered. We find similar bio-metaphysical nonsense even in modern times. Walter B. Cannon's theory of homeostasis (*The Wisdom of the Body*), in which society is compared to the self-regulating human body, is a distant relative of mediaeval thought.

Nowadays, meanwhile, the type of image we use to express society is beginning to change a bit. Pareto, an Italian economist and sociologist, took the capitalist economic system as the model of society in equilibrium; and Talcott Parsons, a Harvard sociology pundit, compares the workings of society to Newtonian mechanics. As our culture has been swept by one great idea after the other, there have always been "men of talent" who happily pin themselves to the coattails of the idea in order to ride to glory. Ardrey is merely one of the latest

in the group. Let us remember that what we read in such writings is nothing but ideology— the unconscious grammar of a self-justifying, status-interested group.

Konrad Lorenz, however, is quite another matter. Much as I sympathize with him, I understand that he is one among the many romantics who, looking now at the "primitive," now at animals, imagine they perceive the ideal of man in a return to some previous state of gentle innocence. Tacitus, Rousseau, Paul Goodman also belong here. These men hunger for what never was and for what can never be. It is a sweet-sad dreaming we do sometimes as we sit in our studies drinking the last wine of man's brief tenure. Nearly two thousand years ago Tacitus, reflecting in the *Annals* on the horror of the reign of Tiberius, imagined a primitive state when man was no Roman, but honest and gentle.

> Primitive man had no evil desires. Being blameless and innocent, his life was free of compulsions and penalties. He also needed no rewards; for he was naturally good. Likewise, where no wrong desires existed, fear imposed no prohibitions.

Paul Goodman seems to think that all this will come true in the simple, philosophic anarchy of the small community. Lorenz sees it in his beloved greylag goose.

So, in conclusion, my friends, let us drink a cup for the romantics, and scatter a little wine on the grass for them, for those who sorrow now, and for those who died in their sorrow; and let us try to feel compassion even for the ideologues, for they walk as blind men and do not know it.

Steinberg

A unique artist, a specialist in the riddles of identity

BY HAROLD ROSENBERG

In his drawings Saul Steinberg records everything about himself but without revealing himself. His art is the autobiography of a man determined to keep his life a secret. A specialist in the riddles of identity, Steinberg knows, of course, that all autobiography is fiction and that those who strive to lay bare "the facts" of their existence are victims of the delusions of Realism. Why commit oneself to incidents merely because they have taken place? In defiance of this era of the couch, Steinberg brushes aside the mirage of the underlying ego and asserts pictorially that one *is* not but only invents. A large exhibition of his works in Paris last spring and a volume of his drawings issued at the same time were called "Masks," a title that points to the artist as an unknown presence behind his screen of images.

Fictions have provided the facts of life for Steinberg. Earlier chapters of his story were the volumes *All in Line, The Passport, The Labyrinth, The New World.* Unreeling the guideline of his draughtsmanship, like the fleeing children of the fairy tale, this pilgrim of the unreal has journeyed through both hemispheres in a landscape of official forms, fingerprints, and bureaucratic detours and blind alleys, to reach at last a legendary frontier of the made-up. His encounters with the dark powers of the mental blank have inspired the insignia by which his graffiti are recognized throughout the world: faked documents, elaborate handwritings in no-language, rubber stamps, spurious signatures, phony terrains, fantastic architecture,

and those representations of the artist, the impassive little man and the nosy cat.

Steinberg's adventures in the bogus began with his birth in Rumania, which he has dubbed "a masquerade country." The moment he opened his eyes he was convinced that his operetta environment, with its peasants and moustachioed cavalrymen, had been set up to trick him. His only recourse was to learn without delay how to put on appearances that would cause him to blend into his surroundings. He became a master of the defensive ruses of childhood, foremost among which is the trick of backing away from one's face and using it as camouflage. As a schoolboy he wore a military uniform. Did this make Steinberg a Rumanian cadet? Much later, he was a wartime officer in the U. S. Naval Intelligence and in the OSS, masquerading professionally and in deadly earnest. The Navy sent him to China disguised as "a weather observer." His actual assignment was to provide a means of communication with the Chinese through his ability to say things in pictures. The hitch was that Steinberg knew no English and couldn't communicate with the Americans. His theory is that his real mission was to confuse enemy intelligence agents by causing them to wonder what this foreigner was doing with the American Navy in China. The fictions within fictions of the intelligence service presented an exemplary Steinbergian situation.

Wearing military uniforms has probably contributed to Steinberg's studied elegance and

IRVING PENN

A magnificent draughtsman, Saul Steinberg is an open-faced enigma, a man of masks. For this mask, Irving Penn first made a passport photograph of Steinberg. Then that photograph was enlarged to slightly more than human size. Afterwards Steinberg, a lover of games, cut the enlargement into a mask, had Penn photograph it on another man without Steinberg. The final mask is when nobody is there.

to his penchant for collecting hats of all nations and trades. But uniforms are only a species of costume, and for people who live in mirrors anything they wear is a uniform. As a young man, Steinberg left Rumania for Italy, a country not without its own operatic emanations, particularly for one who arrived during the reign of Mussolini, when businessmen paraded after hours in black shirts and spurred boots and flaunted the skull and crossbones. Gotten up in the spectacles, moustache, and long hair of the typical Italian professional student, Steinberg spent his twenties in Milan, dividing his time between studying architecture (castles, skyscrapers, monuments, city layouts, and architectural ornaments provide the exotic elements in Steinberg's drawings) and watching the girls go by in the Galleria. It was in Milan that he began his career as an artist by contributing drawings to newspapers and magazines. Even after he had finished his studies, he continued to pass as an architectural student in order to keep his student's visa.

The fall of France and Mussolini's partnership with Hitler forced Steinberg to seek a rapid change of scene and with it a new getup. The place for him, obviously, was America, land of the Revolutionary minuteman, where everyone keeps a spare mask in reserve. To reach the United States, however, was not easy in wartime. Steinberg arrived in Lisbon with a "slightly false" passport—one that had run out but which he had extended by means of faked rubber stamps (Steinberg's studio today contains enough rubber stamps to meet any emergency). At the airport Steinberg was arrested, though not on account of the passport but through a mistake of identity (another Steinberg was wanted or someone who resembled Steinberg physically) and because he enraged the Portuguese police by his denying that he spoke Portuguese, which they took for an insulting pretense. Shipped back to Italy, he managed, after some tough events about which he chooses to remain silent, to make his way to Santo Domingo, where he emerged as a colonial gentleman in a white linen suit and broad-brimmed straw promenading the avenues for the year it took to be admitted to the United States.

In America masks are worn less tightly than in Europe, where they are affixed permanently by class and vocation—"in order," says Stein-

berg, "to make the job of tax collecting easier." In America it is even chic to shift periodically to the mask of anonymity, providing it is transparent and can be seen through by everyone. Thus professors jitterbug to pass as common folk, tycoons address each other as "Joe" and "Frank," and Presidents are headlined in monograms as FDR and LBJ. Conversely, people whom nobody knows disguise themselves in dark glasses in order to pretend to be incognito, that is, Someone who is making an effort to remain unknown.

Individuals unmasking themselves only to reveal other masks, verbal clichés masquerading as things, a countryside that is an amalgam of all styles, conventional and futuristic—America was made to order for Steinberg. In the nation of "The Man Who Was Made Up," as the title of Poe's tale put it, Steinberg's life of ruses and disguises could fulfill itself.

After becoming an American, Steinberg assumed a mask of imperturbable curiosity, that of a species of unofficial inspector, most approximately as inspector of insect life, a mask which in time was divested of its moustache and most of its hair but on which still glitter the old student's eyeglasses. What chiefly occupied the attention of this investigator was the remarkable capacity of his fellow citizens to contrive selves without limit in an environment that was the projection of what each desired to be at the moment. His observations gave rise to the still continuing series of drawings in which a man or a cat draws a line that outlines his own shape and frames him in a scene.

Related researches have produced a parade of personages, furniture, machines, abstract shapes, letters of the alphabet, each staged in a dream of being something else. The effect is of an endless Mardi Gras, an all-embracing Rumania of the imagination, with the Rocky Mountains as a backdrop and the Statute of Liberty, Uncle Sam, The Last of the Mohicans, E PLURIBUS UNUM, and the $ printed on the sky.

With Steinberg the commonly accepted division of the individual into a public identity and a private self does not exist. Self-invention reaches to the roots and it pervades the streets, the living room, the office, the art gallery, nature itself. Steinberg refers to a bird or chipmunk as "he"; even a plant on his lawn is a person, who somehow got the idea of appearing

Steinberg finally made a mask of paper, with the cutouts showing his own eyes and nose. That mask over his face did not look like him. "I feel comfortable behind this shield," Steinberg said.

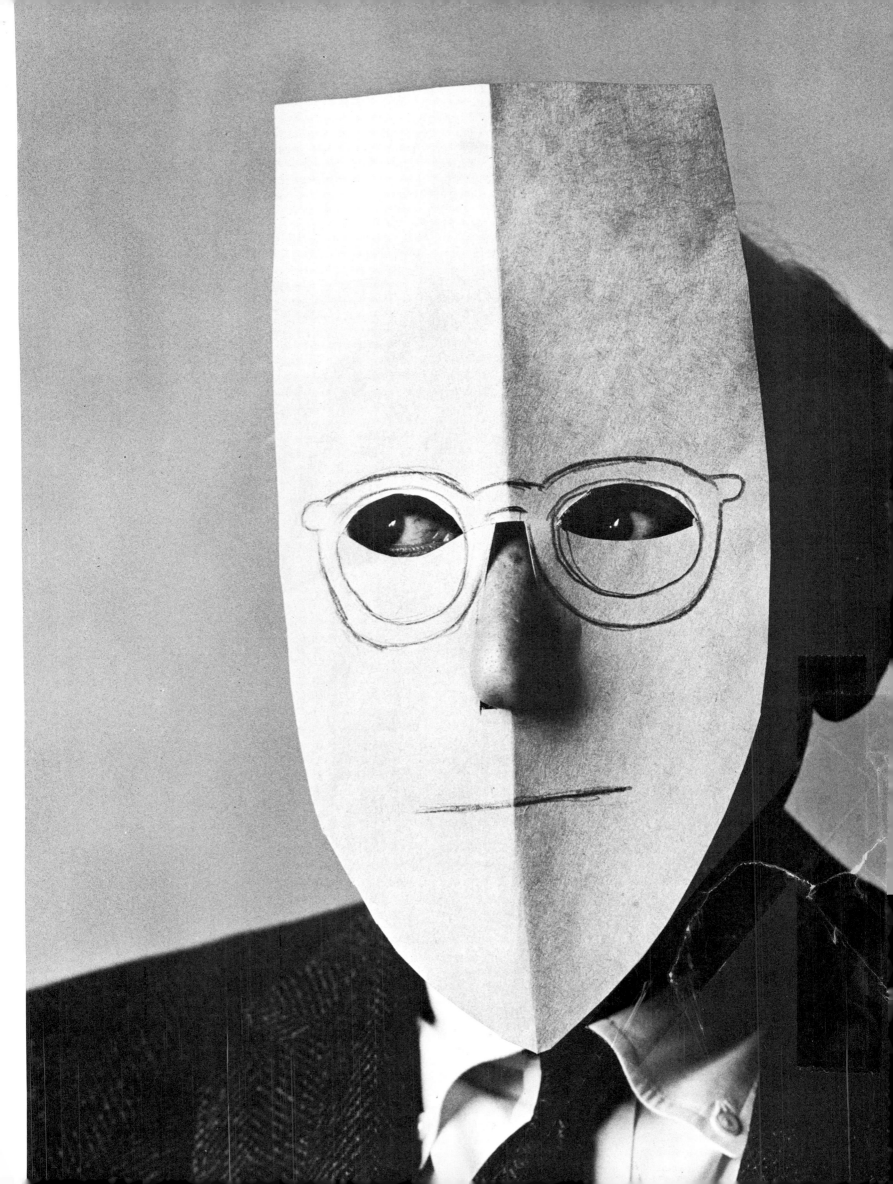

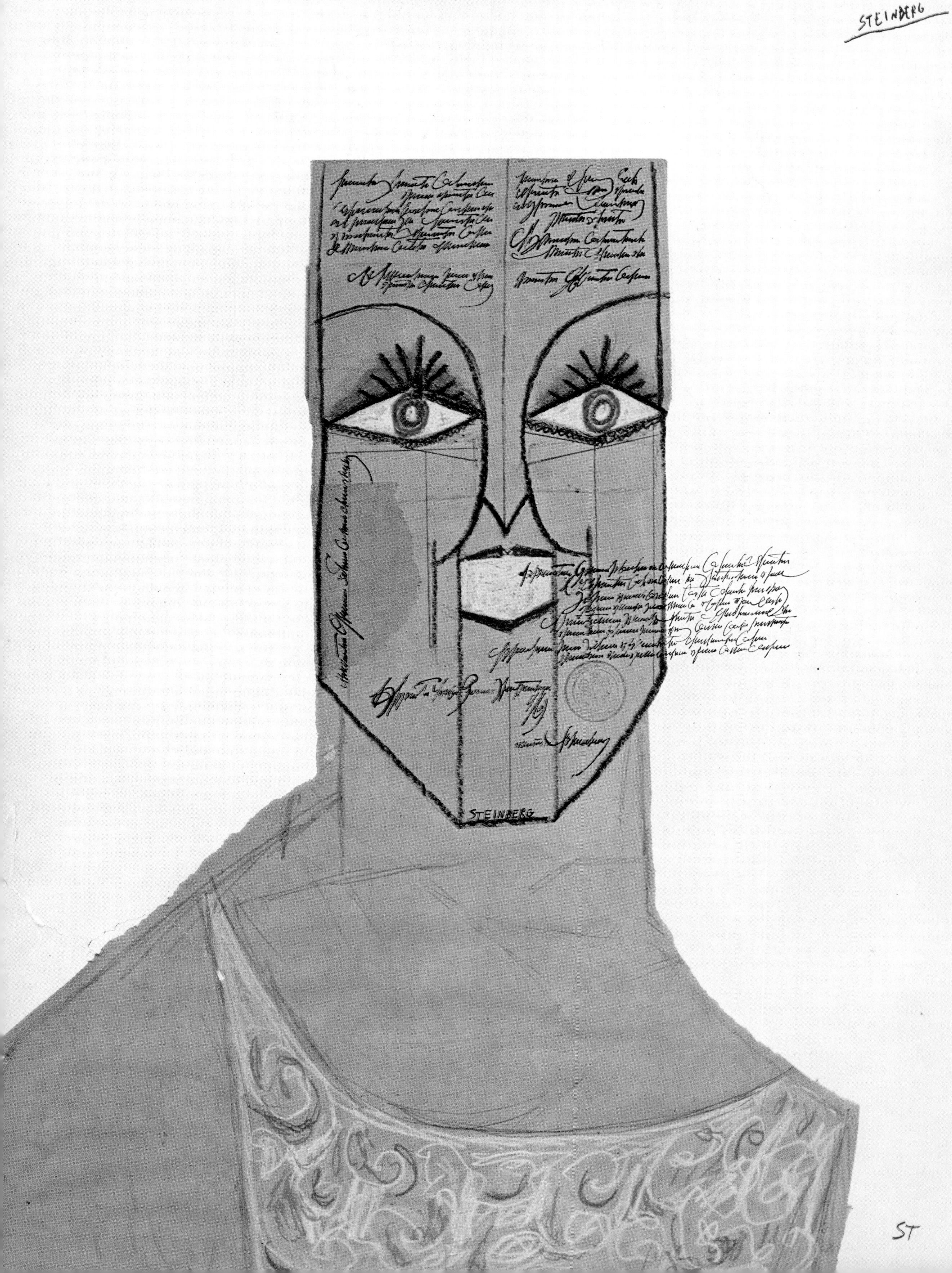

ST

to be green, six inches tall, and to have some petals for a face. Anyone worried about his ego has only to slip it into a stamped, self-addressed envelope and try out a new one until the next mail arrives.

The game of mistaken, misplaced, and half-blended identities goes on continually like modifications in the chemistry of the blood. On the floor of the apartment house where Steinberg lives in New York there are two other Steinbergs—and in East Hampton, where the artist has a house, there is another Saul Steinberg. Steinberg once phoned this gentleman and asked him, "Are you the *real* Saul Steinberg?"

The poor fellow lost his head sufficiently to answer, "No."

"I am the real Saul Steinberg," Steinberg then informed the man, and invited him over for a drink.

Reality in Steinberg's art obligingly presents itself as an endless series of reflections unmarred by the grit of substance—one of his favourite motifs is a work of art examining a work of art. The mouth of a Steinberg figure utters a comic strip balloon larger and more massive than the speaker himself. The human mask as we see it in the mirror or at a cocktail party consists of ovals for eyes and a mouth, some lines for a nose and ears—it would be just as reasonable, suggests a galaxy of Steinberg caricatures, to make it of oblongs and arrows.

Remove the abstract mask and you may find underneath a grinning photograph or a lifelike portrait, which are merely fabrications in a different style. Nature copies art that copies art lovers. A figure examining an abstract painting himself consists of a pile of Impressionist dots. "I think therefore Descartes is," thinks Steinberg's little man, reminding philosophers who claim that the mind can forge a reality that the mind has only produced a platitude.

In Steinberg's world of artifice nothing is real but the act of invention—that is to say, the use of a medium to subject things to continual metamorphosis. The hero of his world of the man-made is, of course, the artist, out of whose pen all things emanate and who reigns absolutely with his wand of illusion. The little man holding the pen can reproduce himself on a gigantic scale; disguised as Uncle Sam, he can scribble an endless prairie; at his own wish he can bring into being the Muse who shall adorn

Steinberg masked, with hat.

Steinberg unmasked, with cap at his country house.

Steinberg's "Western Harpy."

him with laurels. The vicissitudes of the artist on the pedestal have supplied Steinberg with subjects for countless drawings. It is a theme that enables him to unleash his self-consciousness in its fullest range—from the implicit megalomania of the hand of the artist as the hand of God to the most level-headed appraisal of the absurdity and fragility of fame.

The mask of the art historian is Space. For the academic art world the essence of painting consists in the handling of the picture plane in relation to the illusion of depth. It was obvious to Steinberg, however, that today everyone is at home with pictures exploiting all kinds of space concepts, from dribbles on unprimed canvas to actual objects inserted into the composition, so that painting in two dimensions or in three dimensions is simply a matter of the painter's technical apparatus and has no effect on the capacity of the work to create an illusion of reality. Thus Steinberg has kept up a running satire on art dogmas and art devices by crowding many spatial dimensions into a single drawing, as when a sheet of paper drawn on a sheet of paper supplies a head for a man in a bushy overcoat.

The basic Steinberg innovation, however, is his introduction of the one-dimensional, the dot that becomes a line separated from any definable plane and that drifts in the air like a piece of skywriting (few artists since the disappearance of angels from paintings have made such free use of the room above the horizon line). Steinberg's one-dimensional calligraphy is the formal equivalent of his vision of insubstantiality—of a world that can be destroyed or brought into existence by a signature. His drawings negate the flat surface of traditional modernist art by replacing the plane with the void. Steinberg's space is the space of dream, an area of de-identification in which things are pictures, pictures become words, and words act.

In the most literal sense, Steinberg is the poet of the American Dream, including the menace of isolation and emptiness which that dream contains. Isn't the power of the individual to exchange one self for another the deepest meaning of freedom? The myth of the frontier is the myth of drowning one's inherited identity in the waters of forgetfulness and awakening to the greeting of "Howdy, stranger." In his unexcelled vocabulary of visual quick change, studded with sacred clichés and personifications, the immigrant Steinberg has revived the myth of America as the land of possibility, unrestrained to the point of madness. Its non-verbal form and the appeal on all levels of intellect of Steinberg's riddles and exaggerations have made his America accessible throughout the civilized world, with something of the bygone flavour of the America dreamed of in the last century. What could be more fitting than that Steinberg should be now the first artist-in-residence at the Smithsonian Institution?

The Patricians

Rich, aristocratic, "they governed from duty, heritage, and habit—and, as they saw it, from right."

BY BARBARA W. TUCHMAN

EDITOR'S NOTE: *Barbara W. Tuchman, a master of historical mosaic, the author of the famous* The Guns of August, *has written another superb book,* The Proud Tower: A Portrait of the World Before the War—1890 to 1914. *A pulsing, detailed, fascinating look in depth at the Anglo-American and Western European world that has been called by the unknowing the Golden Age,* The Proud Tower *has wit, passion, horror, and amusement.*

LORD SALISBURY

The last government in the Western world to possess all the attributes of aristocracy in working condition took office in England in June of 1895. Great Britain was at the zenith of empire when the Conservatives won the General Election of that year, and the Cabinet they formed was her superb and resplendent image. Its members represented the greater landowners of the country who had been accustomed to govern for generations. As its superior citizens they felt they owed a duty to the State to guard its interests and manage its affairs. They governed from duty, heritage and habit —and, as they saw it, from right.

The Prime Minister was a marquess and lineal descendant of the father and son who had been chief ministers to Queen Elizabeth and James I. The Secretary for War was another marquess who traced his inferior title of baron back to the year 1181, whose great-grandfather had been Prime Minister under George III and whose grandfather had served in six cabinets under three reigns. The Lord President of the Council was a duke who owned 136,000 acres in eleven counties, whose ancestors had served in government since the fourteenth century, who had himself served thirty-four years in the House of Commons and three times refused to be Prime Minister. The Secretary for India was the son of another duke whose family seat was received in 1315 by grant from Robert the Bruce and who had four sons serving in Parliament at the same time. The President of the Local Government Board was a preeminent country squire who had a duke for a brother-in-law, a marquess for son-in-law, an ancestor who had been Lord Mayor of London in the reign of Charles II, and who had himself been a Member of Parliament for twenty-seven years. The Lord Chancellor bore a family name brought to England by a Norman follower of William the Conqueror and maintained thereafter over eight centuries without a title. The Lord Lieutenant for Ireland was an earl, a grandnephew of the Duke of Wellington and

The Third Marquess of Salisbury, 1830-1903, "Epitome of His Class," served three times as Prime Minister to Queen Victoria.

a hereditary trustee of the British Museum. The Cabinet also included a viscount, three barons and two baronets. Of its six commoners, one was a director of the Bank of England, one was a squire whose family had represented the same county in Parliament since the sixteenth century, one—who acted as Leader of the House of Commons—was the Prime Minister's nephew and inheritor of a Scottish fortune of £4,000,000, and one, a notable and disturbing cuckoo in the nest, was a Birmingham manufacturer widely regarded as the most successful man in England.

Besides riches, rank, broad acres and ancient lineage, the new Government also possessed, to the regret of the Liberal Opposition and in the words of one of them, "an almost embarrassing wealth of talent and capacity." Secure in authority, resting comfortably on their electoral majority in the House of Commons and on a permanent majority in the House of Lords, of whom four-fifths were Conservatives, they were in a position, admitted the same opponent, "of unassailable strength."

Enriching their ranks were the Whig aristocrats who had seceded from the Liberal party in 1886 rather than accept Mr. Gladstone's insistence on Home Rule for Ireland. They were for the most part great landowners who, like their natural brothers the Tories, regarded union with Ireland as sacrosanct. Led by the Duke of Devonshire, the Marquess of Lansdowne and Mr. Joseph Chamberlain, they had remained independent until 1895, when they joined with the Conservative party, and the two forces emerged as the Unionist party, in recognition of the policy that had brought them together. With the exception of Mr. Chamberlain, this coalition represented that class in whose blood, training and practice over the centuries, landowning and governing had been inseparable. Ever since Saxon chieftains met to advise the King in the first national assembly, the landowners of England had been sending members to Parliament and performing the duties of High Sheriff, Justice of the Peace and Lord Lieutenant of the Militia in their own counties. They had learned the practice of government from the possession of great estates, and they undertook to manage the affairs of the nation as inevitably and unquestioningly as a beaver builds a dam. It was their ordained rôle and natural task.

But it was threatened. By a rising rumble of protest from below, by the Radicals of the Opposition who talked about taxing unearned increment on land, by Home Rulers who wanted to detach the Irish island from which so much English income came, by Trade Unionists who talked of Labour representation in Parliament and demanded the legal right to strike and otherwise interfere with the free play of economic forces, by Socialists who wanted to nationalize property and Anarchists who wanted to abolish it, by upstart nations and strange challenges from abroad. The rumble was distant, but it spoke with one voice that said Change, and those whose business was government could not help but hear.

Planted firmly across the path of change, operating warily, shrewdly yet with passionate conviction in defense of the existing order, was a peer who was Chancellor of Oxford University for life, had twice held the India Office, twice the Foreign Office and was now Prime Minister for the third time. He was Robert Arthur Talbot Gascoyne-Cecil, Lord Salisbury, ninth Earl and third Marquess of his line.

Lord Salisbury was both the epitome of his class and uncharacteristic of it—except insofar as the freedom to be different was a class characteristic. As a young man, he had been tall, thin, ungainly, stooping and shortsighted, with hair unusually black for an Englishman. Now, at sixty-five, his youthful lankiness had turned to bulk, his shoulders had grown massive and more stooped than ever, and his heavy bald head with full curly grey beard rested on them as if weighted down. Melancholy, intensely intellectual, subject to sleep-walking and fits of depression which he called "nerve storms," caustic, tactless, absent minded, bored by society and fond of solitude, with a penetrating, skeptical, questioning mind, he had been called the Hamlet of English politics. He was above the conventions and refused to live in Downing Street. His devotion was to religion, his interest in science. In his own home he attended private chapel every morning before breakfast, and had fitted up a chemical laboratory where he conducted solitary experiments. He harnessed the river at Hatfield for an electric power plant on his estate and strung up along the old beams of his home one of England's first electric light systems, at which his family threw cushions when the wires sparked and sputtered while they went on talking and arguing, a customary occupation of the Cecils.

Lord Salisbury cared nothing for sport and little for people. His aloofness was enhanced by shortsightedness so intense that he once failed to recognize a member of his own Cabinet, and once, his own butler. At the close of the Boer War he picked up a signed photograph of King Edward and gazing at it pensively, remarked, "Poor Buller [referring to the Commander-in-Chief at the start of the war] what a mess he made of it." On another occasion he was seen in prolonged military conversation with a minor peer under the impression that he was talking to Field Marshal Lord Roberts.

For the upper-class Englishman's alter ego, most intimate companion and constant preoccupation, his horse, Lord Salisbury had no more regard. Riding was to him purely a means of locomotion to which the horse was "a necessary but extremely inconvenient adjunct." Nor was he addicted to shooting. When Parliament rose he did not go north to slaughter grouse upon the moors or stalk deer in Scottish forests, and when protocol required his attendance upon royalty at Balmoral, he would not go for walks and "positively refused," wrote Queen Victoria's Private Secretary, Sir Henry Ponsonby, "to admire the prospect or the deer." Ponsonby was told to have his room in the dismal castle kept "warm"—a minimum temperature of sixty degrees. Otherwise he retired for his holidays to France, where he owned a villa at Beaulieu on the Riviera and where he could exercise his fluent French and lose himself in *The Count of Monte Cristo*, the only book, he once told Dumas *fils*, which allowed him to forget politics.

His acquaintance with games was confined to tennis, but when elderly he invented his own form of exercise, which consisted in riding a tricycle through St. James's Park in the early mornings or along paths cemented for the purpose in the park of his estate at Hatfield. Wearing for the occasion a kind of sombrero hat and a short sleeveless cloak with a hole in the middle in which he resembled a monk, he would be accompanied by a young coachman to push him up the hills. At the downhill slopes, the young man would be told to "jump on behind," and the Prime Minister, with the coachman's hands on his shoulders, would roll away, cloak flying and pedals whirring.

Hatfield, twenty miles north of London in Hertfordshire, had been the home of the Cecils for nearly three hundred years since James I had given it, in 1607, to his Prime Minister, Robert Cecil, first Earl Salisbury, in exchange for a house of Cecil's to which the King had taken a fancy. It was the royal residence where Queen Elizabeth had spent her childhood and where, on receiving news of her accession, she held her first council, to swear in William Cecil, Lord Burghley, as her chief Secretary of State. Its Long Gallery, with intricately carved paneled walls and gold-leaf ceiling, was 180 feet in length. The Marble Hall, named for the black and white marble floor, glowed like a jewel case with painted and gilded ceiling and Brussels tapestries. The red King James Drawing Room was hung with full-length family portraits by Romney and Reynolds and Lawrence. The library was lined from floor to gallery and ceiling with ten thousand volumes bound in leather and vellum. In other rooms were kept the Casket Letters of Mary Queen of Scots, suits of armour taken from men of the Spanish Armada, the cradle of the beheaded King, Charles I, and presentation portraits of James I and George III. Outside were yew hedges clipped in the form of crenellated battlements, and the gardens, of which Pepys wrote that he never saw "so good flowers, nor so great gooseberries as big as nutmegs." Over the entrance hall hung flags captured at Waterloo and presented to Hatfield by the Duke of Wellington, who was a constant visitor and devoted admirer of the Prime Minister's mother, the second Marchioness. In her honour Wellington wore the hunt coat of the Hatfield Hounds when he was on campaign.

The first Marchioness was painted by Sir Joshua Reynolds and hunted till the day she died at eighty-five, when, half-blind and strapped to the saddle, she was accompanied by a groom who would shout, when her horse approached a fence, "Jump, dammit my Lady, jump!"

It was this exceptional person who reinvigorated the Cecil blood, which, after Burghley and his son, had produced no further examples of superior mentality. Rather, the general mediocrity of succeeding generations had been varied only, according to a later Cecil, by instances of "quite exceptional stupidity." But the second Marquess proved a vigorous and able man with a strong sense of public duty who served in several mid-century Tory cabinets. His second son, another Robert Cecil, was the Prime Minister of 1895. He in turn produced five sons who were to distinguish themselves. One became a general, one a bishop, one a minister of state, one M.P. for Oxford, and one, through service to the government, won a peerage in his own right. "In human beings as in horses," Lord Birkenhead was moved to comment on the Cecil record, "there is something to be said for the hereditary principle."

At Oxford in 1850 the contemporaries of young Robert Cecil agreed that he would end as Prime Minister either because or in spite of his remorselessly uncompromising opinions. Throughout life he never bothered to restrain them. His youthful speeches were remarkable for their virulence and insolence; he was not, said Disraeli, "a man who measures his phrases." A "salisbury" became a synonym for a political imprudence. He once compared the Irish in their incapacity for self-government to Hottentots and spoke of an Indian candidate for Parliament as "that black man." In the opinion of Lord Morley his speeches were always a pleasure to read because "they were sure to contain one blazing indiscretion which it is a delight to remember." Whether the indiscretions were altogether accidental is open to question, for though Lord Salisbury delivered his speeches without notes, they were worked out in his head beforehand and emerged clear and perfect in sentence structure. In that time the art of oratory was considered part of the equipment of a statesman and anyone reading from a written speech would have been regarded as pitiable. When Lord Salisbury spoke, "every sentence," said a fellow member, "seemed as essential, as articulate, as vital to the argument as the members of his body to an athlete."

Appearing in public before an audience about whom he cared nothing, Salisbury was awkward; but in the Upper House, where he addressed his equals, he was perfectly and strikingly at home. He spoke sonorously, with an occasional change of tone to icy mockery or withering sarcasm. When a recently ennobled Whig took the floor to lecture the House of Lords in high-flown and solemn Whig sentiments. Salisbury asked a neighbour who the speaker was and on hearing the whispered identification, replied perfectly audibly, "I thought he was dead." When he listened to others he could become easily bored, revealed by a telltale wagging of his leg which seemed to one observer to be saying, "When will all this be over?" Or sometimes, raising his heels off the floor, he would set up a sustained quivering of his knees and legs which could last for half an hour at a time. At home, when made restless by visitors, it shook the floor and made the furniture rattle, and in the House his colleagues on the front bench complained it made them seasick. If his legs were at rest his long fingers would be in motion, incessantly twisting and turning a paper knife or beating a tattoo on his knee or on the arm of his chair.

He never dined out and rarely entertained beyond one or two political receptions at his town house in Arlington Street and an occasional garden party at Hatfield. He avoided the Carlton, official club of the Conservatives, in favour of the Junior Carlton, where a special luncheon table was set aside for him alone and the library was hung with huge placards inscribed SILENCE. He worked from breakfast to one in the morning, returning to his desk after dinner as if he were beginning a new day. His clothes were drab and often untidy. He wore trousers and waistcoat of a dismal gray under a broadcloth frock coat grown shiny. But though careless in dress, he was particular about the trimming of his beard and carefully directed operations in the barber's chair, indicating "just a little more off here" while "artist and subject gazed fixedly in the mirror to judge the result."

Despite his rough tongue and sarcasms, Salisbury exerted a personal charm upon close colleagues and equals which, as one of them said, "was no small asset in the conduct of affairs." He gave detailed attention to party affairs and even sacrificed his exclusiveness for their sake. Once he astonished everyone by accepting an invitation to the traditional dinner for party supporters given by the Leader of the House. He asked to be given in advance biographical details about each expected guest. At the dinner the Prime Minister charmed his neighbour at table, a well-known agriculturist, with his expert knowledge of crop rotation and stockbreeding, chatted amiably afterward with every guest in turn, and before leaving, beckoned to his Private Secretary, saying, "I think I have done them all, but there was someone I have not identified who, you said, made mustard."

Mr. Gladstone, though in political philosophy his bitterest antagonist, acknowledged him "a great gentleman in private society." In private life he was delightful and sympathetic and a complete contrast to his public self. In public acclaim, Salisbury was uninterested, for—since the populace was uninstructed—its opinions, as far as he was concerned, were worthless. He ignored the public and neither possessed nor tried to cultivate the personal touch that makes a political leader a recognizable personality to the man in the street and earns him a nickname like "Pam" or "Dizzy" or the "Grand Old Man." Not in the press, not even in *Punch*, was Lord Salisbury ever called anything but Lord Salisbury. He made no attempt to conceal his dislike for mobs of all kinds, "not excluding the House of Commons." After moving to the Lords, he never returned to the Commons to listen to its debates from the Peers' Gallery or chat with members in the Lobby, and if compelled to allude to them in his own House, would use a tone of airy contempt, to the amusement of visitors from the Commons who came to hear him. But this was merely an outward pose designed to underline his deep inner sense of the patrician. He was not rank-conscious; he was indifferent to honours or any other form of recognition. It was simply that as a Cecil, and a superior one, he was born with a consciousness in his bones and brain cells of ability to rule and saw no reason to make any concessions of this prescriptive right to anyone whatever.

Having entered the House of Commons in the customary manner for peers' sons, from a family-controlled borough in an uncontested election at the age of twenty-three and, during his fifteen years in the House of Commons, having been returned unopposed five times from the same borough, and having for the last twenty-seven years sat in the House of Lords, he had little personal experience of vote-getting. He regarded himself not as responsible *to* the people but as responsible *for* them. They were in his care. What reverence he felt for anyone was directed not down but up—to the monarchy. He revered Queen Victoria who was some ten years his senior, both as her subject and, with chivalry toward her womanhood, as a man. For her he softened his brusqueness even if at Balmoral he could not conceal his boredom. She in turn visited him at Hatfield and had the greatest confidence in him, giving him, as she told Bishop Carpenter, "if not the highest, an equal place with the highest among her ministers," not excepting Disraeli. Salisbury, who was "bad on his legs at any time," was the only man she ever asked to sit down. Unlike in every quality of mind except in their strong sense of rulership, the tiny old Queen and the tall, heavy, aging Prime Minister felt for each other mutual respect and regard.

In unimportant matters of state as in dress, Salisbury was inclined to be casual. Once when two clergymen with similar names were candidates for a vacant bishopric, he appointed the one not recommended by the Archbishop of Canterbury, and this being sorrowfully drawn to his attention, he said, "Oh, I daresay he will do just as well." He reserved high seriousness for serious matters only, and the most serious to him was the maintenance of aristocratic influence and executive power, not for its own sake, but because he believed it to be the only element capable of holding the nation united against the rising forces of democracy, which he saw "splitting it into a bundle of unfriendly and distrustful fragments."

Class war and irreligion were to him the greatest evils and for this reason he detested socialism, less for its menace to property than for its preaching of class war and its basis in materialism, which meant to him a denial of spiritual values. He did not deny the need of social reforms, but believed they could be achieved through the interplay and mutual pressures of existing parties. The Workmen's Compensation Act, for one, making employers liable for work-sustained injuries, though denounced by some of his party as interference with private enterprise, was introduced and passed with his support in 1897.

He fought all proposals designed to increase the political power of the masses. When still a younger son, and not expecting to succeed to the title, he had formulated his political philosophy in a series of some thirty articles which were published in the *Quarterly Review* in the early 1860's, when he was in his thirties. Against the growing demand at that time for a new Reform law to extend the suffrage, Lord Robert Cecil, as he then was, had declared it to be the business of the Conservative party to preserve the rights and privileges of the propertied class as the "single bulwark" against the weight of numbers. To extend the suffrage would be, as he saw it, to give the working classes not merely a voice in Parliament but a preponderating one that would give to "mere numbers a power they ought not to have." He deplored the Liberals' adulation of the working class "as if they were different from other Englishmen" when in fact the only difference was that they had less education and property, and "in proportion as the property is small the danger of misusing the franchise is great." He believed the workings of democracy to be dangerous to liberty, for under democracy "passion is not the exception but the rule" and it was "perfectly impossible" to commend a farsighted passionless policy to "men whose minds are unused to thought and undisciplined to study." To widen the suffrage among the poor while increasing taxes upon the rich would end, he wrote, in a complete divorce of power from responsibility; "the rich would pay all the taxes and the poor make all the laws."

He did not believe in political equality. There was the multitude, he said, and there were "natural" leaders. "Always wealth, in some countries birth, in all countries intellectual power and culture mark out the man to whom, in a healthy state of feeling, a community looks to undertake its government." These men had the leisure for it and the fortune, "so that the struggles for ambition are not defiled by the taint of sordid greed. . . . They are the aristocracy of a country in the original and best sense of the word. . . . The important point is, that the rulers of a country should be taken from among them," and as a class they should retain that "political preponderence to which they have every right that superior fitness can confer."

So sincere and certain was his conviction of that "superior fitness" that in 1867 when the Tory Government espoused the Second Reform Bill, which doubled the electorate and enfranchised working men in the towns, Salisbury at

thirty-seven flung away Cabinet office within a year of first achieving it rather than be party to what he considered a betrayal and surrender of Conservative principles. His party's reversal, engineered by Disraeli in a neat enterprise both to "dish the Whigs" and to meet political realities, was regarded with abhorrence by Lord Cranborne (as Lord Robert Cecil had then become, his elder brother having died in 1865). Though it might ruin his career, he resigned as Secretary for India and in a bitter and serious speech spoke out in the House against the policy of the party's leaders, Lord Derby and Mr. Disraeli. He begged the members not to do for political advantage what would ultimately destroy them as a class. "The wealth, the intelligence, the energy of the community, all that has given you that power which makes you so proud of your nation and which makes the deliberations of this House so important, will be numerically absolutely overmatched." Issues would arise in which the interests of employers and employed would clash and could only be decided by political force; "and in that conflict of political force you are pitting an overwhelming number of employed against a hopeless minority of employers." The outcome would "reduce to political insignificance and extinction the classes which have hitherto contributed so much to the greatness and prosperity of their country."

A year later, on his father's death, he entered the House of Lords as third Marquess of Salisbury. In 1895, after the passage of nearly thirty years, his principles had not shifted an inch. With no belief in change as improvement, nor faith in the future over the present, he dedicated himself with "grim acidity" to preserving the existing order. Believing that "rank, without the power of which it was originally the symbol, was a sham," he was determined, while he lived and governed England, to resist further attack on the power of that class of which rank was still the visible symbol. Watchful of approaching enemies, he stood against the coming age. The pressures of democracy encircled but had not yet closed in around the figure whom Lord Curzon described as "that strange, powerful, inscrutable, brilliant, obstructive deadweight at the top."

American Women of Great Influence

Talent, even genius, generosity, understanding, all to help take the rat out of the race, to make life better, simpler, kinder for the people in the United States and out of the country—that is the uncounted present of American woman to the world. No computer can be given those figures. That colossal sum is missing. In addition to this unnumbered statistic must be added the actual unpaid work by millions of women for the nation's charities. Over so many women the country might well exult.

GIVER

Barbara Linthicum—American Nurse
at the Bac Lieu Hospital in Viet Nam

Barbara Linthicum, a twenty-seven-year-old USAID (Agency for International Development) nurse, is the only American woman in the 210-bed hospital that serves the 280,000 population at Bac Lieu, a provincial capital in the Viet Cong-controlled Delta of South Viet Nam. Since she came to Viet Nam in December 1967—because she wanted to see for herself what was happening, because she wanted to help, and because she is, without heroics or histrionics, a brave woman—she has worked doggedly, exhaustingly, prosaically (for imagination is superfluous here) among scenes like those described in *GI Diary*, David Parks's brilliant new book on his military life in Viet Nam: "One guy came in so badly shot up he tried to kill himself with a knife. . . . An ARVN [one of the Army of the Republic of Viet Nam] came in, with a foot blown off, dripping blood all over the floor. He didn't say anything or cry out. Probably just wondering where he could get another foot."

Each night, Barbara Linthicum helps mothers evacuate their children from the children's ward, because the mothers believe that this ward will be in the direct line of the third attack expected soon. "Our intelligence unit believes so, too," said Nurse Linthicum, who is thankful that in Viet Nam the patient's family customarily moves in to take care of the chores. Some nurses object, but it leaves her free for the more terrible essentials. She had no "culture shock" on arrival at Bac Lieu—such shocks are luxuries when one has to dress a large wound on the leg of a six-day-old baby whose other leg has been blown away and who is being fed from a bottle because his mother's breasts have been torn to rags by the same maiming mortar. Nothing prepared her for Viet Nam's child casualties. Before her arrival in Viet Nam she had worked in the Children's Hospital in Washington, D. C., but in three months' basic training in Hawaii that included Vietnamese language lessons, briefings about the country and its customs, and many photographs of people suffering from unfamiliar diseases, she was never once shown a photograph of a war-wounded child. After her first day in Viet Nam she thought, "My God, don't take off another dressing."

Isolated among the soldiers and Army doctors at Bac Lieu, Miss Linthicum is both overprotected and lonely. "I'm learning a lot," she said, "I've got the same desires as other women, I don't want to do this for the rest of my life, but when I do settle down I hope I'll be a better person for all this." Born in New York, daughter of a Foreign Service official, Barbara Linthicum, who spent her childhood in Shanghai, Holland, Baghdad, and Belgium, has deep courage, a mind of unusual mettle. "I hope by my behaving naturally," she said, "that people here will realize that all Americans are not the same. The other day I ran out of lipstick; one of the Vietnamese nurses said she could get me a tube for three dollars. I knew it cost only one dollar in Saigon, so I told her it was too expensive and I'd do without. She couldn't understand. She kept saying, 'But you have plenty of money. You are American.'"

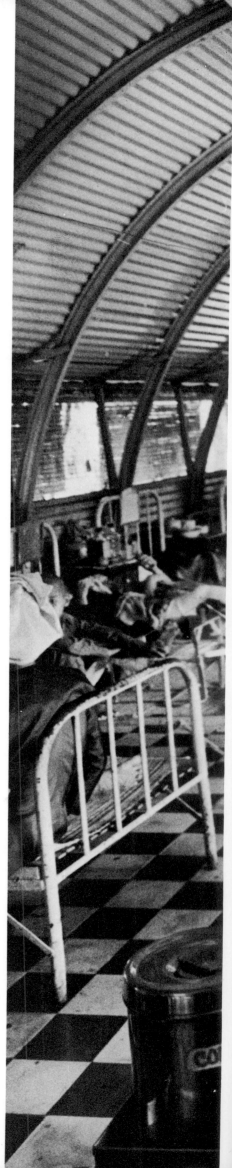

PHILIP JONES GRIFFITH

Barbara Linthicum, who every day gives solace and care in Bac Lieu hospital, where she is the only American nurse.

DOER

Dr. Mamie Phipps Clark, an American woman whose depths of discipline are disguised in charm, and who is the co-founder and director of the oldest mental health out-patient clinic in Harlem.

Dr. Mamie Phipps Clark, a notable doer, has eyes so clear the whites are slightly blue like those of a baby, but she sometimes uses hers like a woman of a wicked age. The effect startles, for, other than these alluring flickers, Dr. Clark disciplines herself to a restrained, unblowable efficiency. She speaks softly, clearly, and without waste. Her voice is light—pretty, really—but it delivers hard facts. Twenty-two years ago Dr. Clark, with her husband, Dr. Kenneth B. Clark, an outstanding authority on Negro affairs, founded in New York the interracial Northside Center for Child Development. At that time the only child guidance service in Harlem, the Center became a national phenomenon. It still is, for it continues to develop new methods of treatment and to serve as a model for other centres. Each year it helps about six hundred children, largely through diagnosis, psychotherapy, and remedial work in education.

Cases are usually referred to Northside Center by public schools, but to succeed the Center concerns itself with all the members of the families and with the intensely personal patterns and problems of the children's lives, down to the food they may not eat, the laws they can not break. Dr. Mamie Clark, the Center's Executive Director, said: "We often find the child referred to us is not the most disturbed member of a family." Her joy: To see most of the children get better, an improvement concretely measurable in school work and family relations. Her challenge: With at least two hundred children of all races on the waiting list, the need to grow and expand.

A ramble of light rooms with brightly painted doors, squashed into the top storey of a private school (somewhat anxious to regain its own territory), Northside Center needs new space, an increased medical staff, legal help for some of the children and their families, an umbrella of services to protect the disadvantaged, even occasional outings for kids who think the world stops at 110th Street. Plainly, the Center needs money. Dr. Clark, who doesn't ruffle but who doesn't yield, doesn't discourage much, either. In fact, her oxygen is her work, which is now largely administrative although she is a trained psychologist who, after undergraduate and postgraduate work at Howard University, took her doctorate at Columbia University. Of her job at Northside Center she said, "When you do a thing like this, your own life seems dull." The Clarks, whose two children are grown, live up the Hudson River in a pleasant town in a pleasant house where Dr. Mamie Clark likes to cook, to garden, and to go a little wild over her new greenhouse. When the chance comes, she likes to travel; if the chance ever should come, she would like to write books for children. But, she said in her glimmery, gentle voice rather as if she were refusing a dessert, "I just never entertain the idea of leisure time."

Dr. Mamie Phipps Clark, with an armload of children, some of them under the guidance of the Northside Center for Child Development in New York.

CHANGER

Marie E. Nyswander, pioneering doctor who treats heroin patients by giving them instead a daily maintenance dose of Methadone to return them to normal life.

SNOWDON

Relaxing in their hospital room, big, airy, with a television set, the two young men talked and laughed with Dr. Nyswander. Both men had been on heroin since they were about fourteen, both had long prison records, both had been stealing about $150 worth of stuff a day which they sold for about $50 to support their $50-a-day habit, buying heroin on the street, their whole lives given over to robbery, a fix, arrest, reform, robbery, a fix. . . . Now off heroin in Rockefeller Hospital, they were given, under strict supervision, a single daily dose, a maintenance dose, of a twenty-year-old drug, methadone, in an orange-flavoured drink, by a nurse. The two young men in their dressing robes would in all probability never go back to heroin—their desire for it was gone. But they would have to observe a new regimen after their six weeks in the hospital. Every day they would have to report to a methadone clinic to be given their liquid methadone and juice; once a week they would have a urinalysis to be sure they have no heroin or any other drug in them. Like a thousand ex-heroin patients using methadone, they will be back with their families, working, going to the movies, with no further thought of heroin. It is too good this way. As long as they remain on methadone, they are safe.

The pioneer in this treatment is a slender, intense, brilliant psychiatrist, easy to talk to, a woman with a close rapport with addicts and ex-addicts, whom she treats with offhand breeziness. She makes no contract with them for gratitude; she laughs off their torrents of self-pity, their guilt. She often finds them infuriating. She has no bedside manner. She has instead a treatment that costs about ten cents a day—some clinicians feel the cost of the medicine in even greater bulk could go down to two cents a day.

In the new, carefully documented book *A Doctor Among the Addicts* by Nat Hentoff, Dr. Nyswander, a brisk, amusing woman, addicted to coffee and cigarettes, explained that drug addiction becomes "a reflection of failure," and sometimes reveals "total despair." She added: "The present situation is so damn senseless and can so often be tragic. Wait, someone put it more accurately: 'The American narcotics problem is an artificial tragedy with real victims.' "

Dr. Nyswander, who has set up seven methadone clinics in New York City, now has funds to drain into society about one thousand addicts a year. (Money is not the problem, attitudes are. Some doctors think that taking addicts from heroin and putting them on methadone is not a cure, but the same doctors will give diabetics stabilizing drugs providing more insulin to their bodies—not a cure but a control, a way of keeping on with a full life.)

Born in Reno, Nevada, in 1919, Marie E. Nyswander has two remarkable parents: her father a retired professor of mathematics; her mother, Dorothy Bird Nyswander, a pioneer in and authority on public health, who has received innumerable honours, remembers when stagecoaches reeled through the dust to her house. Eventually, Marie Nyswander went to Sarah Lawrence where its freedom was like a kite to her, where its president provided instructors for her alone as she was the only premedical student there. (She still has a passionate interest in music and the piano.) With a full choice of medical schools, she chose

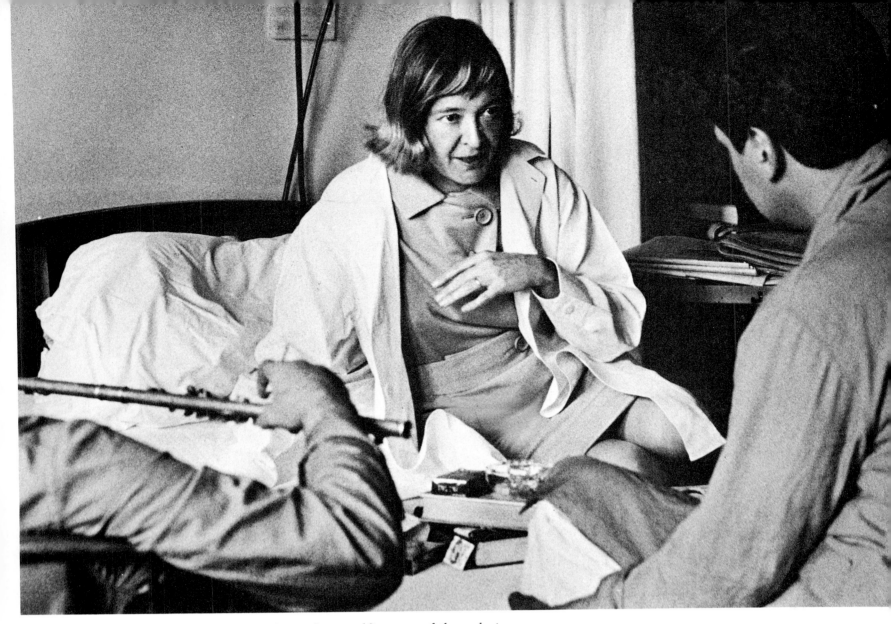

Dr. Nyswander chatting with two patients, former heroin addicts, one of them playing
his flute, at the Rockefeller University Hospital.

Cornell University's Medical College, partly because it is in cahoots with New
York Hospital. She went into the Navy in 1945 as an orthopedic surgeon. Because the Navy didn't want women surgeons she was sent to marine hospitals.
One of these was the narcotics centre at Lexington, Kentucky. Later she became
a Diplomate of the American Board of Psychiatry and Neurology.

When she saw drug addicts treated as criminals, when she saw "cold turkey"
withdrawal methods at Bellevue Hospital in New York, she was horrified. In
1950 the *New England Journal of Medicine* published her first paper, "Withdrawal Treatment of Drug Addiction." (In 1957 she wrote two articles for
Vogue, with a third in 1958.)

Now, Dr. Nyswander has said, there is no problem for her with the Federal
Narcotics Bureau because her research on methadone is done only in hospitals.
She also has said to the consternation of the pious that we all have "a potential
for chemical addiction."

A few years ago Dr. Vincent P. Dole, professor at Rockefeller University,
hired her at the start of the methadone research, and together they developed
the treatment. The New York Narcotic Addiction Commission gave its accredi-
tation to their methods—and gave money. Then the name of the procedure
changed to the Methadone Maintenance Treatment Program which has a list
of eight hundred addicts longing for admission who must wait for two years.
Now Dr. Nyswander, who has disarming candour, enthusiasm, and enormous
attraction, is married to the understanding, big, handsome, and craggy Dr. Dole.

Claude Lévi-Strauss

PHOTOGRAPH BY HENRI CARTIER-BRESSON

Penetrating, thin, dry, brilliant, Claude Lévi-Strauss, the constructor of the theory of structural anthropology, has confused his friends and enraged his enemies, leaving few in the intellectual world untouched by his methods—in fact, he has explained that structural anthropology is not a philosophy but rather a method. He finds out—as do his adherents—what the social facts, the phenomena are and then searches out what they have in common. He arrived at his method partly because he is an almost abnormal skeptic, partly because he is a scholar, and partly because of his massive experience with primitive people. At fifty-nine, Lévi-Strauss is professor of social anthropology at the Collège de France in Paris, looks, in the words of Janet Flanner, "like an intelligent bird, with a voice that is soft but distinct." The author of *The Savage Mind* and eight other books, Lévi-Strauss does not believe that primitive peoples are either backward or retarded. In fact, to him, they may "possess a genius for invention or action that leaves the achievements of civilized people far behind."

Lévi-Strauss has been unsettling almost from his birth in Brussels, Belgium, always skeptical, always questioning. After the Sorbonne where his field was philosophy, primarily because he liked the other subjects less, he eventually wandered into social anthropology, taking a professorship of the University of São Paulo. That led him to the Indians and to the jungle in the interior of Brazil. From then on the Lévi-Strauss speculations have upset anthropology, partly because his reasonings are abstruse, partly because the ideas are fresh, intellectual, and confounding, stretching far away from anthropology into literature, music, and art. He respects all mankind, not just what is called civilized man, for to him primitive man is also learned man, only the learning is different.

Henri Cartier-Bresson is a precise photographer, long recognized for the brilliance of his perception, for the clarity and the implicit significance of his work. Now The Museum of Modern Art in New York has just opened its second Cartier-Bresson exhibition (the first appeared in 1947), with some 150 photographs, including portraits done in the sixties. Later this month Viking will publish *The World of Henri Cartier-Bresson*, a retrospective with some 210 photographs, pointed, marvellous.

In August, 1908, Henri Cartier-Bresson was born in France where he was educated. Early in the 1930's he went to Africa, living for a year in a small village in the Gold Coast (now Ghana) hunting, reading, finding out what he thought. During World War II he was taken prisoner but escaped in 1943. Twice the Louvre has given him one-man shows, the only photographer to be thus honoured. Definite, imperturbable, dry, adamant, Henri Cartier-Bresson waits for the exact moment, photographs, never crops, presenting his subject as it is. No flourishes.

The Private Thoughts of André Malraux

Excerpts from the famous "anti-Memoirs"
of France's Minister of Culture

EDITOR'S NOTE: *Archeologist, soldier, art historian, statesman, novelist, author of some of the most distinguished literature of this century, André Malraux has for ten years been Minister of Culture in the French Cabinet. His new book,* Anti-Memoirs, *translated by Terence Kilmartin and published by Holt, Rinehart and Winston, fuses, as Malraux's life has fused, his extraordinary careers as a man of action and as a man of thought. In this excerpt from* Anti-Memoirs *he describes his capture in 1944 by the Germans when he fought with the French Resistance under the pseudonym of Colonel Berger. This name, chosen for him because it can be either French or German, had for Malraux, curiously, a special resonance: It was the name he had chosen for the family, modelled closely after his own, about whom he wrote a novel,* La Lutte des Anges. *Only a portion of* La Lutte *was ever published, for the rest was destroyed by the Gestapo.*

The French Resistance leader Malraux as Colonel Berger in World War II.

"Freedom must be sought behind prison walls," Gandhi and Nehru had said. Mine had not quite been prisons, or had not been prisons for long. There had been the camp in 1940, from which I had escaped easily, in spite of my shoes being too small: a vast meadow turned into a compound, the pink glow of dawn, carts on the road on the other side of the barbed wire, bloodstained tins of food, shacks built of squat beams, drainpipes, and branches, in which soldiers sat, hunched up like Peruvian mummies, writing letters that would never be sent.

1944 had been more serious. My comrades, arrested by the German security forces, usually the Gestapo, had gone to their deaths by way of the familiar channels; whereas I had been captured in uniform by the tanks of the *Das Reich* division.

My prisons begin with a field. I regained consciousness on a stretcher laid on the grass and held by two German soldiers. Under my legs, the canvas was soaked with blood. They had put together a makeshift dressing over my trousers. The British officer's body had disappeared. In the car were the still bodies of my two comrades. A German was removing the pennant. My stretcher bearers set off for Gramat, escorted by an NCO. It seemed far.

I had gone to arbitrate a dispute between a Buckmaster maquis [Colonel Maurice Buckmaster, head of the French Section of SOE (Special Operations Executive), the British organization responsible for planning resistance in occupied Europe] and an FTP maquis. [*Francs-tireurs et Partisans*: Communist-led resistance network.] On the way back—twenty minutes earlier—we had been dozing as we approached Gramat, with our Cross of Lorraine pennant flapping in the warm breeze. A sudden volley of firing, the rear window shattered, and the car slewed round and plunged into a ditch. The driver had been killed instantaneously by a bullet in the head as he put his foot down hard on the brake. The escort lay slumped over our weapons. The British officer jumped into the road to the right and fell, both hands red with blood clutched to his stomach. I jumped to the left and ran, my legs numb after three hours' driving. A

machine gun was firing at me; the car shielded me from another. A bullet cut through the knee strap of my right legging which flapped loose, still attached by the foot strap. I had to stop to rip it off. A bullet in the right leg. The pain very slight. Only the blood told me I had been hit. Then a terrible wrench in the left leg.

The two men, who were carrying me like a parcel, did not look at all unpleasant. There would be others. It was extraordinarily absurd. How could the Germans be in Gramat?

Everything was going to end here, God knew how, at the end of this road above which the radiant July sky seemed to be fixed in eternity, while the peasants watched me as I went by, their hands crossed on their spade handles, and the women made the sign of the cross as at a funeral procession. I would not see our victory. What was, that would ever be, the meaning of this life? But I was drawn on by a grim curiosity about what lay in store for me.

From the first houses onward, the street was lined with tanks. The French watched me go by with anguish, the Germans with surprise. My porters went into the office of a garage. An NCO questioned the one who was escorting me. Then, "Your papers!"

They were in the pocket of my tunic, and I reached them without difficulty. I held out the wallet and said: "They're false."

Without taking the wallet, he translated. The two NCO's stared at me like a couple of hypnotized hens. The stretcher bearers set off again. This time we went into a small barn. The stretcher was put down on its folding legs. The Germans left. A key turned in the lock. There was a sentry outside the narrow window. I tried to sit up on the stretcher. My left leg was giving me hardly any pain. I felt very dazed. I must have lost a lot of blood, for it was still flowing, in spite of the handkerchiefs knotted round my thighs.

The silhouette of the sentry presented arms. The key turned. And an officer who looked like Buster Keaton came in.

"How sad for your poor family! You are a Catholic, are you not?"

"Yes."

It was not the occasion for a lecture on agnosticism.

"I am the Catholic chaplain."

He looked at the bloodstained handkerchief. "How sad for your poor family!"

"The Passion can't have been very pleasant for Christ's family, Father. Not that I'm Christ."

He looked at me, more stupefied than I was. But in his case it was stupidity. "You have children?" he asked.

"Unfortunately. Am I to be tried or not?"

"I don't know. But if you have need of the consolations of religion, you can call for me."

He opened the door, a black shape against the still dazzling sky. Then, by way of valediction, "All the same, how very sad for your poor family."

A queer sort of chaplain, or a queer sort of religion. A bogus priest would at least have asked questions.

An NCO beckoned me outside. The yard was full of soldiers. I was able to take a few steps. He made me face the wall, hands leaning against the stones above my head. I heard a command: "Achtung," and turned round. I was facing a firing squad.

"Slope arms! Present arms!"

It is customary to present arms to those who are about to be executed. A recent dream came back to me. I was in the cabin of a liner, and the porthole had just been ripped away; water was pouring in; faced with the irremediable fact that my life was over, that it would never be other than what it had been, I burst into an endless peal of laughter (my brother Roland died shortly afterward in the sinking of the "Cap-Arcona"). I had had several brushes with violent death.

"Take aim!"

I stared at the heads bent over the rifle sights. "At ease!"

The soldiers put their rifles under their arms and sauntered off with disappointed smiles.

After all, why could they not have fired *round* me? No one else would have been endangered: I was standing against the wall. Why had I not really believed in death? I had seen it in a much more threatening form on the Gramat road. I had had neither the feeling, which I know well, that someone is going to shoot at me, nor that of imminent separation from life. I remember once telling Saint Exupéry, who had asked me what I thought of courage, that it seemed to me a curious and banal consequence of the feeling of invulnerability. Saint Ex had concurred,

though not without surprise. The comedy in which I had just taken part had not touched this feeling in me. Were its aura, its ceremonial directly associated with death? Perhaps we believe in death only when a companion falls at our side? I went back to my barn, where I was now beginning to feel at home, and lay down again. A second lieutenant came in with two soldiers who picked up the stretcher. We went out. The second lieutenant was not a young officer: over forty, big, erect, red-faced, and rugged-faced, his head shaven. Soon he was walking in front of the stretcher, and I could see only his back.

We were going to the first-aid post. A nurse looked at me with hatred. The medical officer and the orderlies, who had seen others like me, dressed my wound with care. The stretcher moved off again. We went down into a cellar. I knew what cellars were used for. "It will be a hard day," Damiens used to say. [Robert François Damiens was tortured to death for attempted regicide after stabbing Louis XV with a penknife in 1757.] No. We came up again, went on for about half a mile—and Gramat is not a big town. Tanks everywhere. The inhabitants withdrew before the stretcher. We reached a somewhat isolated farm and went into the storage shed. A harrow, rakes, wooden pitchforks. I had seen these ageless storage sheds during the 1940 campaign, but it had not struck me then how much these implements, particularly the harrow, look like instruments of torture. The procession moved off again, stopping twice more in similar places. I had the impression that we were in search of a suitable torture chamber. Evidently the soldiers were assembled, for none were to be seen. Solitude, a town inhabited by sleeping tanks, houses furnished with pitchforks, and harrows to hang corpses on. Five minutes later, my porters stopped.

"Kommandantur," said the second-lieutenant.

It was the Hôtel de France. The maquis had its postbox here. The Germans had just evacuated the reception office, but the manageress was at the pay desk. White hair, regular features, whalebone collar: a boarding school headmistress. I had seen her twice before.

"Do you know him?" the German asked, on the off chance.

"Me? No," she answered absently, almost without looking at me.

"And you?" he asked me.

"The maquis don't put up at hotels, unfortunately!"

The office connected with the little hall through a swing door. The second lieutenant sat down behind the desk. The stretcher bearers put me down on the black and white tiles without unfolding the supports of the stretcher. A soldier came in, notebook in hand, examined me with more curiosity than hostility, and sat down on the officer's left. The street was narrow, and the lamps were already lit. The clerk, with his protruding chin and forehead, looked like a haricot bean; the interrogator like a sparrow—nose in the air, little round mouth. He did not seem very German, except for his close-cropped red hair, completely shorn above his ears, which stuck out from his head. They had both made themselves comfortable.

"Your papers?"

I stood up, took one step forward, and held out my wallet. I lay down again at once: I was beginning to feel faint. Nevertheless, my head was clear, for the game had begun.

"I told your colleague that those papers are false."

The old sparrow looked at them carefully. Identity card, car license, other trivia in the name of Berger. A thousand or so francs in notes. A photograph of my wife and son. He made them into a little pile, which he put next to the wallet.

"You speak German?"

"No."

"Your name, Christian name, rank?"

"Lieutenant Colonel Malraux, André, alias Colonel Berger. I am the military chief of this region."

He threw a puzzled glance at my officer's tunic, which had no badges of rank. What moral did he hope to draw from that? I had been captured in a car that flew a tricolour flag with the Cross of Lorraine.

"What organization?"

"De Gaulle."

"You . . . have some prisoners, have you not?"

He had a North German accent, hard, not at all "Teutonic." His interrogation was menacing but not aggressive.

"In the unit directly under my command, about a hundred."

What a strange game fate was playing! It was the custom, God knows why, to have prisoners taken by the maquis tried by court-martial. I had been present at a trial of this kind in an FTP maquis, with maquis leaders pretending to be judges, an indictment that was acceptable because hate always looks like hate, and a parody of a defense by a kind of clerk who was working off ten years of frustrated ambition by playing the lawyer. In a low, cool room in a château by the Lot, with goats bleating outside in the heat, and yellow flowers. It was to preside over a court-martial the day before that I had put on again the uniform I was wearing. We had already set free some twenty Alsatians —for there were many Alsatians among the troops facing us, as there were in our own maquis groups from which the Alsace-Lorraine brigade would be born. One of our lieutenants, a school-teacher from the Colmar region, had offered to undertake the defense of the German prisoners, and had said, in French and then in German, "None of these men belongs to the SS or the Gestapo. They are soldiers, and you can not shoot soldiers for having been called up and for carrying out the orders they have been given." There were many of our men at the end of the room, and I could sense the anxiety of our Alsatians. It was decided that the prisoners would be handed over to the first Allied unit we came across.

"How are they treated?"

The clerk, who was taking everything down in shorthand, put down his pencil.

"They spend their time playing prisoner's base and eat the same food as our own men. For them, the war is over."

The old sparrow wondered if I was making fun of him but decided that I was not.

"They had been expecting savages in rags," I told him, "and they came across soldiers in uniform."

"Parachuted?"

"No. The French maquis."

"Where are they?"

"Who, the prisoners?"

"It's the same thing!"

"Still, there are more maquisards than prisoners."

"Where are they?"

"I have no idea, fortunately. Let's get this straight. They were in the Siorac woods. For at least two hours my men have known that I'm in your hands. For an hour and a half my successor has been in command, and he is a regular staff officer. By now, not a single soldier, ours or yours, will be left in the camp."

He pondered. "What is your civilian profession?"

"Professor, and writer. I have lectured in your universities. At Marburg, Leipzig, Berlin."

"Professor" sounded serious.

"You obviously speak German. But that is of no importance."

"My first book, *Die Eroberer*, was translated by Max Claus."

It was alleged (falsely, as it later transpired) that Max Claus, having become a Nazi, was some sort of undersecretary of state with Goebbels. My interrogator was growing more and more puzzled. He started playing cat and mouse. After ten minutes:

"Lieutenant," I said, "I think we are wasting each other's time. Usually you interrogate prisoners who say they are innocent or who really are, and you have to make them confess. I have nothing to confess: I have been your opponent since the day of the Armistice."

"But it was Marshal Pétain who signed the Armistice!"

"It certainly wasn't I. So I'm not officially a combatant. So you can have me shot—after you've weighed the consequences. I may tell you that my deputy commanded the Legion in Morocco, and I commanded . . . elsewhere, and we are not playing at soldiers. We have more than one assembly point. We never make contact except on out-of-the-way roads, covered by four lookout men. The German forces have never taken a single one of my men prisoner. I am here because you have just carried out a very brilliant manoeuvre, and I went and threw myself in front of your machine guns like an idiot. But in capturing me you set off the alarm system; up to a hundred kilometres north of here all the command posts have been evacuated. In order to find out the extent of our forces—or the way we treat our prisoners, if it comes to that—you have only to ask the *Milice*. And you could have my men tortured—if you captured any of them—without getting anything out of them, because they know nothing:

our entire organization is based on the assumption that no human being can know what he will do under torture."

"The Wehrmacht does not use torture."

"Furthermore, a unit like yours, if the whole division is grouped together, has other fish to fry."

He asked me where our former command posts were, and I reeled off a list of châteaux abandoned by collaborators, or clearings where he would find listening posts and the remains of fires. No question of mentioning the woods of scrub oaks, which the Germans thought unusable. As for the identity of the leaders of the other maquis groups, the Gestapo and the *Milice* knew their pseudonyms as well as I did, and I was as little aware of their real names as they were. (At least in certain cases.) The old sparrow had certainly received orders to treat me as a prisoner of war. But it was obvious that all this was just a beginning. We continued to talk about the maquis. I exaggerated our numbers. It turned into a conversation.

Eventually the two Germans left—perhaps to dine? A sentry guarded me, on the other side of the swing door: I could only see him up to the knees. Sometimes he chatted: A lot of Germans passed through the little hall. I would have liked to think, but it was only the interrogation that had kept my faculties alert: I sank back, exhausted.

Nine o'clock in the evening. (There was a large wall clock hanging above the desk.) Two other Germans arrived with papers, no doubt a summary of my interrogation. They asked me the questions I had already been asked, and I gave the same answers. To crosscheck? No matter. The two Germans left.

Three quarters of an hour later, there was a great clicking of heels outside. The swing doors, usually pushed open breezily, parted gently, and a colonel came in and sat behind the desk. No secretary. He looked like his predecessors. No, it was because I was not used to looking up at people from ground level. But his hair was white.

"What are you hoping for?" he asked me.

"From our military activities, or from . . . my own fate?"

"From your military activities."

"To slow you up, of course."

He nodded, as if in agreement, or as if to say, "That's what I thought." Then, "Why do you destroy things we can quickly repair?"

"It's part of the plan."

(It was also, on occasion, because we could not do any better.)

"You didn't fight in the last war?"

"I was too young. My identity card is false, but the date of birth is correct—1901."

"You fought in this one?"

"Yes."

"In what branch?"

"Tanks."

(And what tanks! But that was none of his business. I had envied his, then.) He glanced through my papers absently, as if to give his hands something to do.

"Your maquis has antitank weapons?"

"Yes."

The Gestapo could not be unaware that London had been dropping bazookas by parachute for over a month. Therefore he knew this or, more precisely, was afraid of it. For in wooded country tanks can only be covered by infantry. German armoured divisions had motorized infantry at their disposal, but if it stayed in its trucks it could not protect the tanks against the bazookas, and if it protected the tanks by patrolling both sides of the road, the latter would be reduced to walking speed. My interrogator did not seem surprised or even very interested. Curious, rather. Had he simply wanted to see an officer of this mysterious maquis that was all round him? Was he rediscovering the French army, the "pigheads" of Verdun?

He put back the little pile of papers beside the empty wallet, got up, and came round to the front of the desk. As he passed in front of me, he picked up my wallet from the desk and handed it to me. I could feel at once that it was no longer empty. The colonel left. The sentry outside clicked his heels. The German had put back the photograph of my wife and son in one of the wallet pockets.

No one came after him. Finished for the night? The hotel was dropping off to sleep. The electric light in the office was still on. I thought I would be unable to sleep. I was wrong. Sleep overcame me as it used to do in Spain, when a meal followed an air battle: dead asleep, as we say dead-drunk.

Dawn. Daylight. A slamming of doors upstairs and the clatter of swing doors on the ground floor. Sounds of water. The crop-headed sparrow came back and sat down behind the desk without saying a word. Boots clumping on the stairs, and the hubbub of a hotel, of a barrack room, and above all of departure. Why does the German language, when shouted, always sound as if it is expressing anger? The voices went back and forth:

"Matâme: Have you any butter?"

"No!"

"Any chocolate?"

"No!"

"Matâme! Have you any bread?"

"Only in exchange for coupons."

Then they stopped asking. The manageress must have left the pay desk. An interval. Boots going upstairs, accompanied by a clink of messtins. Then from the upper floors came a strange clamour which grew louder as it came nearer: the noise children make when the Christmas tree is uncovered before their eyes. The swing doors parted, pushed by a tray on which were set a steaming bowl of coffee and some huge slices of bread and butter. Behind it came the manageress. Her white hair was very carefully done; she had put on a black dress, as if to go to Mass, but was wearing a white apron because she had come from the kitchen. She looked at the blood-stained tiles (my wounds had bled during the night), came toward me, knelt down —first one leg, then the other. It is not easy for an elderly woman to kneel down while carrying a tray. She placed it on my chest, got up again, went toward the swing door, turned round—two big red stains on the white apron, where she had knelt—and said, in the tone which she must often have used forty years earlier to say, "I'll trouble you not to pinch your brothers' bread and butter," but with an almost imperceptible hint of solemnity now. "It's for the wounded French officer!" Then she went back upstairs to the sound of boots shuffling aside.

My sparrow was staring at me with his beak open. To snatch bread from a wounded man would have been ridiculous, but how provoking it all was!

"Let's share it," I said.

He got up, went out and came back with a glass. Took one of my pieces of bread and put it on the desk. Took the bowl to pour half the coffee into his glass—and burned himself. Put the glass on the desk, took hold of the bowl again with his handkerchief, and poured, measuring carefully. Then gave me the bowl back. On the white tiles there were now two sets of bloody footprints, big ones to and from the desk, and small ones to and from the door.

Around eight o'clock, we left. The manageress was back.

"Thank you, Madame. You were admirable: the personification of France."

She stopped writing. Her features remained immobile, and her gaze followed me until the hotel door closed.

I was taken to the sick bay, where my dressings were changed. I would now be able to stand up, and perhaps take a few steps. No need. I was shut into an armoured van—an ambulance, perhaps. To the rear, a double door, bolted from the outside. Four partitions. I was alone. Lying down, I could see, through a little barred window in the door, a line of trucks, and the countryside flashing by. Would the maquis attack? I hardly thought so, for though the area was fairly mountainous, it was not wooded. To my knowledge there were no maquis units of any importance this side of the Garonne. No doubt the German armoured division was engaged on some punitive expedition: Above the road and its riverbends our villages burned beneath long, slanting trails of smoke.

When the column halted, I was allowed to get out.

At Figeac (where Roger Martin du Gard lived), a peasant brought me a walking stick and disappeared.

Every French glance told me that I was a condemned man. I did not think so—at least, not yet. I assumed I was destined for another interrogation, or a trial. But something was bound to happen.

At Villefranche-de-Rouergue, where I recognized the almost Spanish church I had used as a setting for some episodes in L'Espoir, the column halted for the night. I was put up at the convent. As soon as I was in bed, the Mother Superior brought me some coffee. She was no more than forty years old, and she was beautiful. As she went by, she smiled at the soldier who was guarding me, an inaccessible smile.

I had sometimes wondered what the Gospel would mean to one in the face of death.

"Mother Superior, could you lend me the Gospel according to St. John?"

"Oh of course!"

She brought a Bible and went out again. I searched for the text of St. John, but the book fell open at the marker that she must have just put there. I might have been killed many times, in Asia, in Spain, at home; the idea that I could have stayed behind, instead of attending a court-martial or an execution at the edge of a ditch, seemed to me laughable. Even that night, dying seemed banal to me. What interested me was death.

But it was not in the face of death that I had encountered St. John. It was at Ephesus, and above all in the Byzantine and Slav world which had venerated his tomb no less than Christ's. Through him, my memory retained a fairly complex image of Jesus: convincing and near, like that of St. Francis of Assisi, yet curiously hazy in this text where John refers to himself only as "He whom Jesus loved." I remembered the sellers of doves driven from the Temple, and certain phrases which made the Gospel a sort of incantation: ". . . for his hour was not yet come . . ." and the dark tone of "Father, deliver me from this hour . . ." and the words spoken to Judas, "That thou doest, do quickly." I remembered the story of the woman taken in adultery, which is so often related as a judgment, whereas Christ in fact turns neither to the accusers nor to the woman, and says, "He that is without sin among you . . ." while continuing to draw figures in the sand. I discovered again, "For God so loved the world, that he gave his only begotten Son, that whosoever believeth in him should not perish, but have everlasting life. For God sent not his Son into the world to condemn the world; but that the world through him might be saved." I had not believed in the burlesque firing squad at Gramat, but I would probably meet one soon that would not be burlesque. On the road, I might have received the bullets in the head, like the driver, instead of in the legs. I felt strongly that all faith dissolves life into the eternal, and I was cut off from the eternal. My life was one of those human adventures which Shakespeare justifies by calling dreams and which are not dreams. A human destiny coming to an end in front of a dozen rifles, among so many other destinies as ephemeral as the earth. What was about to befall me was of passionate concern to a worthless part of myself, like the urge to escape from the water when one is drowning. But I did not seek the meaning of the world in a thrashing of the limbs. The genius of Christianity is to have proclaimed that the path to the deepest mystery is the path of love. A love which is not confined to men's feelings, but transcends them like the soul of the world, more powerful than death and more powerful than justice: "For God did not send his son into the world to judge the world through him might be saved." I had belief; I had a great respect for the Christian message which had pervaded this earth in which I would doubtless soon be lying, but I did not believe in it. The memory of St. John is more powerful against misfortune than his presence is against death. . . . It was all as though my supreme value was Truth—and yet what did Truth matter to me that night?

My past, my biographical life, was of no importance. I did not think of my childhood. I did not think of my family. I thought of the atheist peasant women who saluted my wounds with the sign of the cross, of the stick brought to me by the frightened peasant, of the coffee from the manageress of the Hôtel de France and from the Mother Superior. All that remained in my memory was fraternity. In this convent silence probably filled with prayers for me, and broken by the distant clattering of a tank on the move, what lived as profoundly in my mind as the approach of death—even when I thought of the scorpions of Babylon—was the despairing caress that closes the eyes of the dead.

Faulkner
at West Point

William Faulkner Nobel Prize-winner, at West Point said, "Writing, it don't get any easier . . . and I'm the oldest living sixth grader."

BY ALLENE TALMEY

At West Point, the Military Academy, that spring evening had the delicate air of a watercolour. The cadets in their dress greys, their faces so young and untouched, flowed without much noise into the Point's old riding academy into which a big new auditorium had been inserted, its glossy yellow wood walls the colour of curly maple. When the boys had filled the sharply raked, comfortable seats, everyone waited, including a small group of photographers and reporters up from New York.

A newsreel cameraman said: "Who we photographing tonight?"

One of the cadets answered: "William Faulkner."

"Who's he?" asked the cameraman.

At that point, Lieutenant Colonel Joel B. Stephens, the Point's Information officer, a jovial bouncing man with four rows of ribbons on his dress blue uniform (with a gold stripe down the trouser legs), suggested in the tone of an order to the cadets that they clap and yell as though this pre-talk time was post-talk time. It was only for the benefit of the television cameramen who seem to prefer the shell of reality to actuality. They couldn't wait for the real end of Faulkner's talk to record what their imagination and experience told them would happen. The boys dutifully clapped and yelled. It was unsatisfactory. They clapped and yelled again with more enthusiasm. At the true end of the talk they clapped but did not yell.

A man came over to the ABC-TV man to ask: "You interested in thirty Vassar girls?"

"Not me," said the television man.

"They came over in buses," added the first man persuasively.

Suddenly a definite wave of silence rippled over the audience. Four men marched down the aisle as solemnly as though they were the prelude to a firing squad. In front, in dress blues, walked Major General W. E. Westmoreland, Superintendent of the Point, with William Faulkner, short, white-haired, broad-shouldered,

242

wearing a superbly fitting dinner jacket, the red rosette of the French Legion of Honour on his lapel. His country face, ruddy, tanned, thin, looked precise, controlled, and a little lost. Two officers followed them. The General led Faulkner up the side steps to the stage and lectern, and said, after the usual salutation in which he gracefully mentioned the Pulitzer Prize of 1955, the Gold Medal of the National Institute of Arts and Letters of 1962, and the Nobel Prize of 1949, that the speaker had come "to read from his works and to converse with you."

At that Faulkner put on heavy tortoise glasses over his squirrel-bright black eyes, touched his cuffs, stepped to the microphone, greeted the General, "the Gentlemen of the Faculty, the Gentlemen of the Corps" . . . and said "I have been given permission to read from the book I have just finished. I will have to skip about a little to read about a horse race which to me is one of the funniest horse races I've ever heard of. . . ." Without mentioning that his new book is *The Reivers*, Faulkner was hurriedly off and away, like the race.

He started off in so deeply a Southern accent that the audience at first had great difficulty understanding him. Fairly soon, however, we caught on and from that moment for the next thirty or so minutes, everyone laughed at the twists, enjoying with the author the funniest race he had ever read. As he came to the last sentence, he pulled off his glasses and stood ready to answer cadet questions. A boy toward the rear stood up, zipped close his jacket, and asked about a writer's dedication and "do you, sir, think you have fulfilled it?"

Faulkner answered: "It's possible that I hadn't. I think that it is the writer's privilege, his dedication, to uplift man's heart by showing the record of the experiences of the human heart, the travail of man living and dying with his fellows . . . in such moving times that the lesson of honesty and courage are evident. I think that that's the reason possibly the poet, the writer writes. Whether he is successful or not is something else. However, the only reason the poet ever writes another poem is that the one he just finished didn't quite serve that purpose, wasn't good enough. So he writes another one."

Down in front a boy stood up, zipped close his jacket, and read from a small piece of paper the question: "Out of all the books you've written, which one do you think is the best?"

After a pause, Faulkner said: "That goes back to the answer I just gave. . . . If the writer ever wrote one which suited him completely, nothing would remain but to go and quit. In my own case, the one that is closest to me would be the one that failed the most, that gave me the most trouble. . . . So I'd have to answer that the one that cost me the most anguish and that I still don't like is the one called *The Sound and the Fury*."

A cadet stood up, zipped close his jacket, and asked a question about Ernest Hemingway's death. To that Faulkner said: "I think that Hemingway was too good a man to be the victim of accidents. Only the weak are victims of accidents unless a house falls on them. I think that that was a deliberate pattern which he followed just as all his work was a deliberate pattern. I think that every man wants to be at least as good as what he writes, and I'm inclined to think that Ernest felt that at that time this was the right thing in grace and dignity to do. I don't agree with him. I think that no man can say until the end of his life whether he's written out or not. It probably occurs to almost everybody at some time that he had done his best, that this is when he would like to write finis to his life. I think that Hemingway was wrong."

As soon as he paused, another cadet asked a question that led Faulkner to say: "The primary job that any writer faces is to tell you a story, a story out of human experience—I mean by that universal mutual experience . . . of the human heart without regard to race or time or condition . . . I think that no writer's got time to be drawing a picture of a region or preaching anything; if he's trying to preach a sermon, he's a propagandist which is another horse. The writer is simply trying to tell a story of the human heart in conflict with itself or with others or with environment, in a moving way.

Absorbed by the immediacy of Faulkner's opinions, by the fountain of phrases, by the charm of his voice, slurring over some syllables, clipping others, pronouncing heart as "hot" or cowardice as "cowar-dice," the audience bent towards him, then twitched around in their seats to catch the cadets' questions. When Faulkner said: "If a spirit of nationalism gets

into literature, it stops being literature," the body of cadets applauded vigorously, happily. Faulkner smiled with pleasure at the sound.

A cadet in the rear stood up and asked: "Who is your favourite author?"—that most obvious of questions, put forth by radio and television interviewers. Faulkner sensibly said: "That's a question that really doesn't make much sense to a writer because the writer is not concerned with who wrote the book but what he wrote. To me, anyway, characters are the thing—the people that I know and love are Don Quixote and Sairey Gamp, some of Conrad's people, a lot of Dickens' people, Balzac's people, but not Balzac especially because I think Balzac's writing is bad writing. . . ."

That stirred the boys, who were even more stirred up by the next question: "Sir, since your books show perversions and corruptions and wickedness, how do you think this uplifts your readers?" Briskly Faulkner shot back, slightly irritated: "My books may show them what I think they shouldn't do. One must show man not when he's dressed up for Sunday, but in all his phases, his conditions, his base attitudes and spirit—that he goes on, he continues, he has outlived the dinosaur, he has outlived the atom bomb, and I'm convinced in time he can even outlive the wheel. There is something that makes him endure. . . ."

After several more questions, Colonel R. K. Alspach, chairman of the department of English, announced that there would be time for only one more question. A tall cadet immediately stood up, zipped his jacket, and asked: "What works would you consider as furthering the naturalistic movement in America?" Quickly Faulkner said: "I don't know what naturalism means. Can you be more specific?" Instantly the drama of a student asking a pedantic question, and being fought back, engaged the audience, expecting the cadet to fall on his academic face. The cadet quickly said: "I mean Sinclair Lewis, *Sister Carrie*." The audience moved with pleasure, neighbour nodding to neighbour. The boy had come through with instant accuracy. Everyone relaxed, especially Colonel Alspach.

In Faulkner's reply he said: "Yes, yes, I see what you mean. I still think that the job of the writer is to tell you a moving story of the human heart in conflict. I would say that Dreiser [author of *Sister Carrie*] used the best material he had, the best method, the best skill he had which wasn't very much. He was a bad writer. But he had a tremendous drive to tell you of the conflict of the human spirit and that's what I meant by saying that I didn't know what a naturalist writer was. . . . The writer uses naturalism, romanticism as the tools to his hand—just as the carpenter uses the hammer . . . the eternal verities haven't changed too much since man first found how to record."

He stopped The audience applauded, deeply pleased. Quickly Faulkner left the stage, and, escorted by officers, walked over to a library in Building 600 followed hastily by the photographers and reporters. While the television cameramen arranged their lights to focus on the armchair where Faulkner would sit, Captain Winfield A. Holt, a thin, tall instructor in the English department, talked with a group of reporters. One of them asked if the Captain had been teaching long at the Point. "No," said Captain Holt, "I'm a rifleman." Then Colonel Stephen added that Holt, a 1952 graduate of the Point, after a tour of duty in the Far East, had been sent to Columbia University to get a master's degree in American literature in a quick nine months before coming back to teach.

In about ten minutes the amenities were over. Faulkner leaned back in the easy chair, took out his pipe, jabbed it a bit, and tensed up. His face, with its thin lips, almost hidden by a grey-black moustache that looks like those on Confederate generals, had the ruddy sheen of health. Somehow the reporters' questions failed in precision in the studied knowledge of Faulkner's work that the cadets' questions had. Recognizing this, Faulkner said that the boys' questions had a discipline behind them; the cadets were in top gear.

When someone asked him about the difficulty of writing, he replied: "What I like best is fox hunting." He jabbed again at his pipe, adding, "Writing, it don't get any easier." The questions dribbled off until Faulkner at last said, with what nineteenth-century novelists would have called a "merry twinkle in his sparkling eyes," that "I'm the oldest living sixth grader."

With that he bounced up from his chair, straightened his shoulders, smiled again, and walked out of the room, followed by some of the Gentlemen of the Faculty in their dress blues.

The next morning at 7:55 Faulkner began conversing again with the students, this time in their classrooms. Later in the day, with his son-in-law, Paul Summers, Jr., a former West Point officer, class of 1951, who had arranged the visit, William Faulkner dressed in a rough tweed suit with umbrella and derby left for home. He looked like a Southern cross between Charlie Chaplin and the elegant King Edward, the Seventh.

HENRI CARTIER-BRESSON